Professional Cloud Google Cloud Certification Guide

A handy guide to designing, developing, and managing enterprise-grade GCP cloud solutions

Konrad Cłapa
Brian Gerrard

BIRMINGHAM - MUMBAI

Professional Cloud Architect – Google Cloud Certification Guide

Commissioning Editor: Karan Sadawana
Acquisition Editor: Rahul Nair
Content Development Editor: Ronn Kurien
Senior Editor: Rahul Dsouza
Technical Editor: Mohd Riyan Khan
Copy Editor: Safis Editing
Project Coordinator: Vaidehi Sawant
Proofreader: Safis Editing
Indexer: Priyanka Dhadke
Production Designer: Arvindkumar Gupta

First published: October 2019

Production reference: 1171019

Published by Packt Publishing Ltd.
Livery Place
35 Livery Street
Birmingham
B3 2PB, UK.

ISBN 978-1-83855-527-6

www.packt.com

To my parents, for their constant support.

– Konrad Cłapa

To Linda, for her constant support and understanding.

– Brian Gerrard

Packt.com

Subscribe to our online digital library for full access to over 7,000 books and videos, as well as industry leading tools to help you plan your personal development and advance your career. For more information, please visit our website.

Why subscribe?

- Spend less time learning and more time coding with practical eBooks and Videos from over 4,000 industry professionals

- Improve your learning with Skill Plans built especially for you

- Get a free eBook or video every month

- Fully searchable for easy access to vital information

- Copy and paste, print, and bookmark content

Did you know that Packt offers eBook versions of every book published, with PDF and ePub files available? You can upgrade to the eBook version at www.packt.com and as a print book customer, you are entitled to a discount on the eBook copy. Get in touch with us at customercare@packtpub.com for more details.

At www.packt.com, you can also read a collection of free technical articles, sign up for a range of free newsletters, and receive exclusive discounts and offers on Packt books and eBooks.

Foreword

In 2016, the year in which I obtained all of my Amazon Web Services certificates, I heard the news about Google launching a certification program. Believing that the future is multi-cloud, I wanted to learn Google Cloud Platform. After attending the Google Cloud Next conference in San Francisco, I decided to become a certified Google Cloud Architect. Whilst preparing for the certification, I found that there were no books on the topic, and online documentations were the only source available. Three years later, I finally had this book in my hands. I wish I'd had this book when I was starting my journey!

Having passed all 6 Google Cloud Profession exams and being an author myself, I understand what it takes to pass this professional level certification. Having all of your resources in one place is irreplaceable when preparing for the certification. By buying this book, you can seize the opportunity to have all you need at your fingertips.

If you are still wondering whether you should start your journey with the help of Brian and Konrad, do not hesitate. I can assure you that the Google Cloud Architect certification is becoming one of the hottest on the market. Once a niche platform, Google Cloud is now on a path to truly shine, and is thus attracting more and more companies. With Google Cloud's focus on Machine Learning, Cloud Native applications development, and Data Processing services, the demand for certified specialists is growing by the day.

Don't wait any longer. Read this book, start using Google Cloud, and get certified.

A bright future is waiting for you!

Yujun Liang
Google Certified Cloud Architect

Contributors

About the authors

Konrad Cłapa is a lead cloud automation architect working for Atos R&D. He has over 10 years' experience in the IT industry. He holds over 30 IT certifications, including all 6 Google Cloud Platform certifications. He is also listed among 30 individuals who hold double VMware Certified Design Expert certifications. Sharing knowledge has always been important to him, so he contributes to the community by acting as a leader for a local Google Cloud Developer group and an AWS user group in Poland.

Brian Gerrard is a technical engineer from Scotland with over 10 years' experience in the IT industry. Currently working for Atos, he holds the Google Certified Professional Architect certification, as well as all three AWS Certified Associate certifications. In addition to this, Brian has a number of advanced certifications in infrastructure and private cloud technologies, including two VMware Certified Implementation Expert certifications. Brian is a firm believer in lifelong learning, and you will regularly find him contributing to his local user groups.

About the reviewers

Antonio Gulli has a passion for establishing and managing global technological talent for innovation and execution. His core expertise is in cloud computing, deep learning, and search engines. Currently, he serves as the Engineer Director for the Office of the CTO, Google Cloud. Previously, he served as the Google Warsaw site leader, doubling the size of the engineering site.

So far, Antonio has been lucky enough to gain professional experience in four countries in Europe and has managed teams in six countries in EMEA and the US. In Amsterdam, he was the vice president for Elsevier, a leading scientific publisher; in London, he was a site lead for Microsoft, working on Bing, Search; in Italy and the UK, he was the CTO, Europe and UK, for Ask.com and also worked in several co-funded start-ups, including one of the first web search companies in Europe.

Antonio has co-invented a number of technologies for searching, smart energy, and AI, with more than 20 patents issued/applied for. Additionally, he has published several books about coding and machine learning, which have been translated into Japanese and Chinese. Antonio speaks Spanish, English, and Italian, and he is currently learning Polish and French. Antonio is the proud father of two boys, Lorenzo, who's 18, and Leonardo, who's 13; and a little queen, Aurora, who's 9 years old.

Jaroslaw Gajewski holds a technical lead architect position at Atos. He is responsible for designing private and multi-cloud solutions for cloud-agnostic and cloud-native services. His technical knowledge is backed by multiple industry-standard certificates. He is already a Google Cloud Certified Professional and VMware, DELL, Microsoft, and AWS certified, and is also recognized by Atos as a senior expert in the cloud and automation domain. Being passionate about the cloud, outside work, he is an active community speaker and one of the Google Developer Group leads for GDG Bydgoszcz.

In his spare time, he loves spending time with his wife, two daughters, and one son; he enjoys board games and is constantly striving to further his knowledge.

Packt is searching for authors like you

If you're interested in becoming an author for Packt, please visit `authors.packtpub.com` and apply today. We have worked with thousands of developers and tech professionals, just like you, to help them share their insight with the global tech community. You can make a general application, apply for a specific hot topic that we are recruiting an author for, or submit your own idea.

Table of Contents

Section 4: Managing Implementation

Section 5: Ensuring Solution and Operations Reliability

Section 6: Exam Focus

Preface

Google Cloud Platform (**GCP**) is a leading cloud offering that has grown exponentially year on year. GCP offers an array of services that can be leveraged by various organizations in order to bring the best out of their infrastructure. This book is a complete guide to GCP and will teach you various methods of how to effectively utilize GCP services for your business needs. You will also become acquainted with the topics required to pass Google's Professional Cloud Architect certification exam.

Following the Professional Cloud Architect certification's official exam syllabus, first, you will be introduced to GCP. You will then be taught about the core services that GCP offers, such as computing, storage, and network. Additionally, you will learn methods of how to scale and automate your cloud infrastructure and make it compliant and secure. Finally, you will also learn how to process big data and embrace **machine learning** (**ML**) services.

By the end of this book, you will have all the information required to ace Google's Professional Cloud Architect exam and become an expert in GCP services.

Who this book is for

If you are a cloud architect, cloud engineer, administrator, or anyone who would like to learn different ways to implement Google Cloud services in your organization, as well as get yourself certified with the Professional Cloud Architect's certificate, then this is the book for you.

What this book covers

Chapter 1, *GCP Cloud Architect Professional*, discusses the benefits of becoming a certified architect, how to register for the exam, and what to expect when you are in the test center.

Chapter 2, *Getting Started with Google Cloud Platform*, covers the basics of GCP and how it positions itself on the market. You will learn about all the major GCP services that are available.

Chapter 3, *Google Cloud Platform Core Services*, examines the most important GCP services, including computing, storage, networking, big data, and machine learning.

Chapter 4, *Working with Google Compute Engine*, examines how to create and run virtual machine instances on top of the **Google Compute Engine (GCE)** service.

Chapter 5, *Managing Kubernetes Clusters with Google Kubernetes Engine*, explains the basis of containers and microservices. It looks at running and managing Kubernetes clusters on the **Google Kubernetes Engine (GKE)** service.

Chapter 6, *Exploring Google App Engine as a Compute Option*, discusses how to define and run applications on Google App Engine.

Chapter 7, *Running Serverless Functions with Google Cloud Functions*, looks into running serverless functions on Google Cloud Functions.

Chapter 8, *Networking Options in GCP*, discusses Google's networking services. Understanding networking is key to successfully completing the architect exam. We will introduce you to concepts such as **Virtual Private Cloud (VPC)**, before diving further into other concepts such as **Virtual Private Network (VPN)**, networks, subnetworks, and routes.

Chapter 9, *Exploring Storage Options in GCP – Part 1*, considers different storage options. This will allow us to choose the right storage for a given use case. We will discuss object storage alongside relational and non-relational databases.

Chapter 10, *Exploring Storage Options in GCP – Part 2*, looks at storage options such as Cloud Spanner and Bigtable.

Chapter 11, *Analyzing Big Data Options*, discusses how big data is another key topic in the architect exam. Understanding what big data is, and what services GCP offers to handle the complexities of data analytics, will really help you in the test center when taking the exam. In this chapter, we will look at the various services that are available, and when we might choose one over the other.

Chapter 12, *Putting Machine Learning to Work*, examines machine learning in general as well as GCP-related services. This will allow us to understand the use cases and possible implementations of ML using Google Cloud.

Chapter 13, *Security and Compliance*, covers security, which is a feature of all GCP services. In this chapter, we will cover IAM in more detail than we have in previous chapters, to allow you to understand custom roles and service accounts. Additionally, we will look at Google's commitments to compliance; for example, through the **Payment Card Industry (PCI)** regulations.

Chapter 14, *Google Cloud Management Options*, shows you that there are a number of ways to manage your GCP infrastructure and its services. In this chapter, we will look at how to manage your GCP infrastructure and the key management options that are available, including Cloud Shell, SDK, and gcloud, and the steps that are needed to access or install these tools.

Chapter 15, *Monitoring Your Infrastructure*, looks at monitoring your infrastructure using Stackdriver.

Chapter 16, *Case Studies*, discusses how, in the exam, some questions may refer you to several case studies. You should be familiar with these case studies before you take the exam. These involve hypothetical business and solution concepts. In this chapter, we will cover how to find these case studies; additionally, we will also take a look at an example case study and analyze it in order to design an appropriate solution.

Chapter 17, *Test your Knowledge*, goes through exam tips and sample tests.

To get the most out of this book

As the practical examples throughout the book involve the use of GCP, a GCP free-tier account is required.

Download the color images

We also provide a PDF file that has color images of the screenshots/diagrams used in this book. You can download it here: https://static.packt-cdn.com/downloads/ 9781838555276_ColorImages.pdf.

Code in Action

Visit the following link to check out videos of the code being run: http://bit.ly/31i6wpz

Conventions used

There are a number of text conventions used throughout this book.

`CodeInText`: Indicates code words in text, database table names, folder names, filenames, file extensions, pathnames, dummy URLs, user input, and Twitter handles. Here is an example: "It automatically creates one subnet per region with predefined IP ranges with the `/20` mask from the `10.128.0.0/9` CIDR block."

A block of code is set as follows:

```
<INSTANCE_NAME>.c.<PROJECT_ID>.internal
```

When we wish to draw your attention to a particular part of a code block, the relevant lines or items are set in bold:

```
resources:
- name: {{ properties["name"] }}
  type: compute.v1.instance
```

Any command-line input or output is written as follows:

```
gcloud deployment-manager deployments create networking --config
config.yaml
```

Bold: Indicates a new term, an important word, or words that you see on screen. For example, words in menus or dialog boxes appear in the text like this. Here is an example: "Navigate to **Network Services** and then **Load Balancing**."

Warnings or important notes appear like this.

Tips and tricks appear like this.

Get in touch

Feedback from our readers is always welcome.

General feedback: If you have questions about any aspect of this book, mention the book title in the subject of your message and email us at `customercare@packtpub.com`.

Errata: Although we have taken every care to ensure the accuracy of our content, mistakes do happen. If you have found a mistake in this book, we would be grateful if you would report this to us. Please visit `www.packtpub.com/support/errata`, selecting your book, clicking on the Errata Submission Form link, and entering the details.

Piracy: If you come across any illegal copies of our works in any form on the internet, we would be grateful if you would provide us with the location address or website name. Please contact us at `copyright@packt.com` with a link to the material.

If you are interested in becoming an author: If there is a topic that you have expertise in and you are interested in either writing or contributing to a book, please visit `authors.packtpub.com`.

Reviews

Please leave a review. Once you have read and used this book, why not leave a review on the site that you purchased it from? Potential readers can then see and use your unbiased opinion to make purchase decisions, we at Packt can understand what you think about our products, and our authors can see your feedback on their book. Thank you!

For more information about Packt, please visit `packt.com`.

Section 1: Introduction to GCP

This section will introduce you to the **Google Cloud Platform (GCP)** and outline the Professional Cloud Architect exam.

This section contains the following chapters:

- Chapter 1, *GCP Cloud Architect Professional*
- Chapter 2, *Getting Started with Google Cloud Platform*
- Chapter 3, *Google Cloud Platform Core Services*

1
GCP Cloud Architect Professional

The shift to the cloud is not a new thing, and for many years, companies have been utilizing cost-effective solutions from public cloud vendors to move away from traditional on-premises architecture. The speed at which technology is moving now makes it increasingly difficult for companies managing their own infrastructure to get the most out of their IT systems.

While **Amazon Web Services (AWS)** and Microsoft Azure currently lead the race with enterprise-scale companies, **Google Cloud Platform (GCP)** is emerging as one of the most popular solutions among IT professionals, and interest is steadily increasing. It seems that Google is playing the long game very well. In Q3 2018, ex-CEO of Google Cloud, Diane Greene, estimated that only 10% of workloads are in the public cloud, showing the massive scope for market share still available. Furthermore, in Q4 2018, CEO of Google, Sundar Pichai, said that GCP was the fastest-growing major public cloud provider in the world. Given that companies are continuously moving to split cloud solutions, this means that IT cloud architects and engineers need to understand more than just the current top two providers.

This book, of course, will focus on Google technologies. Many of our readers may have experience of other public cloud vendors—for example, AWS or Microsoft Azure; however, we also cater to those who are new to the public cloud. The ultimate goal of this book is to help you to pass the Google Professional Cloud Architect exam. This book is suitable for both levels of experience. In this chapter, we will look at why you would take this exam, inform you about how to register for the exam, and brief you on what to expect from the exam.

We will cover the following topics in this chapter:

- The benefits of being a certified architect
- Registering for the exam
- What to expect from the exam
- Some tips

The benefits of being a certified architect

Studying for an exam can be a daunting prospect. Many hours need to be spent to achieve a certification, and it's not always an easy decision to dedicate a lot of personal time to achieve this goal. That said, if you currently work in the IT industry, you will know that the landscape has changed over several years. The public cloud is no longer something that worries companies, and more enterprises are shifting away from traditional on-premises solutions, meaning that the time you invest in learning new technologies will only be beneficial to your career.

But *why take the exam?* There are several reasons why you would take this exam, such as the following:

- You have used GCP for some time and want to have an industry-recognized certification that reflects your current skillset
- You want to achieve a new role or promotion and show that you can dedicate your own time to learning new skills that you don't get to use day to day
- There is no better way to showcase your skills than having industry-led certifications
- You want to get acquainted with modern stack development technologies

 A Forbes article recently showed that the Google Cloud Certified Professional Cloud Architect is the highest-paid certification of 2019. You can read it at https://www.forbes.com/sites/louiscolumbus/2019/02/11/15-top-paying-it-certifications-in-2019/#a7923023e7cd.

Whatever your reason for taking the exam, it is important to be realistic about your expectations.

Registering for the exam

The cost of the GCP Professional Architect exam is 200 USD, and it can be booked in several languages, such as English, Japanese, Spanish, and Portuguese. You can register for the exam by going through the following steps:

1. The first step is to visit the Google certification web page at `https://cloud.google.com/certification/`.

2. You will see that there are many certification paths you can take. Click on the **REGISTER** link under **Professional Cloud Architect**, as highlighted in the following screenshot:

3. Next, you will need a Webassessor account to book the exam. You can create a new account using the hyperlink in the **WELCOME** page:

WELCOME

- The Professional Cloud Architect exam is now available in <u>Spanish</u> and <u>Portuguese</u>.
- The Professional Data Engineer exam is now available in <u>Spanish</u> and <u>Portuguese</u>.
- The Associate Cloud Engineer exam is now available in <u>Japanese</u>, <u>Spanish</u>, <u>Portuguese</u>, <u>German</u>, and <u>French</u>.

Please login with your existing Google Cloud Webassessor account to see our catalog and register for an exam. If you do not have a Google Cloud Webassessor account, you can create a new account <u>here</u>.

 If you have ever attempted another Google exam, for example, the Associate Cloud Engineer exam, then you can use the same credentials.

4. Next, click on **REGISTER FOR AN EXAM**, as shown in the following screenshot:

Shopping Cart | Edit Profile | Change Password | Help | Log Out
Welcome, **Brian Gerrard**

Google Cloud

Receipts   Register For An Exam   My Assessments   **Home**

You last logged in 09 May 2019 at 12.46AM MST.

REGISTER FOR AN EXAM

<u>Privacy Policy</u> | <u>Terms of Service</u>   © 2019   KRYTERION, Inc. and KRYTERION, Limited - All Rights Reserved   **KRYTERION™**

5. Select your testing center, as shown in the following screenshot:

6. Next, select a date, as shown in the following screenshot:

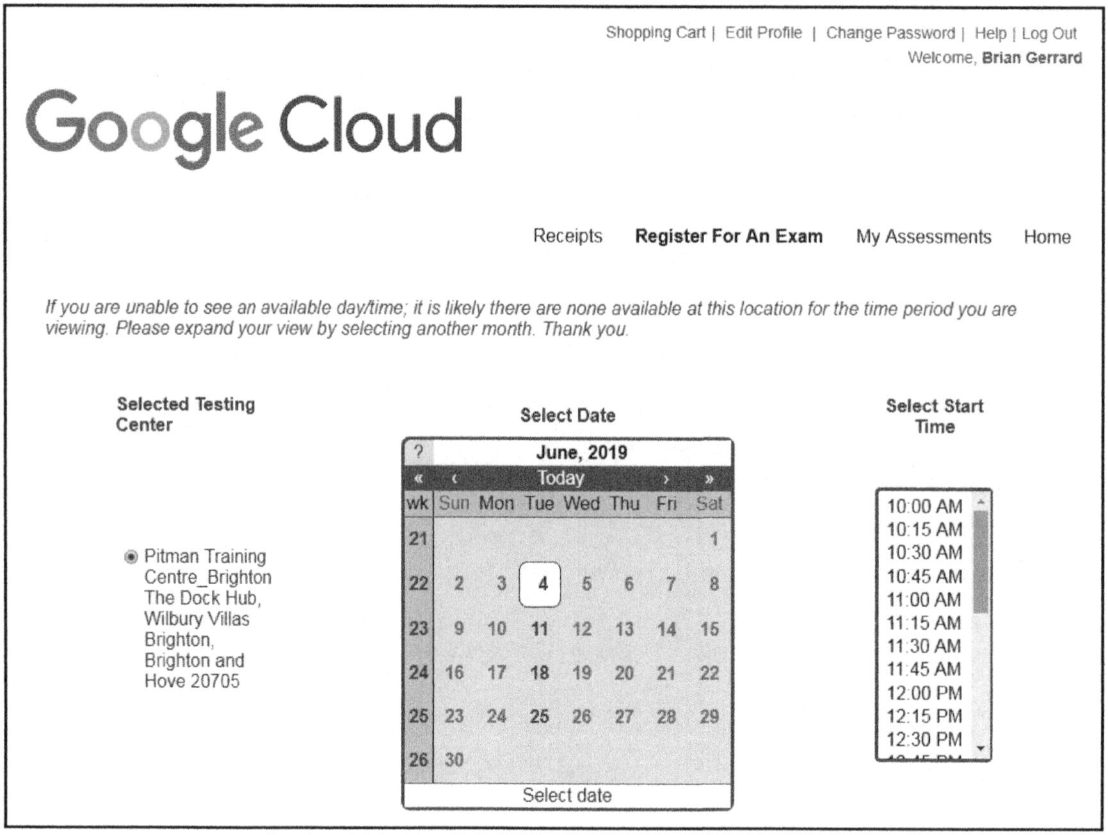

Shopping Cart | Edit Profile | Change Password | Help | Log Out
Welcome, **Brian Gerrard**

Google Cloud

Receipts   **Register For An Exam**   My Assessments   Home

If you are unable to see an available day/time; it is likely there are none available at this location for the time period you are viewing. Please expand your view by selecting another month. Thank you.

Selected Testing Center

Select Date

Select Start Time

⦿ Pitman Training Centre_Brighton The Dock Hub, Wilbury Villas Brighton, Brighton and Hove 20705

?		June, 2019					
«	‹	Today			›	»	
wk	Sun	Mon	Tue	Wed	Thu	Fri	Sat
21							1
22	2	3	4	5	6	7	8
23	9	10	11	12	13	14	15
24	16	17	18	19	20	21	22
25	23	24	25	26	27	28	29
26	30						

Select date

10:00 AM
10:15 AM
10:30 AM
10:45 AM
11:00 AM
11:15 AM
11:30 AM
11:45 AM
12:00 PM
12:15 PM
12:30 PM

7. Finally, review and click **Check Out**. Pay for the exam and you are ready to go. Submit the coupon or voucher code if you have one:

Shopping Cart | Edit Profile | Change Password | Help | Log Out
Welcome, **Brian Gerrard**

Google Cloud

Receipts   **Register For An Exam**   My Assessments   Home

Exam	Details	Price	Actions
Exam: Google Cloud Certified - Professional Cloud Architect (English) Length : 120 minutes	Schedule : Tuesday, 04 June 2019 Start Time : 10:30 (UTC+01:00) Location : [Change] Pitman Training Centre_Brighton The Dock Hub, Wilbury Villas Brighton, Brighton and Hove 20705	200.00	Remove

Coupon/Voucher Code: [   ]   Submit

Subtotal: 200.00

Total Price: **USD 200.00**

*Charges are made in USD, currency conversion fees may apply

Empty Cart   Add Another Exam   Return Home   Check Out

Please bear in mind that you can change the selected date after the exam is booked up to 72 hours before the scheduled date at no extra cost. Note that a rescheduling fee will be charged for any changes made within 72 hours of your scheduled exam time.

What to expect from the exam

There are several resources that Google advises you to take advantage of to prepare for the exam. These consist of online training courses, instructor-led training, and practical labs. All of this information can be found on the cloud architect web page at `https://cloud.google.com/certification/cloud-architect`.

In addition, by visiting the exam guide web page at `https://cloud.google.com/certification/guides/professional-cloud-architect/`, you can see the expected subject knowledge of the exam applicants. The exam blueprint is critical for any exam, and GCP Architect is no different. You should review this guide and make sure you understand each section.

Like most exams, some real-life experience will also help you. The exam is created with cloud architects in mind who have experience with software development and multi-cloud/hybrid-cloud environments. That being said, there is no reason that you cannot pass this exam with the correct amount of study, even if you don't have practical, hands-on experience.

Google offers Qwiklabs that can be used to gain experience in the services offered. It is recommended that you sign up to these to familiarize yourself with the GCP layout and services. Qwiklabs can be paid for either through a monthly subscription, which will give you unlimited access to the labs, or by purchasing credits. Each lab will have a certain number of credits depending on the complexity of the lab. The typical cost of 10 credits is 10 USD. GCP Essentials gives a great introduction to GCP and can be found at `https://google.qwiklabs.com/quests/23?utm_source=gcputm_medium=siteutm_campaign=certification`. It takes around five hours to complete this lab.

Once you are prepared for the exam and have successfully scheduled it, you will need to visit one of the registered test centers. You will be expected to arrive around 15 minutes before the exam and take two forms of identification with you. All of this will be explained in your exam confirmation email. The exam itself will consist of multiple-choice questions that will require one or more answers to be selected. In addition to this, you will be quizzed on case studies of fictional companies. You will, however, have access to these case studies before the exam, and you can refer to them during the exam. In Chapter 16, *Case Studies*, we will go over these in more detail. There will be around 60 questions in the exam, and you will have two hours to complete them. You will receive only a pass or fail, with no indication of your score.

Some tips

In the exam, we recommend that you make use of the fact that you can mark questions for review and come back to them later. It is a personal preference, of course, but we suggest that you don't puzzle over a question for too long. You will have around two minutes per question to provide an answer. Some of the answers to the questions will jump straight out of the screen at you, and others will take you more time to determine the correct answer. If you are spending too long on a question, then mark it for review and move on, as it's important to get to the end of the test to ensure that the maximum number of marks are scored.

We also recommend booking the exam to give you an incentive. It is easy to procrastinate or worry too much that you are not fully prepared. This is a natural feeling, but having an end date in sight gives you focus and determination. We recommend that you print out the exam guide and work through these points to ensure that you have an understanding of each objective.

Additionally, two hours is a long time to be in the exam center. Ensure that you book the exam at a time of day that you are most alert, to give yourself the best chance of success.

Summary

In this chapter, we covered what to expect from the exam and how to actually register for the exam, as well as the benefits of being a GCP. Throughout this book, we will introduce you to the services that are needed for a successful outcome. This book's ultimate goal is to assist you in passing the exam; however, we encourage you to do more reading if you wish to deep dive into a particular topic or service that you encounter while reading this book.

In the next chapter, we will get started with the GCP.

Further reading

Read the following article for more information:

- **Google Cloud Certificate**: https://cloud.google.com/certification

Getting Started with Google Cloud Platform

2

In this chapter, we will introduce the concept of cloud computing to better understand what **Google Cloud Platform (GCP)** is. We will take a look at GCP resources and their hierarchy. After that, we will create our first account and set up a project. The billing options will be discussed. We will see how to create a billing account and associate it with the project. Finally, we will take a look at how to export the billing information. It is important to have this introduction before we start talking about GCP services. This will both help you to pass the exam and to perform the basic setup of GCP for real-life scenarios before you can even use the services.

We will cover the following topics in this chapter:

- Introducing the cloud
- Understanding GCP
- Understanding GCP infrastructure
- Basic GCP configuration

Exam tips: Having a good understanding of GCP resources is absolutely a must to pass the GCP Cloud Architect exam. Make sure that you go through this chapter with full attention. Read it multiple times if required and play with the creation of projects and billing accounts using your free tier account. Try exporting billing data both to files and BigQuery. You must remember individual **Identify and Access Management (IAM)** roles for billing. Make sure you understand the scope of the services.

Introducing the cloud

Before we jump into GCP, let's first learn what the cloud is:

It is true—*there is no cloud: it's just someone else's computer*. With the cloud, what we are actually doing is accessing resources and consuming services that are hosted on someone else's computer. If we want to be more precise, the cloud is a pool of computers.

Now, let's look at a more accurate and professional definition used by Google that comes from the United States National Institute of Standards and Technology (https://csrc. nist.gov/publications/detail/sp/800-145/final):

> *"Cloud computing is a model for enabling ubiquitous, convenient, on-demand network access to a shared pool of configurable computing resources (for example, networks, servers, storage, applications, and services) that can be rapidly provisioned and released with minimal management effort or service provider interaction. This cloud model is composed of five essential characteristics, three service models, and four deployment models."*

The five essential characteristics of the cloud are as follows:

- **On-demand self-service**: Services are provisioned automatically without manual provider intervention.
- **Broad network access**: Resources are available through the network.
- **Resource pooling**: Resources are pooled from a shared pool, giving the user a sense of location independence. For some of the resources, the location might be restricted.
- **Rapid elasticity**: Services can be elastically provisioned and deprovisioned with capacity being managed by the provider.
- **Measured service**: Resource usage is monitored and can be reported on.

The four deployment models are as follows:

- **Private cloud**: Used by specific organizations, but can be managed by third parties
- **Public cloud**: Used by the general public
- **Community cloud**: Used by specific communities
- **Hybrid cloud**: Composed of two or more different clouds

When we look at GCP, it fulfills all of the five characteristics and fits into the public cloud deployment model. In the next section, we will have a look at GCP itself.

Understanding GCP

Google has been developing its own tools to deliver services such as Gmail, YouTube, Google Drive, and Google+ for years. These tools have been converted into services that can be consumed by others. Consumers are given the amazing scalability that Google has to use for their own purposes. GCP lets you choose from computing, storage, networking, big data, and **machine learning** (**ML**) services to build your application on top of them. The number of services is growing constantly, and new announcements are made on an almost weekly basis. New services and features are released, first as alpha then as beta versions, and finally, are made available globally. The early releases are available even earlier for selected customers and partners. This allows the services to be tested by external parties even before the official release!

Google supports several service models, including the following:

- **Infrastructure as a Service (IaaS)**
- **Platform as a Service (PaaS)**
- **Container as a Service (CaaS)**
- **Function as a Service (FaaS)**
- **Managed services**

As we can see, the range of services in GCP is very broad. Looking at the following diagram, we will analyze this range of services offered by GCP:

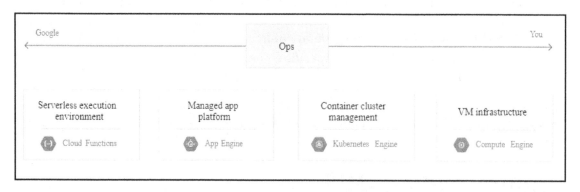

We can start from very simple IaaS, such as a traditional data center, and end up using functions as services and managed services. The choice of service depends on our requirements. To put it simply, if we need flexibility and control over our **virtual machines (VMs)**, we would simply use **Compute Engine**. This service allows us to provision VM instances or simply lift and shift machines from our existing environment. The trade-off, however, that is you are responsible for managing all of the layers above the VM container. That includes the operating system, any middleware, and any applications on top of it.

When we move to the left of the diagram, the burden of maintaining the infrastructure is taken away from us. With **Cloud Functions**, all we really care about is the coding of a function in a language supported by GCP. Once it's done and published, we access it through the HTTP protocol.

Finally, as we move to managed services, we start to simply consume services that bring us particular business value without having to worry about any underlying parts. They can be used in **Software as a Service (SaaS)** models and consumed through APIs. An example of this **Dataprep**, which is a data service that allows you to clean up and prepare your data for further analysis. Another example is the pretrained ML model, **Vision API**. Developers can consume this service using the RESTful API to analyze images without having to write any code, except for the call itself.

Hopefully, now you understand that GCP is much more than just a hosting service. It provides you with sets of tools, services, and resources that will help you to develop and deliver your applications. The choice of the services you will use depends entirely on the set of requirements you have. If that feels overwhelming, don't worry. This book is written to help you to go through GCP step by step.

In Chapter 3, *Google Cloud Platform Core Services*, you will get an overview of the most important GCP services. In the following chapters, we will dive into each of them in more detail to get you prepared for the exam.

GCP differentiators

Every cloud provider has something that differentiates it from others. Each provider has its own strategy for how to deliver value to customers, and the same is true for GCP. Let's have a look at what the key GCP features are that make it stand out from the crowd:

- **Developer focused**: GCP was built with a focus on developers. If you look at the history of GCP, it started in 2008 with a preview release of App Engine, which is a fully serverless platform, allowing developers to run their applications written in languages such as Python, Java, and Go. It provides out-of-the-box load balancing and autoscaling. Developers just need to choose the platform they want to develop on and they can start coding. Also, if you look at **Stackdriver** (a GCP monitoring tool) itself, it provides several tools that can be directly integrated with an application. This allows the developer to use them to monitor and debug their application. Google makes it very clear that GCP was created for developers to help them with their challenges. Having achieved this goal, they are now aiming at large enterprises.
- **The Google Network**: The Google Network is something that differentiates GCP from other cloud providers. Google claims that around 40% of the world's internet traffic is carried by the Google Network, making it the largest network on the globe. This allows the Google Network to provide responses with very low latency as close to the end user as possible.
- **Global scope**: GCP was developed with global availability in mind. You will see services such as load balancing available globally rather than regionally, unlike other providers. This allows the client to concentrate on development and embrace out-of-the-box high availability and elasticity.

- **ML**: GCP offers a great number of ML services for both data scientists and regular developers who have limited knowledge of the topic. ML allows pretrained models to be used, as well as offering AutoML services. The latter allows you to train ML models without knowing how they are actually created. The portfolio of these services is growing very quickly. The key goal of Google is to enable enterprises with ML to make faster and smarter decisions.
- **Pricing**: The VM instances are priced per second with a minimum run time of one minute. This allows you to run the machines for short tests and not have to pay for a full hour of use.
- **Service-level agreement (SLA)**: GCP services provide monthly uptime percentage **Service-level objectives (SLOs)**. If the SLO is not met, the customer is eligible for financial credits. Note that this percentage depends on the service and that alpha and beta features are not included with any SLA.
- **Security**: Google uses its 15 years of experience in running services such as Gmail in GCP. Your data is always encrypted with a choice of Google or customer-managed keys.
- **Carbon neutral**: This might not be the most important feature when it comes to functionality, but it is worth knowing. Google data centers are carbon neutral, meaning that 100% of the energy used to power them comes from renewable energy. This includes the GCP data centers.

GCP locations

As we have already mentioned, GCP has a global footprint that includes North America, South America, Europe, Asia, and Australia. The locations are further split into regions and zones.

It is your decision where your application should be located to provide low latency and high availability:

- **A region** is defined by Google as an independent geographic area that is divided into multiple zones. Locations within regions should have round-trip network latencies of under 1 ms in 95% of cases.
- **A zone** is a deployment area for GCP resources. Note that a zone does not correspond to a single data center; it can consist of multiple buildings. Even though a zone provides a certain amount of fault protections, a zone is considered a **single point of failure (SPOF)**. Therefore, you should consider placing your application across multiple zones to provide fault tolerance.
- **Network edge locations** are connections to GCP services located in a particular metropolitan area.

At the time of writing, GCP has the following:

- 20 regions
- 61 zones
- 134 network edge locations

These numbers are quickly growing and, while this book was being written, Google announced an additional two regions at the Google Cloud Next conference. For the most up-to-date information, refer to `https://cloud.google.com/about/locations`. The following map shows the current and future regions and zones across the globe:

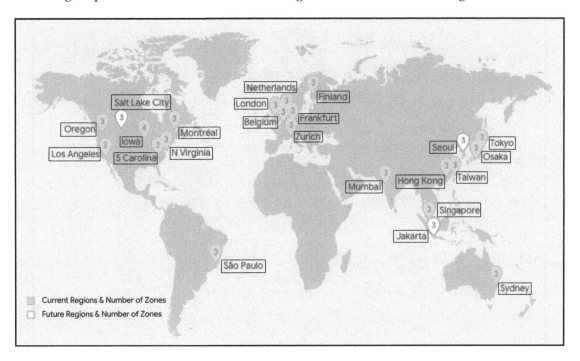

Source: https://cloud.google.com/about/locations/

The preceding map shows current regions in blue and planned regions in white. It should also be noted that not all services are available in each region. As an example, Cloud Functions, after being made available globally, was introduced only to a limited number of locations.

Resource manager

GCP consists of containers such as organizations, folders, and projects to hierarchically group your resources. This allows you to manage their configuration and access control. The resources can be managed programmatically using APIs. Google also provides tools such as Google Cloud Console and command-line utilities, which are wrappers around the API calls. Let's now have a look at the hierarchy presented in the following diagram and familiarize ourselves with each of the resources:

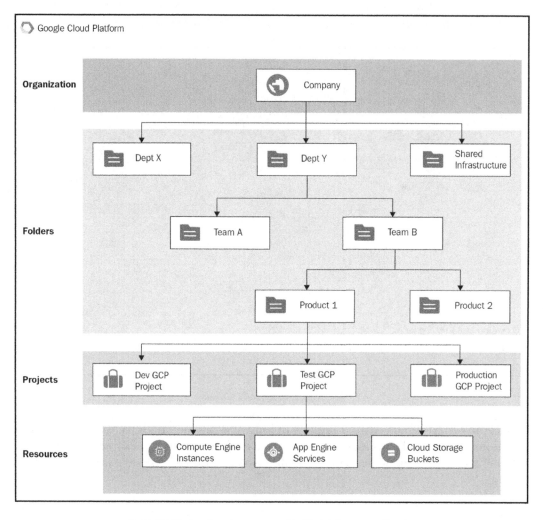

Source: https://cloud.google.com/resource-manager/docs/cloud-platform-resource-hierarchy
License: https://creativecommons.org/licenses/by/4.0/legalcode

The preceding diagram shows the resource manager hierarchy. Starting from the top, we have an **Organization** that can be mapped to a company. Next, we have **Folders** that can represent a company's departments. Next, we have **Projects**, which further divide the actual company projects or environments, such as development and production. Finally, under **Projects**, we have GCP **Resources**.

Organizations

At the top of the hierarchy, we have the organization. You need to note, however, that this is an optional resource and you can use GCP very well without it. The organization is only available to users of **G Suite** and **Cloud Identity**, which are products outside of GCP.

To provide some context, G Suite is a bundle of collaboration tools including Gmail, Google Drive, Hangouts, and Google Docs. Users use these tools, which are stored in the G Suite Domain.

Cloud Identity is an **Identity-as-a-Service (IDaaS)** offering. It similarly allows you to create a domain and to manage your users, applications, and device accounts from a single point. You can learn more about Cloud Identity in Chapter 13, *Security and Compliance*.

A single G Suite or Cloud Identity account can be associated only with a single organization. This implies that the organization is bound to one domain only. In both G Suite and Cloud Identity, there is a defined role of super administrators. When you create the organization, those users will have very high privileges in the organization and underlying resources. Make sure that this account is not used for day-to-day operations.

Instead, the super admin should assign the role of organization administrator to designated users. This role is further used to define IAM policies, resource hierarchy, and delegate permissions using IAM roles.

 With the creation of a new organization, all users from the domain get project creator and Billing Account Creator IAM roles. This allows them to create new projects in that organization. Again, we will have a closer look at this Chapter 13, *Security and Compliance.*

Folders

Folders are logical containers that can group projects or other folders. They can be used to assign IAM policies. Again, the use of folders is optional and is available only when an organization resource exists. The use case for using folders is to group projects that will use the same IAM policies.

Projects

Projects are the smallest logical containers that group resources. Every resource within GCP needs to belong to exactly one project. Each project is managed separately, and IAM roles can be assigned per project to control the access in a fine-grained way.

Projects have three identification attributes:

- **Project ID**: A globally unique immutable ID generated by Google
- **Project name**: A unique name provided by a user
- **Project number**: A globally unique number generated by Google

In most cases, you will use the project ID to identify your project. To manage resources within GCP, you will always need to identify which project they belong to by either project ID or project number. You can create multiple projects, but there is a quota that limits the number of projects per account. If you reach the quota, you will need to submit a request to extend it.

Resources scope

Now that we know the physical and logical separation of GCP resources, let's have a look at their scope. The resources can be either global, regional, or zonal. That indicates how accessible the resource is for other resources. For example, a global image can be used in any region to provision VMs. On the other hand, a VM that needs to belong to a particular subnet must reside in the same region for which the subnet was configured.

Even though the resources have a narrow scope, keep in mind that they still need to have unique names within the project, meaning you can't have two VMs with the same name within one project.

OK, let's have a look at the resources and their scope. You might not be fully familiar with the following resources, but don't worry: they will be explained in more detail in the coming chapters.

Global resources

Global resources are globally available within the same project and can be accessed from any zone. These include the following objects:

- **Addresses**: These are reserved external IP addresses and can be used by global load balancers.
- **Images**: These are either predefined or user customized. They can be used for provisioning VMs.
- **Snapshots**: Snapshots of a persistent disk allow the creation of new disks and VMs. Note that you can also expose a snapshot to a different project.
- **Instance templates**: These can be used for the creation of managed instance groups.
- **Virtual Private Cloud (VPC) networks**: These are virtual networks that you can connect your workloads to.
- **Firewall**: These are, in fact, defined per VPC, but are accessible globally.
- **Routes**: Routes allow you to direct your network traffic and are assigned to VPCs, but are also considered global.

Regional resources

Regional resources are accessible by other resources only within the same region. These include the following objects:

- **Addresses**: Static, external IP addresses can only be used by instances that are in the same region.
- **Subnets**: These are associated with VPC networks and allow the assignment of IP addresses to VMs.
- **Regional managed instance groups**: These allow you to scale groups of instances. The scope can be set to either regions or zones.
- **Regional persistent disks**: These provide replicated, persistent storage to VM instances. They can also be shared between projects for the creation of snapshots and images, but not disk attachments.

Zonal resources

Zonal resources are only accessible by other resources within the same zone. These include the following objects:

- **VM instances**: These reside in a particular zone.
- **Zonal persistent disks**: These provide persistent storage to VM instances. They can also be shared as disks between projects for the creation of snapshots and images, but not disk attachments.
- **Machine types**: These define the hardware configuration for your VM instances and are defined for any particular zone.
- **Zonal managed instance groups**: These allow you to autoscale groups of instances. The scope can be set to either regions or zones.

Now that we understand the theory, let's have a look at how we create a project.

Managing projects

To create a new project, follow these steps:

1. Log in to the GCP console at `https://console.cloud.google.com` and click on the drop-down arrow next to the name of the project you are currently logged into. A **Select a project** window will pop up. Click on **NEW PROJECT** in the top-right corner:

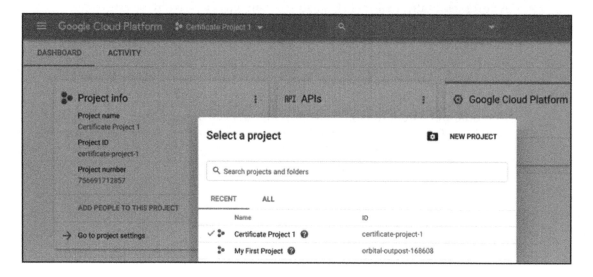

2. Fill in the name and choose the billing account. You can attach the project to an organization or a folder. Choose the default billing account. In the following steps, we will show you how to create a new billing account and associate it with the project we are now creating. Click on the **CREATE** button, as shown in the following screenshot:

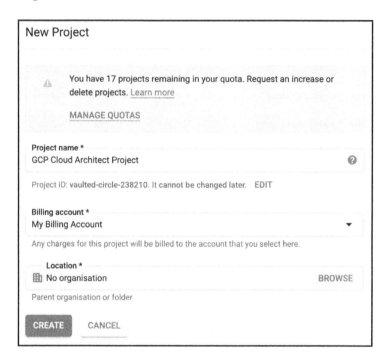

3. The new project has been created. You can now manage it from the GCP console:

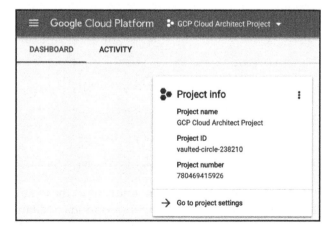

4. To start using the GCP services, click on the hamburger icon. A menu will pop up. You can access all GCP services from here, as shown in the following screenshot:

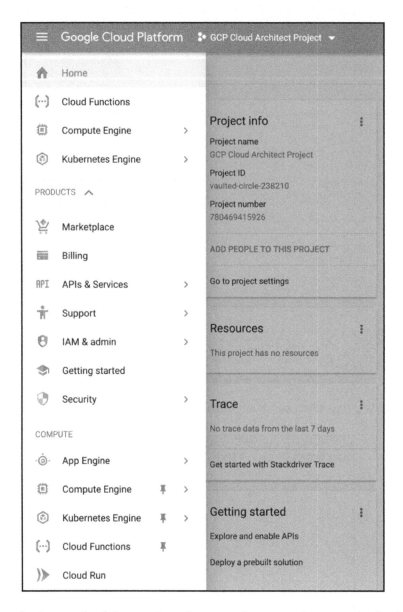

We will have a look at each of the services that are relevant to the exam in the following chapter of this book. Don't get scared by the number of options available.

Granting permissions

In the *Identity and Access Management (IAM)* section of `Chapter 13`, *Security and Compliance*, you will find more details about assigning permissions to your GCP resources.

For the sake of this introduction, we will now learn how to add a member and assign previously-defined roles to them. Roles are basically sets of permissions.

The following are the step-by-step instructions to grant permission:

1. To add a new member to your project, go to the **IAM** section of the **IAM & admin** pane.
2. Select the **MEMBERS** tab and click on **ADD**. Now, select a member and choose a role. Click on **Save** to confirm:

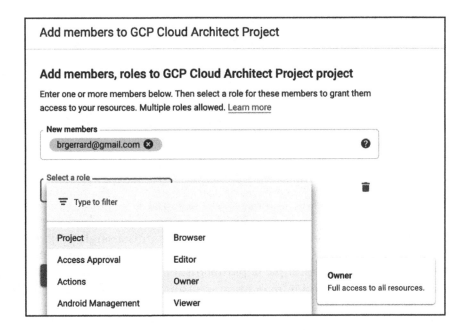

3. The user has been added and has the permissions as per the defined role:

`Brian Gerrard` has been sent an invitation to join the project as an **Owner**. The triangle with an exclamation mark will be displayed until the invitation is accepted.

Billing

Depending on your company structure, you might have different requirements as regards billing. With GCP, you have the possibility of creating a single or multiple billing accounts. As shown in the following diagram, the billing accounts can be associated with one or more projects. The actual payment details are created in the payment profiles that are attached to the billing account:

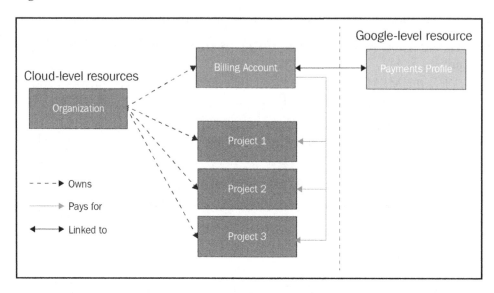

We can see here that the smallest entity that you are billed for is a single project. Therefore, you cannot split your bill inside the project. This affects how you can split the billing within your organization. Do you have multiple departments that need separate billing—for example, finance, engineering, and human resources—or do you manage it centrally?

In the first scenario, you might want multiple projects with multiple billing accounts, but in the latter scenario, you might need multiple projects with a single billing account.

Managing billing accounts

The first billing account will be created upon the creation of your GCP account. However, as we have just learned, you might need multiple billing accounts.

To create a new billing account, follow these steps:

1. Go to the GCP console and choose **Billing** from the left navigation pane.
2. You will be presented with the existing billing accounts. Click on **Create account**:

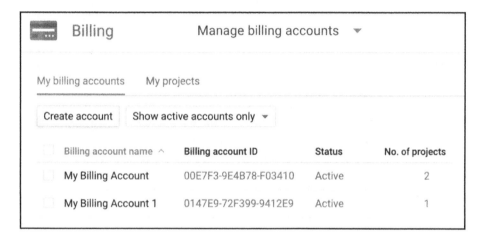

3. In the next window, name your billing account, as shown in the following screenshot:

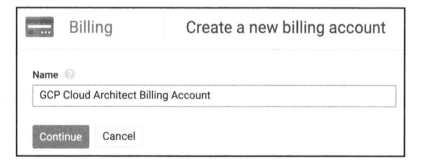

4. Choose the country and the currency will be presented for you. Click on the **Confirm** button:

5. Now, you can choose an existing payment profile or create a new one. Note that we do not see any existing profiles. This is because my existing payment profiles are set for Polish PLN, while the new billing profile is set for USD. Fill in the customer information and scroll down to **Payment method**:

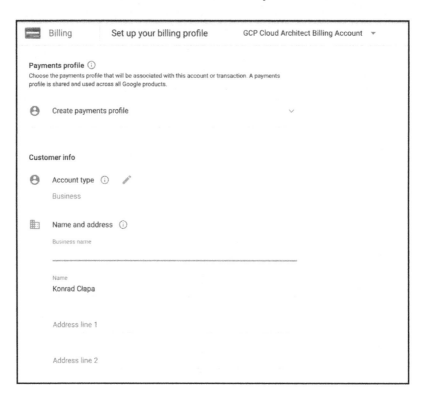

6. Fill in your payment details and click on the **Submit and enable billing** button:

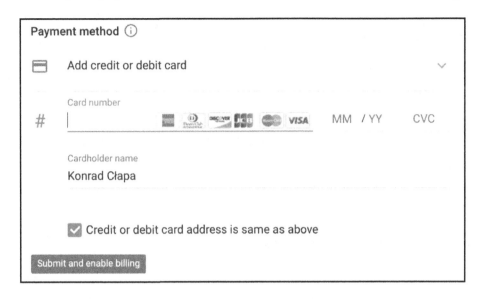

7. Now, your billing account has been created and you can manage it from the **Billing** window:

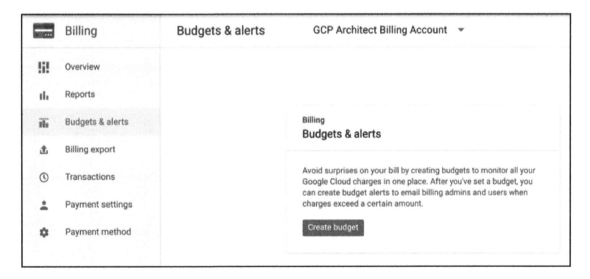

We can now assign a project to the newly created billing account.

Assigning a project to a billing account

As we have already said, you can assign multiple projects to one billing account. In the following screenshot, you can see that we now have three billing accounts and multiple projects assigned to them. Our newly created billing account has no project assigned to it, so let's therefore move our GCP Cloud Architect project to that billing account, as follows:

1. First, we need to click on **My billing accounts**, as this is where the project is attached:

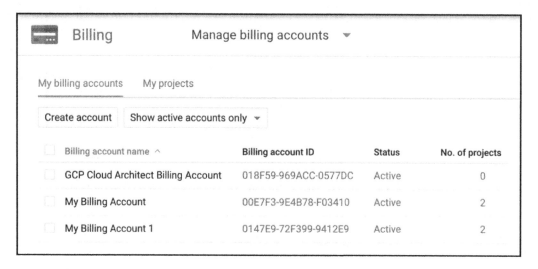

2. This brings us to the **Overview** page. Now, we click on the three-dots icon next to the **Project name** and choose **Change billing**:

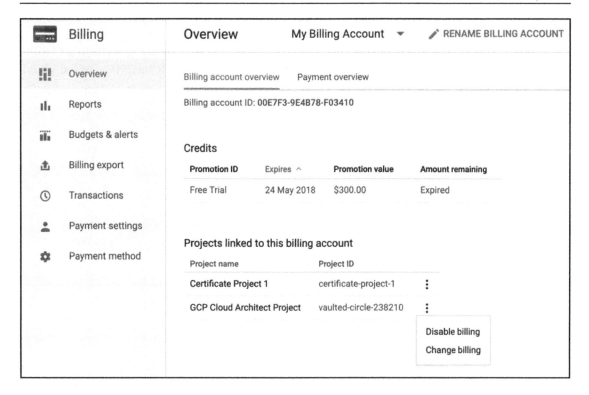

3. In the next window, we choose the billing account we want the project to be attached to and click on **SET ACCOUNT**:

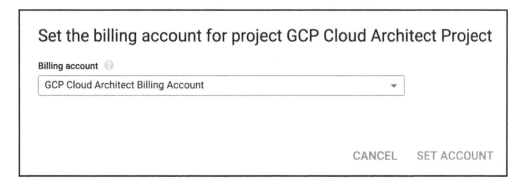

The project is now attached to its proper billing account.

Exporting billing

GCP allows you to export the billing information to a **BigQuery** dataset or a file in a **Cloud Storage** bucket. This can be useful for preparing reports and an analysis of the cost of your cloud consumption.

 We will learn about BigQuery and Google Storage in the big data and storage chapters of this book. To understand billing exports, you just need to know that BigQuery is a GCP data-warehouse service and Cloud Storage is an object-storage service.

To perform the export, follow these steps:

1. Go to **Billing** and choose **Billing export**. You will be presented with both options. Select the type of export, fill in the information about the dataset or bucket, and click on **SAVE**:

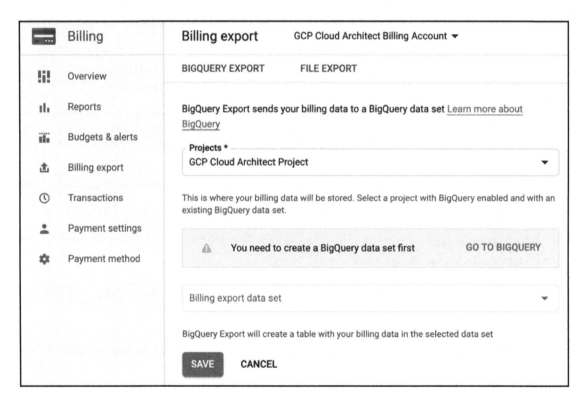

2. After the data is exported to BigQuery, you can perform queries on it. As an example, you can check which service has generated the most costs:

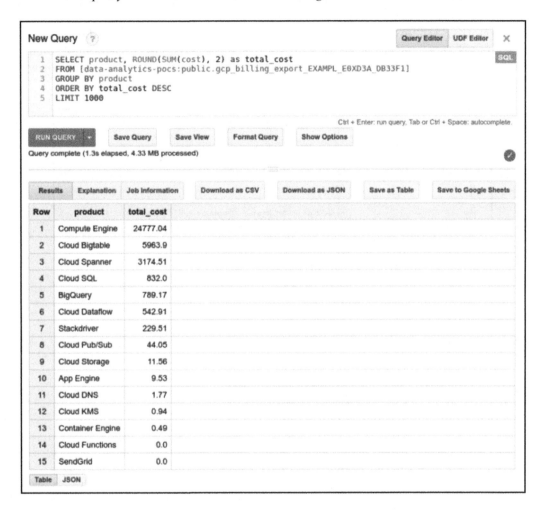

This information is very useful for creating all sorts of billing reports. On top of the reporting, we would also like to be informed upfront whether we are exceeding our budget. Let's have a look at how this can be done in the next section.

Budgets and alerts

Budgets and alerts can be set for each billing account or project. You can set up a specific threshold. Once the amount spent is higher than the defined threshold, billing administrators and billing account users will be notified. This will not stop the usage of any services, and charges will continue to apply for the running resources. By default, there are three alert thresholds: **50%**, **90%**, and **100%**. Both the number of thresholds and their values can be modified:

Exam tip: If the alerts and budgets are attached to a billing account and you have multiple projects attached to the alerts, this would count toward the total cost generated in all of those projects together. Remember the default thresholds for the alerts.

Billing account roles

You would surely want to have control over who has access to your billing and who can manage the payments. The following list shows the roles that can be used to control the billing:

- **Billing Account Creator**: This is used for the initial billing setup, including signing up for GCP with a credit card.
- **Billing Account Administrator**: This is the owner of a billing account. This role is allowed to link and unlink projects and manage other users' roles for the billing account. This role can manage payment instruments, billing exports, and view cost information.
- **Billing Account User**: In combination with the project creator role, the Billing Account User role is allowed to create new projects linked to the billing account on which the role is granted.
- **Billing Account Viewer**: This role allows access to view the billing information. It can be used by the finance team.
- **Project Billing Manager**: This role enables the attachment of the project to a billing account without rights to resources.

Exam tip: Make sure you understand the billing roles; especially, make sure you understand who can manage new billing accounts and who can only view the data.

Summary

In this chapter, we learned the basics of GCP. We talked about resources and their scopes and hierarchies. We set up our first account, created permissions for other users to access it, and configured billing. We also learned how to export billing information. Finally, we learned how to set up alert and budgets to control the cost of GCP usage.

In the next chapter, we will have a look at GCP core services, and, in the chapters that follow, we will continue to deep dive into each of them.

Further reading

For more information on GCP billing and security, read the following articles:

- **IAM**: https://cloud.google.com/billing/docs/how-to/billing-access
- **Visualizing billing**: https://cloud.google.com/billing/docs/how-to/visualize-data?hl=pl
- **SLA**: https://cloud.google.com/terms/sla/
- **Security in GCP**: https://cloud.google.com/security/

3
Google Cloud Platform Core Services

Before we do a deep dive into **Google Cloud Platform** (**GCP**) services, let's have a tour to introduce all of the most important core services. This will help us to understand the overall picture in a much better way. It is important to be familiar with all of the core services, not only for the sake of the exam—as it will also allow you to choose the best fit for your use case. Google divides the services into the following logical groups:

- Computing and hosting services
- Storage services
- Networking services
- Big data services
- **Machine learning** (**ML**) services
- Identity services

We will have a look at each of these in this chapter.

 Exam tip: As a cloud architect, you need to understand how most of the services work from a high level. This chapter should allow you to answer 20% of the questions in the exam. Note that Google releases new services very often; however, there is always a delay between a new service release and the exam being updated with new content.

Computing and hosting services

We are given a variety of options when it comes to computing in GCP. Depending on our requirements and flexibility, we can choose from one of the following four options, which we will be looking into in the upcoming sections:

- **Infrastructure as a Service (IaaS): Google Compute Engine (GCE)**
- **Container as a Service (CaaS): Google Kubernetes Engine (GKE)**
- **Platform as a Service (PaaS): Google App Engine (GAE)**
- **Function as a Service (FaaS): Cloud Functions**

Exam tip: Note that there are additional compute options that might not yet appear on the exam but have been announced in 2019. **GKE On-Prem** is a GKE service that can be installed on your local environment and managed from your Google Console. **Cloud Run** is an FaaS offering that allows you to define containers that will listen for HTTP requests. This allows you to use languages that are not supported by Cloud Functions. To read more about these services, check the *Further reading* links.

The choice we make can depend on several factors. For example, do we need full control over our infrastructure, or do we want a fully managed service? Starting with Compute Engine, we have control from a **virtual machine** (**VM**) container. This gives us the most flexibility but also implies that we need to take care of the stack above it. With Cloud Functions, we are very much constrained by the supported programming languages (JavaScript, Python, and Go). The advantage of Cloud Functions is that you don't need to worry about infrastructure and scaling. You only concentrate on developing your functions. If you need to use a language that is not supported by Cloud Functions, you will not be able to use it.

The computing options in GCP are as shown in the following diagram:

IaaS	CaaS	PaaS	FaaS	
Function	Function	Function	Function	User Managed
Application	Application	Application	Application	User Managed (scalable unit)
Runtime	Runtime	Runtime	Runtime	Service Provided managed
Container (optional)	Container (optional)	Container (optional)	Container (optional)	
OS	OS	OS	OS	
Virtualization	Virtualization	Virtualization	Virtualization	
Hardware	Hardware	Hardware	Hardware	

Let's have a look at each of the compute options and see what is managed by Google for us against the flexibility that we are given:

- **GCE**: GCE is an IaaS offering. It allows the most flexibility as it provides compute infrastructure to provision VM instances. This means that you have full control of the instance hardware and operating system. You can use standard GCP images or your own custom image. You can control where your VMs and storage are located in terms of regions and zones. You have granular control over the network, including firewalls and load balancing. With the use of an instance group, you can autoscale your control and your capacity as needed. Compute Engine is suitable in most cases, but might not be an optimal solution.
- **GKE**: GKE is a CaaS offering. It allows you to create Kubernetes clusters on demand, which takes away all of the heavy lifting of installing the clusters yourself. It leverages Compute Engine for hosting the cluster nodes, but the customer does not need to bother with the infrastructure and can concentrate on writing the code. The provision cluster can be automatically updated and scaled. The GCP software-defined networks are integrated with GKE and allow users to create network objects, such as load balancers, on demand when the application is deployed. Several services integrate with GKE, such as a container repository, which allows you to store and scan your container images.

- **GAE**: GAE is a PaaS offering. It allows you to concentrate on writing your code, while Google takes care of hosting, scaling, monitoring, and updates. It is targeted at developers who do not need to understand the complexity of the infrastructure. GAE offers two types of environments, as follows:
  - **Standard**: With sets of common languages supported
  - **Flexible**: Even more languages, with the possibility of creating a custom runtime

  With a flexible environment, you lose some out-of-the-box integration, but you gain more flexibility. GAE is tightly integrated with GCP services, including databases and storage. It allows versioning of your application for easy rollouts and rollbacks.

- **Cloud Functions**: Cloud Functions is an FaaS offering. It allows you to concentrate on writing your functions in one of the supported languages. It is ideal for executing simple tasks for data processing, mobile backends, and IoT. This service is completely serverless and all of the layers below it are managed by Google. The functions can be executed using an event trigger or HTTP endpoint.

Now that we have studied computing services, let's have a look at storage services in the next section.

Storage services

Storage is an essential part of cloud computing as it saves the data and state of your applications. GCP offers a wide variety of storage, from object storage to managed databases. The different storage services that we will be looking at are as follows:

- **Cloud Storage**: Cloud Storage is a fully managed, object-oriented storage service with infinite capacity. It allows the creation of buckets that store your data and allow access through APIs and other tools such as `gsutil`. It comes with different flavors to best suit your needs in terms of how often your data will be accessed and where it should be located. Keep in mind that the price differs for each tier. Making a conscious decision will allow you to cut costs. You can choose from the following options:
  - **Multi-regional**: The highest availability in multiple geolocations
  - **Regional**: High availability with fixed locations
  - **Nearline**: Low-cost, for data accessed less than once a month
  - **Coldline**: The lowest cost for backup and disaster recovery

With Cloud Storage, you do not need to worry about running out of capacity.

- **Filestore**: Cloud Filestore is a managed file storage service. It allows users to provision a **Network Attached Storage (NAS)** service that can be integrated with GCE and GKE. It comes with two performance tiers—**standard** and **premium**, which offer different **Input/Output operations Per Second (IOPS)** and throughputs.
- **Cloud SQL**: Cloud SQL is a fully-managed relational database service providing either a MySQL or PostgreSQL database. It offers data replication, backups, data exports, and monitoring. It is ideal when you need to move your current instances from on-premises and want to delegate the maintenance of the database to Google.
- **Cloud Datastore**: Cloud Datastore is a fully managed non-SQL database. It is ideal for applications that rely on highly available structured data at scale. The scaling and high availability is achieved by distributed architecture and is abstracted from the user. There is only one database available per project. Cloud Datastore offers SQL-like language to query your data.
- **Firestore:** Firestore is the next generation of Cloud Datastore with several enhanced features. It can run in Native or Datastore mode. The former is compatible with Cloud Datastore. Google has announced that all Datastore clients will be automatically moved to Firestore without any downtime or any user intervention. All new projects should be created in Firestore instead of Datastore.
- **Cloud Spanner**: Cloud Spanner is a fully managed, globally distributed, and highly consistent database service. It is a strong and consistent relational database with non-relational database scaling capabilities. Users can define a schema and leverage industry-standard **American National Standards Institute (ANSI)** 2011 SQL. It is very high-performing, with a 99.999% availability **Service Level Agreement (SLA)**, meaning there is almost no downtime applicable. Cloud Spanners are aimed at use cases such as financial trading, insurance, global call centers, telecoms, gaming, and e-commerce. Global consistency makes it ideal for globally accessible applications.

- **Bigtable**: Bigtable is a fully managed, massive scale, non-SQL database with sub-10 ms latency. It is used by Google to deliver services such as Gmail and Google Maps. It is ideal for fintech, IoT, and ML storage use cases. It integrates easily with big data product families such as **Dataproc** and **Dataflow**. It is based on open source Apache HBase, enabling the use of its API. The cost of Bigtable is much higher than Datastore, so the database should be chosen with great care.
- **Custom databases**: You can also choose to use Compute Engine to install a database of your choice, such as MongoDB; however, that would be an unmanaged service.

With this, we conclude our look at the storage services; let's have a look at the networking services in the next section.

Networking services

GCP networking is based on **Software-Defined Networks** (**SDNs**), which allows users to deliver all networking services programmatically. All of the services are fully managed, leaving users with the task of configuring them according to their requirements. The networking services that we will be looking at are as follows:

- **Virtual Private Cloud (VPC)**: The VPC is the foundation of GCP networking. Each GCP project has a default VPC network created, but the user can also create new networks. You can think of it as a cloud version of a physical network. A VPC can contain one or more regional subnets. A VPC creates a global logical boundary that allows communication between VMs within the same VPC. To allow communication between VPCs, traffic needs to traverse the internet or via VPC peering.
- **Load balancer**: Load balancer allows the distribution of traffic between your workloads. It is available for GCE, GAE, and GKE. For GCE, you can choose from load balancers with global or regional scopes. The choice will also depend on the network type. The following load balancers are available to choose from:
  - HTTP(S) load balancer
  - SSL proxy load balancer
  - TCP proxy load balancer
  - Network load balancer
  - Internal TCP/UDP load balancer

- **Virtual Private Network (VPN)**: VPNs allow a connection between your on-premises network and GCP VPC through an IPsec tunnel over the internet. Only site-to-site VPNs are supported. To establish a VPN connection, there needs to be two gateways on each side of the tunnel. The traffic in transit is encrypted. Both static and dynamic routing are supported, with the former requiring a cloud router. Using a VPN should be the first method of connecting your environment to GCP as it entails the lowest cost. If there are low-latency and high-bandwidth requirements, then Cloud Interconnect should be considered.
- **Cloud Interconnect**: If there is a need for low latency and a highly available connection, then interconnect should be considered. In this case, the traffic does not traverse the internet. There are two interconnect options, which are as follows:
  - **Dedicated Interconnect**: 10 Gbps piped directly to a Google datacenter
  - **Partner Interconnect**: 50 Mbps-10 Gbps piped through a Google partner

Multiple pipelines can be used to multiply the bandwidth.

- **Cloud Router**: Cloud Router is a service that allows for dynamic routing exchange between Compute Engine, VPNs, and external networks. It eliminates the need for the creation of static routes.
- **Cloud DNS**: Cloud DNS is a managed DNS service with a 100% SLA. It translates domains into IP addresses. Millions of zones and records can be managed. Cloud DNS can also host private zones accessible only from your GCP network. It can be integrated on-premises, where your local DNS is authorized and Cloud DNS is responsible for caching.
- **Cloud Content Delivery Network (CDN)**: Cloud CDN is a service that allows the caching of HTTP(S) load balanced content, including Cloud Storage bucket objects. Caching reduces content delivery time and cost. It can also protect you from a **Distributed Denial-of-Service (DDoS)** attack. Data is cached on Google's globally distributed edge points. On the first request, when content is not cached, data is retrieved from a backend service. The next call data will be served directly from the cache until the expiration time is reached.
- **Cloud NAT**: Cloud NAT is a regional service that allows VMs without external IPs to communicate with the internet. It is a fully managed service with built-in autoscalability. It works with both GCE and GKE. It is a better alternative for NAT instances that need to be managed by users.

- **Firewall:** GCP Firewall is a service that allows for micro-segmentation. Firewall rules are created per VPC and can be based on IPs, IP ranges, tags, and service accounts. Several firewall rules are created by default but can be modified.
- **Identity Aware Proxy (IAP)**: IAP is a service that replaces the VPN when a user is working from an untrusted network. It controls access to your application based on user identity, device status, and IP address. It is part of Google's BeyondCorp security model.
- **Cloud Armor**: Cloud Armor is a service that allows protection against infrastructure DDoS attacks using Google's global infrastructure and security systems. It integrates with global HTTP(S) load balancers and blocks traffic based on IP addresses or ranges. Preview mode allows users to analyze the attack pattern without cutting off regular users.

Phew! We have covered a lot about networking services. Now, let's look at big data services in the following section.

Big data services

Big data services enable the user to process large amounts of data to provide answers to complex problems. GCP offers many services that tightly integrate to create an **End-to-End (E2E)** data analysis pipeline. These services are as follows:

- **BigQuery**: BigQuery is a highly scalable and fully managed cloud data warehouse. It allows users to perform analytics operations with built-in ML. BigQuery is completely serverless and can host petabytes of data. The underlying infrastructure scales seamlessly and allows parallel data processing. The data can be stored in BigQuery Storage, Cloud Storage, Bigtable, Sheets, or Google Drive. The user defines datasets containing tables. BigQuery uses familiar ANSI-compliant SQL for queries and provides ODBC and JDBC drivers. Users can choose from two types of payment models—one is flexible and involves paying for storage and queries, and the other involves a flat rate with stable monthly costs. It is ideal for use cases such as predictive analysis, IoT, and log analysis, and integrates with GCP's big data product family.
- **Pub/Sub**: This is a fully managed asynchronous messaging service that allows you to loosely couple your application components. It is serverless with global availability. Your application can publish messages to a topic or subscribe to it to pull messages. Pub/Sub can also push messages to **Webhooks**.

- **Dataproc:** Dataproc is a fully managed **Apache Spark** and **Hadoop** cluster. It allows users to create clusters on demand and use them only when data processing is needed. It is billed per second. It allows users to move already existing, on-premises clusters to the cloud without refactoring the code. The use of pre-emptible instances can further lower the cost.
- **Dataflow:** Cloud Dataflow is a fully-managed service for processing data in streams and batches. It is based on open source Apache Beam, is completely serverless, and offers almost limitless capacity. It will manage resources and job balancing for the user. It can be used for use cases such as online fraud analytics, IoT, healthcare, and logistics.
- **Dataprep:** This is a tool that can be used to perform data visualization and exploring without any coding skills being required. Data can be interactively prepared for further analysis.
- **Datalab:** Datalab is a built-in tool on **Jupyter** (formerly **IPython**) that allows users to explore, analyze, and transform data. It also allows users to build ML data models and leverages Compute Engine.
- **Data Studio**: This a tool that allows you to consume data from sources and visualize it in the form of reports and dashboards.
- **Cloud Composer**: This is a fully managed service based on open source **Apache Airflow**. It allows you to create and orchestrate big data pipelines.

Finally, let's study the ML services in the next section.

ML services

One of the strongest points of Google is its long-term experience with ML. GCP offers several services around ML. You can choose between a pre-trained model or training the model yourself. The various services included under ML are as follows:

- **Cloud ML Engine**: ML Engine is a managed service that allows you to train and host your ML models in GCP. It leverages the **TensorFlow** application for the training process. The underlying infrastructure is managed by Google, while users can choose from different hardware options. The trained model can be accessed through APIs to perform predictions.
- **Pretrained APIs**: ML APIs are services that allow you to leverage several pre-trained models, enabling you to analyze a video. Currently, the following APIs are available:
  - Google Cloud Video Intelligence
  - Google Cloud Speech

- Google Cloud Vision
- Google Cloud Natural Language
- Google Cloud Translation

These models can be used without any background knowledge of how they work. As an example, we can analyze text for sentiment analysis.

- **AutoML**: AutoML is a service that can be used by developers to train models without having extensive knowledge of data science. As an example, by providing labeled samples to AutoML, it can be trained to recognize objects that are not recognizable by Vision API. The following are the labeled samples of AutoML:
  - AutoML Translation
  - AutoML Natural Language and Vision
- **Dialogflow**: This is a service that allows you to build conversation applications that can interact with human beings. The interface can interact with many compatible platforms, such as Slack or Google Assistant. It can also integrate with **Firebase** functions to integrate with third-party platforms using common APIs.

Identity services

Identity and Access Management (IAM) is one of the

most important aspects of any cloud. It allows you to control who has access to the cloud but can also provide identity services to your applications. In short, this is achieved by a combination of roles and permissions. The roles are assigned to either users or groups. Let's have a look at the options we have in GCP:

- **IAM**: IAM allows the GCP admin to control authorization to GCP services. Administrators can create roles with granular permissions. Roles can then be assigned to users, or preferably, a group of users.
- **Cloud Identity**: Cloud Identity is an
- **Identity as a Service (IDaaS)** offering. It sits outside of GCP but can be easily integrated with GCP. It allows you to create organizations, groups, and users, and manage them centrally. If you already have an existing user catalog, you can synchronize it with Cloud Identity.

Summary

In this chapter, we learned about GCP services and gathered them in specific groups: computing and hosting, storage, networking, big data, ML, and identity services. This allowed us to get a broad overview of what GCP offers us. That should give you a little bit more confidence in what GCP actually is, but you probably also understand that there is quite some work ahead of us. But don't worry, we'll get there together!

Once you finished going through this chapter, let's switch to Chapter 4, *Working with Google Compute Engine*, where we will finally get some hands-on experience with deploying our first services to GCP. This is getting exciting!

Further reading

- **GCP core services and products:** https://cloud.google.com/products/.
- **Cloud Run:** https://cloud.google.com/run/
- **GKE On-Prem:** https://cloud.google.com/gke-on-prem/

2
Section 2: Managing, Designing, and Planning a Cloud Solution Architecture

In this section, we will focus on the various GCP services in more detail. By examining these services, we will demonstrate how to manage, design, and plan solutions based on GCP.

This section contains the following chapters:

Working with Google Compute Engine

4

Google Compute Engine (GCE) is one of the fundamental services inside **Google Cloud Platform (GCP)**. While the public cloud continues to move on from traditional **Virtual Machines (VMs)**, there are still use cases for these machines and, just like other vendors, GCE allows us to create and run VMs on our GCP platform. Google refers to a VM in GCP as a Compute Engine instance. Compute Engine makes it easy to find the VM to match our requirements whether it is a small-sized VM or a large data processing VM.

GCE is a purely **Infrastructure as a Service (IaaS)** solution, therefore, you will need to manage and scale your VM as necessary, but this makes it an ideal solution for **lift and shift** migration from on-premises into the public cloud. You can use your own customized OS as you do within your own datacenter or you can use some predefined Google, Windows, or Linux images. Throughout the GCE section of this chapter, we will look at how we can deploy a simple GCE instance, the options available to us when we deploy, and more complex solutions that enable us to scale out at ease.

GCE provides VMs and is GCP's IaaS offering. In this chapter, we will take a deeper look into Compute Engine. Specifically, we will cover the following topics:

- Deploying our first GCE instance
- Deployment options
- Instance templates and instance groups
- Autoscaling
- Autohealing
- Quotas and limits
- IAM roles
- Pricing

Code in Action

Check out the following video to see the Code in Action:
`http://bit.ly/31i6wpz`

Deploying our first GCE instance

Let's begin this chapter with the basics of provisioning a new VM. We can do this from the GCP console. In this section, we will look at the very basics needed to deploy a VM. We will look at the deployment options in more detail in the next section of this chapter:

1. Browse to the navigation menu and go to **Compute Engine | VM instances**, as shown in the following screenshot:

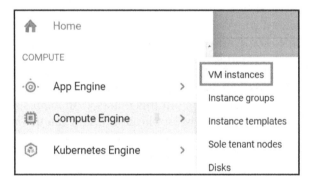

2. Click **Create**, as shown in the following screenshot:

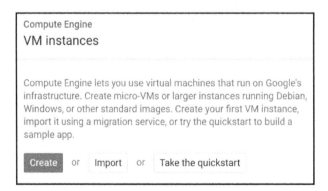

3. Give your VM a name in this example, we called it `cloudarchitect`. We can select a **Region** and a **Zone** along with the size of the machine. Some zones are more expensive than others and you will notice that, depending on the zone and machine type, we can see the estimation of the cost of our instance change:

4. If we click on the drop-down menu under **Machine type**, we can select several predefined sizes:

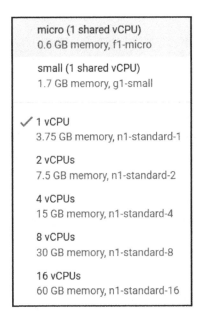

5. However, if this does not meet our requirements, we can also click the **Customize** button and select the exact resources we need. We should think of 1 vCPU as 1 hyper-threaded core:

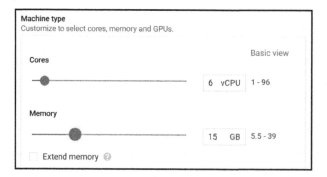

6. The boot disk selection allows us to select the image we require. For now, let's select **Windows Server 2016 Datacenter**, as shown in the following screenshot:

7. Leave everything else as default; we will look at other settings in more detail shortly in this section. Click **Create** to begin the deployment.
8. Now that we have a VM, we need to connect to it. Within the **Compute Instance** section, we will now see our new VM. Simply click on the arrow beside **RDP** and select **Set Windows Password**. Once we set our password, click on the **RDP** button:

 RDP (short for **Remote Desktop Protocol**) allows us to connect to another Windows server over a network connection.

9. Click **SET**, as shown in the following screenshot:

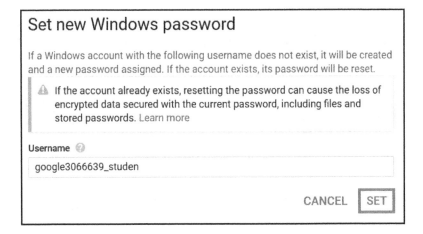

One feature to note is, following the aforementioned process to create a VM from the GUI, underneath the **Create** button, you will find the **Equivalent REST or command line** options, as shown in the following screenshot:

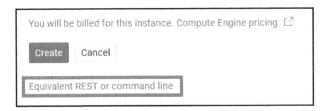

2. Click on the **command line** option to open up the exact CLI you would need to create this using `gcloud` commands:

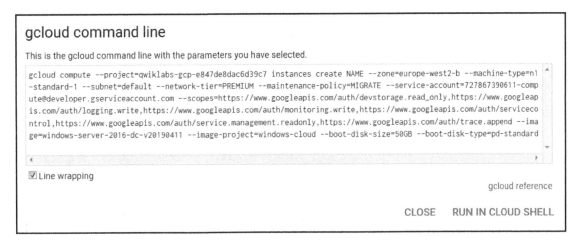

You can copy the text or click **RUN IN CLOUD SHELL**, which will activate your cloud shell instance and execute the request.

Deployment options

You will notice that there are some options we left as default. Let's look at these in a bit more detail to make sure we understand all of the settings required to create a Compute Engine instance.

Region

Regions are geographical locations that are made up of one or more zones. We need to select a region where we can run our VM. The requirements may be related to where most traffic is expected. As we have mentioned, some regions are more expensive than others:

asia-east1 (Taiwan)
asia-east2 (Hong Kong)
asia-northeast1 (Tokyo)
asia-northeast2 (Osaka)
asia-south1 (Mumbai)
asia-southeast1 (Singapore)
australia-southeast1 (Sydney)
europe-north1 (Finland)
europe-west1 (Belgium)
europe-west2 (London)
europe-west3 (Frankfurt)
europe-west4 (Netherlands)
europe-west6 (Zürich)
northamerica-northeast1 (Montréal)
southamerica-east1 (São Paulo)
us-central1 (Iowa)
us-east1 (South Carolina)
us-east4 (Northern Virginia)
us-west1 (Oregon)
us-west2 (Los Angeles)

Make sure the selected region makes sense based on your requirements.

Zone

Many regions will have multiple zones to select from. Make sure you select a zone that suits your requirements. Consider network latency and select a region or zone close to your point of service:

All zones in a region are connected through fast networking—usually below 5 ms for a roundtrip between each zone.

Boot disk

We have already seen that many predefined images can be selected. The default storage for these images is a standard persistent disk (block storage), but this can be changed to SSD if more IOPS is required. The default size will change depending on the OS image selected, but this can be adjusted:

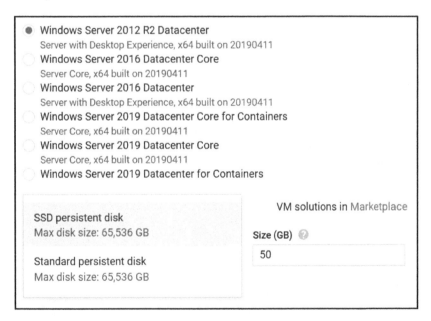

Changes from the default will again impact the cost of your instance.

Application images

Application images can be used if you require Microsoft SQL Server pre-installed on your Windows Server:

Boot disk

Select an image or snapshot to create a boot disk; or attach an existing disk

OS images   **Application images**   Custom images   Snapshots   Existing disks

○ SQL Server 2012 Enterprise on Windows Server 2012 R2 Datacenter
    x64 built on 20190411
○ SQL Server 2012 Standard on Windows Server 2012 R2 Datacenter
    x64 built on 20190411
● SQL Server 2012 Web on Windows Server 2012 R2 Datacenter
    x64 built on 20190411

Custom images are available per project where an image has already been created from a boot disk.

Snapshots

It is possible to snapshot a persistent disk and use this as part of a new instance creation even if they are still attached to a running instance. It is recommended to have a snapshot schedule to reduce data loss. Snapshots are also global resources, which means it would be accessible by any resource in the same project.

To create a snapshot from the console, we should browse to the hamburger menu and go to **Compute Engine** | **Snapshots**. Then, we must give our snapshot a name and select the source disk we wish to work with. Lastly, we can select the location we wish to store the snapshot, as shown in the following screenshot:

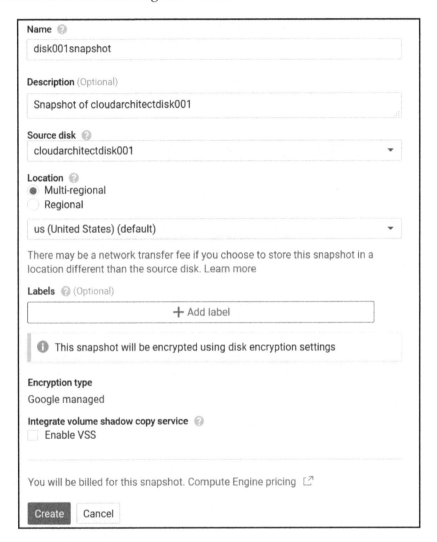

The following diagram shows how the process of multiple snapshots works. The first snapshot will be a full snapshot of all the data on the disk and subsequent snapshots will be incremental:

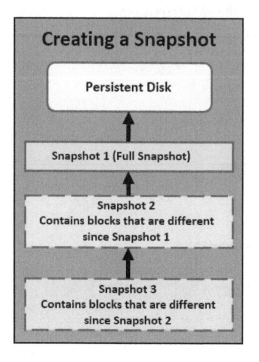

 Snapshots are incremental, therefore, will contain blocks that are different from the previous snapshot. If you, therefore, perform regular snapshots, the cost is less than performing a regular full image of the disk. Each snapshot is stored across multiple locations within GCP for redundancy. Snapshots can be stored across projects with the correct permissions.

Existing disks

Existing disks can also be attached to a new instance. To create a new disk, we can browse to the hamburger menu and go to **Compute Engine** | **Disk**. The following screenshot shows us creating a new blank disk:

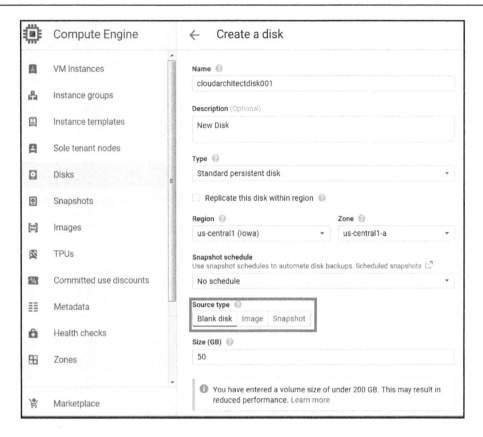

Once successfully created, we can use this new disk when we deploy a new Compute Engine instance. The following screenshot shows how this would look when we click on the **Existing disks** tab. We can see all of the disks available to us:

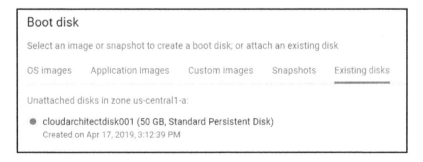

We can also see, from the preceding screenshot, that we can use a snapshot of a disk as our boot disk. We discussed how to take snapshots earlier in this chapter.

Management | Labels

To group related resources, it can be beneficial to label your VM instances. This can help with organizing and filtering for billing and reporting. Labels work with key-value pairs and can be used, for example, to differentiate between projects, environments, and much more:

The preceding screenshot is an example of this, where we are tagging this instance as the production environment.

Management | Deletion protection

Enable this to prevent your GCE instance from accidental deletion. Checking this box will set the `deletionProtection` property on the instance resource. Usually, only critical VM instances that need to stay running indefinitely would have this option checked. Even after this is checked, instances can still be reset, stopped, or even removed after a project is terminated. Only users who have `compute.instance.create` permissions can modify this flag to allow a protected VM to be deleted.

Management | Metadata

Adding metadata to your GCE instance allows for future queries to pull information about the instance. Metadata is stored on a metadata server and can be queried from the Compute Engine API or from the instance itself. We can pull information such as hostname, instance ID, or any custom metadata we apply. We can also provide configuration information to applications using metadata, which will negate the need to store this data in the application itself.

We also use metadata to reference the startup script to be executed during our instance deployment. Let's assume we host our startup script called `startup.sh` on a Cloud Storage bucket called `deployments`. To ensure it is executed, we need to add the path to our bucket and the startup script:

The preceding screenshot shows how this would look in the console.

Management | Startup scripts

When populating the variables for a GCE deployment, we can also set a startup script if we wish. This is a script that will run when your instance boots up or restarts. Common examples would be to install specific software or ensure services are started. These scripts are specified through the same metadata server we previously mentioned and use the startup script metadata keys. Again, these scripts can be added via gcloud commands as well as at the console. Let's look at the example commands from the CLI. This is installing `apache2` and populating the main page:

```
gcloud compute instances create cloudarchitect --tags http-server \
--metadata startup-script='#! /bin/bash
# Installs apache and a custom homepage
sudo su -
apt-get update
apt-get install -y apache2
cat <<EOF > /var/www/html/index.html
<html><body><h1>Hello World</h1>
<p>This page was created from a simple start up script!</p>
</body></html>
EOF'
```

It is also possible to specify a script that resides on Google Cloud Storage. Again, from the gcloud CLI, we can specify our bucket location. In this example, our bucket is called `cloudarchitectbucket`:

```
gcloud compute instances create example-instance --scopes storage-ro \
    --metadata startup-script-
url=gs://cloudarchitectbucket/startupscript.sh
```

Exam tip
If we want to specify a shutdown script, then we will browse to the metadata section and add `shutdown-script` as the key and add the contents of the script as the value.

Management | Preemptibilty

Preemptibility brings the cost of an instance down but will generally only last a maximum of 24 hours before it is terminated. Certain actions such as stopping and starting an instance will reset this counter. It might sound strange to deploy VMs that have such a limited lifecycle, but if we have fault tolerance at an application level, then utilizing preemptible instances can result in significant cost savings. Let's take the example of batch processing jobs.

These could run on preemptible instances and if some of the instances are terminated, then the process will slow down but not stop entirely. This allows for batch processing to occur without any additional workload on existing instances. We should note, however, that due to the nature of preemptible instances, there is no GCP SLA applied and can be removed by the provider with only 30 seconds notification.

To set up a preemptible instance, simply set to **On** under the **Availability policy** while creating a new instance:

Management | Availability policy

Google will perform maintenance on its infrastructure, which may require your VM instances to be moved to another host. GCE will live migrate your instance if the instance's availability policy was set to use this feature. As a result, your applications will not suffer from any downtime but may witness some performance degradation. Live migration is the default setting for an instance.

Alternatively, if you have built-in high availability at the application level, then you may wish to change this setting to terminate and restart on another host. This setting means that your instance would be shut down cleanly and restarted on a fresh host. Google will report any maintenance issues and how it affects your instance depending on the setting selected.

Management | Automatic restart

If underlying hardware causes your instance to crash, then GCE offers a setting to automatically restart the instance by setting the `automaticRestart` field to `true`. Google will report any automatic restart:

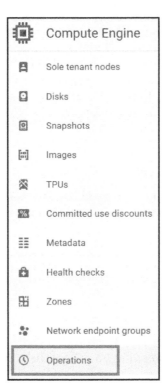

These reports can be found under **Operations** from the **Compute Engine** menu, as shown in the preceding screenshot:

Operations					
Operations are REST requests that affect resources at the global, region, or zone level Learn more					
Operation summary	Target	User		Time (GMT)	Status
✓ compute.projects.setCommonInstanceMetadata	qwiklabs-gcp-37865da19b691f65	qwiklabs-gcp-37865da19b691f65@qwiklabs-gcp-37865da19b691f65.iam.gserviceaccount.com		Start: Jun 7, 2019, 8:19:22 PM End: Jun 7, 2019, 8:19:28 PM	Done
✓ compute.projects.setCommonInstanceMetadata	qwiklabs-gcp-37865da19b691f65	qwiklabs-gcp-37865da19b691f65@qwiklabs-gcp-37865da19b691f65.iam.gserviceaccount.com		Start: Jun 7, 2019, 8:19:18 PM End: Jun 7, 2019, 8:19:22 PM	Done

The preceding screenshot shows what these alerts would look like from the **Operations** screen.

Security | Shielded VM

GCP offers the ability to harden your VM instance with security controls, which will defend against rootkits, bootkits, and kernel-level malware. GCP uses a **virtual Trusted Platform Module (vTPM)** to provide a virtual root-of-trust to verify the identity of the VM and ensure they are part of a specified project or region. vTPM generates and stores encryption keys on the guest OS level. It should be noted that this does not add any extra cost to your VM deployment.

Disks | Deletion rule

This option allows us to keep the boot disk on instance termination. By default, this is not enabled and can cause unexpected billing if there is an assumption the boot disk has been deleted:

Management	Security	Disks	Networking	Sole Tenancy

Boot disk
Deletion rule
☑ Delete boot disk when instance is deleted

If there are specific use cases for keeping your boot disk, then make sure the checkbox is removed.

Sole tenancy | Node affinity labels

Sole tenancy was introduced to GCE in 2018 and is physical Compute Engine server designed for your dedicated use. In other words, the underlying host hardware and hypervisor handles only your GCE instances. A use case for this setup could be security requirements. Many companies have compliance or regulations that require a physical separation of their compute resources.

The following diagram shows this split. We can see that, on the left-hand side, different customers share the same hardware but, on the right-hand side, we have dedicated hardware for this specific customer and only their VMs reside on it:

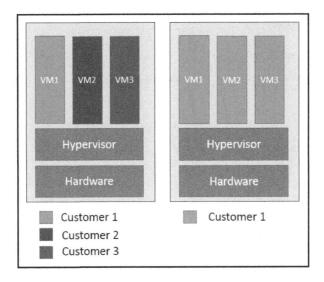

VMs will still have the same live migration functionality and shared instances but there are cost implications. Not all regions and zones support sole tenancy.

When we create a VM, we have the option to add a label that would define where the new instance would be deployed. To use sole tenancy, we first have to create a sole tenant node from the console under **Compute Engine | Sole tenant nodes**. Note, we could also use gcloud commands for this. Click on **Create a node template**, and select **Region** and **Node type**. The following screenshot shows the different options available. We can also utilize labels to give a key/pair value, for example, `Environment:HighSecureArea`:

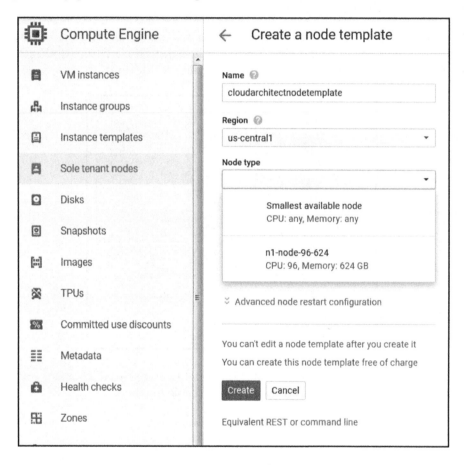

Once created, on the same menu page, we can now create a sole tenant node. Again, we can give a name, select a region and a template, and define the number of nodes we need. Note that the region needs to match the region you created the template in:

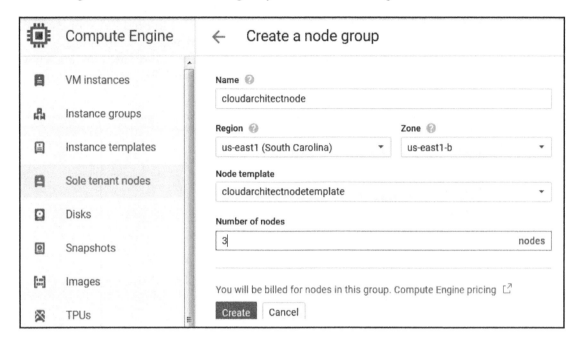

We can now create a VM from within the sole tenancy. Some more advanced settings can be made, but we will look at these in more depth in the coming chapters:

- For firewalls, refer to Chapter 11, *Analyzing Big Data Options*.
- For security and encryption settings, refer to Chapter 13, *Security and Compliance*.

GPUs and TPUs

Along with standard vCPUs, Compute Engine also offers **Graphics Processing Units (GPUs)**. These can be used on graphics-intensive workloads such as 3D rendering or virtual applications. We should note here that GPUs can only be attached to predefined or custom machine types and are only available in certain zones. They are also still eligible for sustained use discounts that we receive from standard vCPUs. When we are creating a new instance, we can add a GPU by expanding the **CPU platform and GPU** section, as shown in the following screenshot:

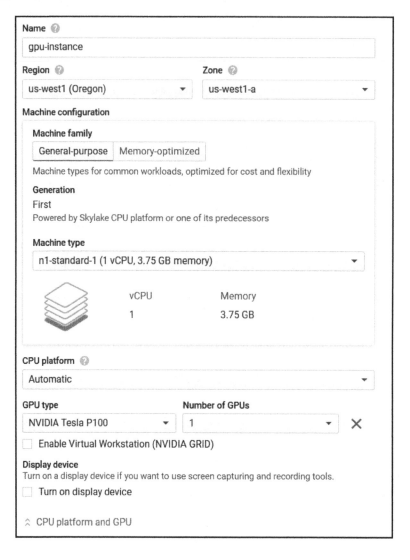

Tensor Processing Units (TPUs) are custom designed using Google's experience in **machine learning (ML)** and can be used to maximize performance and flexibility in building TensorFlow compute clusters and other ML workloads. We can access TPUs from the hamburger menu and go to **Compute Engine | TPUs**. Once we enable the API, we can create our first TPU node. From the following screenshot, you can see that we can assign **Zone**, **TPU type**, **TPU software version**, **Network**, and **IP address range**. The TPU should be in the same zone as the Compute Engine instance you wish to connect from:

As shown, we can also enable preemptibility on TPU nodes.

Instance templates and instance groups

Even when we think of on-premises architecture, many of the key requirements were around high availability and scalability. Of course, this does not change when we architect in the public cloud, but these do become a lot easier and cheaper to do!

We have previously seen how we can deploy single GCE instances, but not many organizations will move to the public cloud to host only one VM. Business needs depend on the ability to react to demand and react to any instance failures.

Each of the VM instances deployed into the instance group comes from the same instance template, which defines the machine type, boot disk images, labels, and other instance properties that we spoke about previously in this chapter. Instance templates are global resources, which means they are not tied to a specific zone or region. Zonal resources in the template itself will restrict the template to the zone where that resource resides. For example, the template may include a disk that is tied to a specific zone.

It's important to understand that there are two types of instance groups:

- **Managed instance groups**: This type of instance group allows your workloads to be scalable and highly available via automated services in the groups such as autoscaling or autohealing. Google recommends using this type of group unless it is unavoidable due to pre-existing configurations or a requirement to group dissimilar instances.
- **Unmanaged instance groups**: This type of instance group allows for load balancing across a fleet of VMs that are not identical. These are self-managed, and autoscaling or autohealing are not supported.

Let's look at an example of creating a new instance template and group:

1. First, we need to browse to **Compute Engine | Instance templates**:

2. We can name and update settings as if we were creating a new VM instance. In previous examples, we set a startup script from gcloud commands but, in this example, let's set it up from the console. We add this under the **Metadata** options and use the `startup-script-url` key and `gs://cloudarchitect/startup.sh` as our value:

3. Click on **Instance groups**, then create a new instance group:

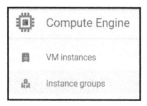

Let's look at the different options that we can specify when creating an instance group.

Setting the location

Here, we can set whether we want multi- or single zones. This selection will be based on your availability requirements. If you require a higher availability, then it's best to go with multiple zones; however, you should note that this restricts your group type to managed only:

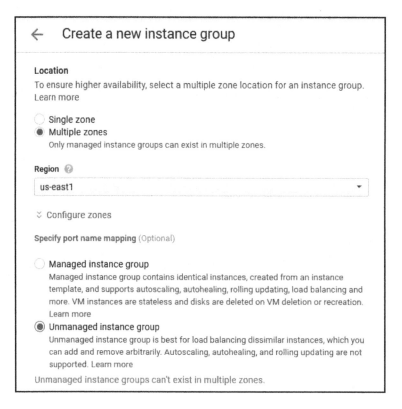

We can see in the preceding screenshot that, with **Multiple zones** selected, we get an error message when we also select the **Unmanaged instance group** type.

Port name mapping

This is an option we can utilize. We would use this in conjunction with a load balancer. We will speak about load balancers in the next section. We can specify a port name and associated port number and map incoming traffic to this specific number.

Of course, we also need to specify the instance template we want to use for this managed group. This option is only available if we select a managed instance group under the group type options. We also need to select the number of instances to be deployed by the instance group.

We can select whether we want to turn autoscaling on and off. Autoscaling allows for the dynamic growth or, indeed, deletion of your VM instances as demand increases or decreases. We will also speak more on autoscaling in this chapter as it's key to understanding its capabilities.

When we have populated everything we need, we can click **Create**. The group will now create the number of VMs we have specified in the instance group. Under **Compute Engine | Instance groups**, we can see the running instances connected to the instance group.

Autoscaling

We mentioned autoscaling earlier and this deserves a full section to itself. Autoscaling is a fundamental principle of cloud computing. It allows infrastructures to be elastic and will increase and decrease based on demand. As a reminder, we can only use autoscaling with managed instance groups. This is because only managed instance groups will use a dedicated template, which, in turn, can create a pool of homogeneous VM instances.

Once autoscaling is enabled in our instance group, it also enables many settings under an **Autoscaling policy**. These policies can be based on CPU usage, HTTP load balancing usage, or Stackdriver metrics. We should also note here that it is possible to autoscale based on custom metrics so we are not reliant only on out-of-the-box metrics.

The following example is based on CPU usage, which is the simplest form of autoscaling. The autoscaler will the collect CPU utilization of instances in a group and decide whether it is necessary to scale the group or whether it should maintain the current number of VM instances.

Looking at the following screenshot, let's take a look at the settings we should populate:

- **Target CPU usage**: This is set at 60%. This means the autoscaler should keep an average CPU usage of 60% among all vCPUs in the instance group.
- **Minimum number of instances**: This is the minimum instances that the autoscaler should scale down.
- **Maximum number of instances**: This is the maximum instances that the autoscaler should scale out.
- **Cool down period**: This number indicates the number of seconds the autoscaler will wait after a VM instance has started before the autoscaler starts collecting information from it. Generally, this is the time you expect your VM instance to boot. The default time is 60 seconds and anything below this could be deemed to give false information to the autoscaler:

We should also understand that, as our managed instance group grows, the impact of adding the same sized VM decreases. Let's clarify what we mean here. Say we have set a CPU utilization of 75% and a minimum of three instances in our group. The autoscaler is checking to see whether the aggregate of the VM instances averages above 75%. If the autoscaler adds a fourth VM, it adds a 25% increased capacity to the group.

If we have a maximum of 10 VMs in our group, then the 10th VM is only contributing 10% more capacity—so the impact of the 10th node is not the same as the 4th node. We should keep this in mind when setting utilization and maximum capacity. It's also important to note that autoscaling will always act conservatively and round up the statistics. It would start an extra VM instance that isn't really needed rather than possibly running out of resources.

Scaling based on HTTP load balancing will scale based on the load of your VM instances. A load balancer will spread the load over backend services that are configured when you create an HTTP load balancer. As part of the configuration, you can define load balancing serving capacity based on CPU utilization, maximum requests per second per VM instance, or maximum requests per second of the entire group. This setting will depend on whether the load balancer serving capacity of the instance groups is defined as requests per second or CPU utilization.

The **Target HTTP load balancing usage** in the **Autoscaling policy** should be a fraction of what is configured in your load balancer setting. For example, if you set the policy to 100 requests per second, then it would be sensible to scale slightly below this and set the usage in the policy to maybe 80 requests per second (80%):

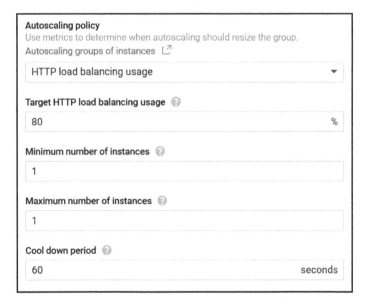

 We will discuss load balancers in more detail in Chapter 8, *Networking Options in GCP*.

We also can scale on Stackdriver metrics, where the selected metric will provide data for each instance in the managed instance group or the entire group. These metrics can either be out-the-box or custom metrics you have created.

> If you have a requirement to scale down to zero instances from time to time, then you should use per-group metrics.

Let's look at another example using a custom metric that Google offers as a demonstration metric, called `custom.googleapis.com/appdemo_queue_depth_01`.

The **Utilization target type** is set to **Gauge** in this example because this will tell the autoscaler to compute the average value of the data collected over the last few minutes and compare it to the target value. We also set a minimum and maximum number of instances:

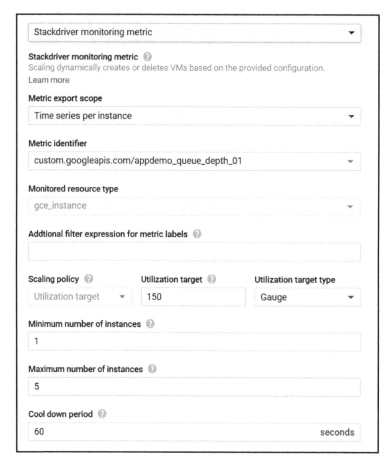

Let's assume we now have a startup script on our instance template, which will invoke another script responsible for generating these custom metrics. We can see, from the charts monitoring tab within our instance group, that the load started to increase on our instance groups around 5:55 p.m. but dropped again around 6 p.m.:

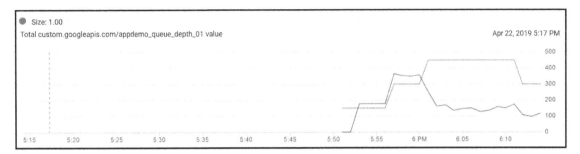

Given the spike in our queue depth, we can expect that the **Autoscaling policy** would have generated a new instance. If we check the autoscaler logs, we can confirm this. It then added a third instance before reducing back to two instances when the demand dropped again:

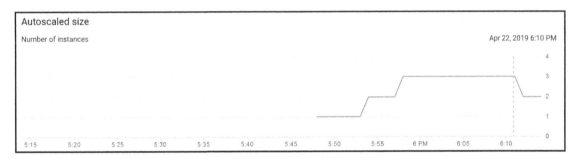

This is true elastic computing! These are small examples of how autoscaling works and we advise that you ensure you can create your own policies and replicate any load that's responsible for increasing and decreasing your machine instances.

 You can only create one autoscaler per managed instance group.

Autohealing

Autohealing is also part of the managed instance group settings but merits its own section in order to discuss it further. GCPs managed instance groups are responsible for validating whether each VM instance in our group is running and ready to accept client requests. To perform this validation, it needs a **health check**, which is basically a probe that contacts each member of the instance group to check their current health. The policy can be based on certain protocols, namely HTTP(S), TCP, or SSL.

We also need to configure the criteria to inform the health check how often to check the instance, the acceptable amount of time that it can get a no response, and the number of consecutive failures to its probe. These settings define when a VM would be classified as unhealthy. If that specific instance is no longer healthy, the autoscaler will add a new instance:

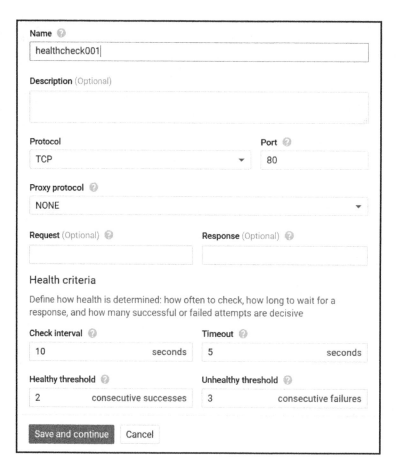

Within the health checks, we also have to specify the health threshold in which the autoscaler will check the newly created instance before it directs traffic to it.

We can then apply this health check as an autohealing policy in our instance group. The following screenshot shows this health check selected in this example:

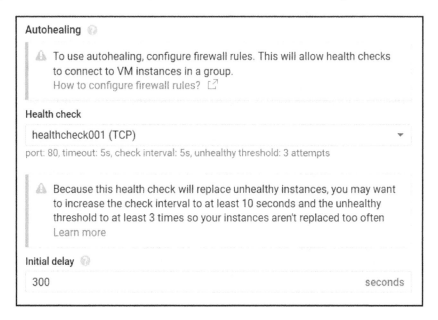

Autohealing policies can also improve the availability of your application.

Quotas and limits

Compute Engine comes with a predefined quota. These default quotas can be changed in the console via the hamburger menu and go to **IAM & Admin | Quotas**. From this menu, we can review the current quotas and request an increase to these limits. We recommend you are aware of the limits for each service as this can have an impact on your scalability:

- There is a default limit of 24 CPUs.
- There is a default limit of 4,096 GB of persistent disk storage.
- There is a default limit of 15,000 instances per network.

IAM roles

Access to GCE is secured with IAMs. Let's have a look at the list of predefined roles, together with a short description for each:

- **Compute Admin Role**: This has the right to access all Compute Engine resources.
- **Compute Image User Role**: This has the right to list and read images.
- **Compute Instance Admin (v1) Role**: This has the right to access full management of Compute Engine instances, instance groups, disks, snapshots, and images. It also has read access to all Compute Engine networking resources.
- **Compute Instance Admin (beta) Role**: This has the right to create, modify, and delete VM instances. Additionally, it has the right to create, modify, and delete disks and to configure shielded VM settings.
- **Compute Load Balancer Admin Role**: This has the right to create, modify, and delete load balancers and associated resources.
- **Compute Network Admin Role**: This has the right to create, modify, and delete networking resources, except for firewall rules and SSL certificates. Additionally, this role has read-only rights to firewall rules, SSL certificates, and instances (to view their ephemeral IP addresses). With this role, you cannot create, start, stop, or delete instances.
- **Compute Network User Role**: This has the right to access a shared VPC network.
- **Compute Network Viewer Role**: This has read-only rights over all networking resources.
- **Compute OS Admin Login Role**: This has the right to log on to a Compute Engine instance as an administrator.
- **Compute OS Login Role**: This has the right to log on to a Compute Engine instance as an administrator.
- **Compute Security Admin Role**: This has the right to create, modify, and delete firewall rules and SSL certificates. This role also has the right to configure shielded VM settings.
- **Compute Storage Admin Role**: This has the right to create, modify, and delete disks, images, and snapshots.
- **Compute Viewer Role**: This has read-only access to list Compute Engine resources. It does not have the right to read the data stored on them.
- **Compute Shared VPC Admin Role**: This has the right to administer a shared VPC host project. This role is on the organization by an organization admin.
- **DNS Administrator Role**: This has read-only rights to all cloud DNS resources.

- **DNS Peer Role**: This has the right to target networks with DNS peering zones. Note, at the time of writing, this is in beta.
- **DNS Reader Role**: This has read-only access to all cloud DNS resources.
- **Service Account Admin Role**: This has the right to create and manage service accounts.
- **Create Service Account Role**: This has the right to create service accounts.
- **Delete Service Account Role**: This has the right to delete service accounts.
- **Service Account Key Admin Role**: This has the right to create and manage service account keys. The role has the right to rotate keys.
- **Service Account Token Creator Role**: This has the right to impersonate service accounts.
- **Service Account User Role**: This has the right to run operations as the service account.

For less granular access, you can also use primitive roles of owner, editor, and viewer, but we should always use the principle of least privilege.

Exam tip

If you want to debug an issue in a VM instance, grant the compute instance admin role and not the compute admin role. The latter has full control of all Compute Engine resources, whereas the former has less privilege.

Pricing

Google's billing model means that you are charged for vCPUs, GPUs, and GB of memory per 1 minute. If you run a VM for only 30 seconds, you will still be charged for the full 1 minute of usage. However, Google also offers the opportunity to significantly reduce monthly billing. Sustained use discounts reduce the cost of running specific GCE resources.

Predefined machine types are a fixed collection of resources with a preset number of vCPUs and amount of memory and are charged at a set price.

Custom machine types can be used if the predefined types don't map to your requirements. As you would expect, we can, therefore, specify the number of vCPUs and memory. This may be because the workload requirements need more memory or processing power.

Sole tenant nodes will also receive discounts. We have spoken in more detail about these in the preceding sections.

If we run one of the preceding resources for more than 25% of a month, then GCE will discount every incremental minute you use for the instance automatically. Discounts will increase with usage and anything up to a 30% discount per month can be expected. This size of discount can only be taken advantage of if VM instances are created on the first day of the month as discounts are reset at the beginning of each month. If we deployed instances around the middle of the month, then we would expect a discount of around 10%.

One key thing to note is how the billing is calculated. At a high level, let's take a look at an example. Let's say we are running an `n1-standard-4` instance from the beginning of the month until halfway through the month. This translates to an instance of size 4 vCPUs and 30 GB of memory. Secondly, we add an `n1-standard-16` instance halfway through the month until the end of the month. As sustained billing organizes the instances into individual vCPU and memory resources, it will break them down to the following:

- 4 vCPUs for the full month
- 12 vCPUs for half the month (sustained billing is still using the 4 vCPUs from the first half of the month)
- 15 GB of memory for the full month
- 45 GB of memory for half the month (sustained billing is still using the 15 GB of memory from the first half of the month)

Another method offered for discounts is **committed use** discounts, whereby we can purchase a specific amount of vCPU and memory for an agreed term of 1 or 3 years. Discounts can reach 57% for most custom machine types or even 70% for more memory-focused instances. There are no upfront costs and discounts are applied to your monthly billing. You will be billed for the selected vCPU and memory each month for the agreed term.

Discounts are applied via purchase commitments. Let's say, for example, we make a commitment for 8 cores but run 16 cores for 10 hours. We would receive the discount on the 8 cores for the 10 hours but we would be billed as standard for the remaining 8 cores. The remaining 8 cores would, however, qualify for sustained use discounts. Likewise, if we did not use the 8 committed cores in a monthly cycle, we would still be billed for them, so we should ensure that we only commit to what we will use. There are some other important caveats to committed use discounts.

Discounts can only be applied to general-purpose machine types between 0.9 GB and 6.5 GB of memory per vCPU or memory-optimized machine types between 14 GB and 40 GB of memory per vCPU.

Discounts are applied to resources in the following order:

- Custom machine types
- Sole-tenant node groups
- Predefined machine types

Let's take another example to make this clearer. We have an inventory of 5 custom machine type vCPUs and 30 GB of custom type memory along with a single predefined machine. If we purchase 10 vCPUs and 15 GB of memory for committed use, the discount would apply first to our 5 vCPUs of the custom machine type and the remaining 5 discounted vCPUs would be applied to the predefined machine type. Likewise, the discount for the full 15 GB of committed use memory would be applied to our custom type memory and the remaining 15 GB of memory would be eligible for a sustained use discount.

Summary

In this chapter, we introduced GCP's IaaS offering—Compute Engine. This is a basic offering by Google and aligns with a traditional VM. We discussed how to deploy an instance and how to add to instance groups to scale our services automatically.

In the next chapter, we will move away from IaaS and introduce **Google Kubernetes Engine (GKE)**.

Further reading

- We recommend that you review the following URL for further information: `https://cloud.google.com/compute/docs/`

5
Managing Kubernetes Clusters with Google Kubernetes Engine

In the previous chapter, we took a deep dive into Google Compute Engine, which provides Infrastructure as a Service. In this chapter, we will look at a **Container as a Service (CaaS)** offering. **Google Kubernetes Engine (GKE)** allows us to create managed Kubernetes clusters on demand. Before we start talking about GKE, we need to understand a few concepts, such as microservices, containers, and Kubernetes (K8s) itself.

Exam tips: GKE is heavily tested in the cloud architect exam. Make sure you understand the basic concepts of containers, microservices, Kubernetes, and GKE-specific topics. Pay special attention to the Kubernetes section itself. A lot of questions are related to Kubernetes rather than being GKE-specific. Make sure you understand the Kubernetes architecture and objects, pay special attention to networking and services so that you know how the applications are accessed, understand how you can secure clusters with IAM and RBAC, and finally, understand how you can manage, scale, and upgrade GKE clusters.

If you have never heard of these before, don't worry—we will take you through all the basic concepts. We will go through the following topics in this chapter:

- An introduction to microservices
- Containers
- Docker
- Kubernetes
- Google Kubernetes Engine

An introduction to microservices

Let's start by going over the concept of microservices. In the legacy world, applications were delivered in a monolithic architecture. This meant that multiple services were hosted together on a single node. In the microservice architecture, the application is divided into a number of microservices, each hosted on a separate node, like so:

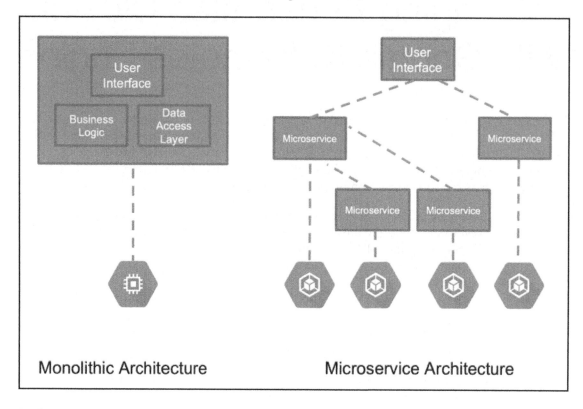

Each microservice is responsible for a single functionality. The microservices are loosely coupled and can be developed and managed separately. They communicate with each other using APIs. Thanks to that, each microservice can even be developed in a different programming language. When you need to upgrade your application, you can upgrade a single node without affecting other components. By splitting the application into microservices, you also have control when you scale your application. You can granularly scale the services that require scaling without touching the others. Finally, microservices allow you to embrace CI/CD and deliver functionalities faster as deployments can be rolled out in a very controlled way.

Continuous integration and continuous delivery and/or continuous deployment (CI/CD) is a methodology of streamlining software delivery. **Continuous integration** is a practice where developers frequently submit code to a common repository. The code is reviewed and tested. After validation, automatic builds are triggered. **Continuous delivery** allows for the automation of the release process so that the software can be deployed to the target environment at any point in time. In **continuous deployment**, any changes that are made by a developer that pass all the tests are automatically deployed to the production environment.

Containers

To understand containers, let's compare them with virtual machines. While virtual machines virtualize hardware, containers virtualize the operating system. They abstract the application, along with all its dependencies, into one unit. Multiple containers can be hosted on one operating system running as an isolated process:

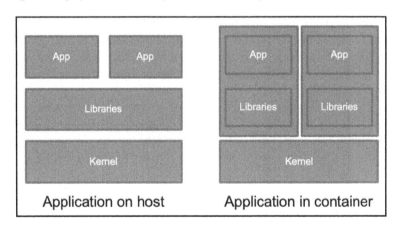

Containers bring the following advantages:

- **Isolation**: Applications can use their own libraries without conflicting with libraries from other applications.
- **Resource limitation**: Applications can be limited to the resource's usage.
- **Portability**: Applications are self-contained with all dependencies and are not tied to an OS or a cloud provider.
- **Lightweight**: The footprint of the application is much smaller as the containers share a kernel.

Docker

There are multiple container formats available on the market. GKE supports the most popular one, which is Docker. Docker is an open platform and allows you to develop and run containerized applications. It can run on multiple Linux images offered in GCP as they have the same kernel. Docker images are created using a definition called a **Dockerfile**. Google Cloud Platform offers a service called Google Container Registry, which allows you to host your Docker images securely, as well as to access them from your Kubernetes cluster.

Kubernetes

Kubernetes, also known as K8s, is an open source container orchestrator that was initially developed by Google and donated to the Cloud Native Computing Foundation. It allows you to deploy, scale, and manage containerized applications. As an open source platform, it can run on multiple platforms both on-premise as well as in the public cloud. It is suitable for both stateless as well as stateful applications.

Exam tip: Kubernetes is an important exam topic. Fortunately, the exam does not require you to have in-depth knowledge of it. In this section, we will talk about both the management layer and Kubernetes objects. We want you to understand the management layer because it is necessary to understand GKE itself. When it comes to Kubernetes objects, make sure that you understand at least the ones we mention in this book, including Pods, deployments, services, and namespaces. Kubernetes itself deserves its own book, and there are many available on the market. If you feel like you want to learn more, refer to the *Further reading* section.

Kubernetes architecture

In the following diagram, we can see the basic architecture of a Kubernetes cluster. The cluster consists of multiple nodes. From a high level, the master nodes are responsible for the management of the cluster, while the worker nodes host the workloads. The worker nodes host so-called Pods, which are the most atomic units of Kubernetes. These Pods can contain one or more containers. Access to the containers in the Pods is provided using services. In the following diagram, we can see a Kubernetes cluster and the services that are hosted on each type of node:

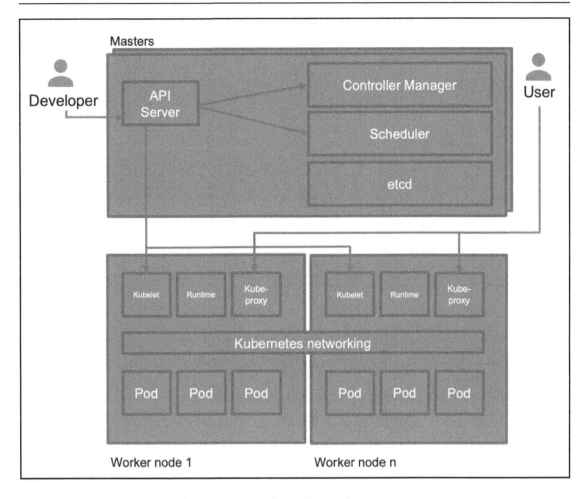

Now, let's have a closer look at master and worker nodes.

The master node

The master node takes care of maintaining the desired state of the cluster. It monitors the Kubernetes object definitions (YAML files) and makes sure that they are scheduled on the worker nodes.

YAML Ain't Markup Language (YAML) is a human-friendly data serialization standard, mainly used for configuration files. It is an alternative for formats such as XML or JSON.

It is essentially a control plane for the cluster. It works as follows:

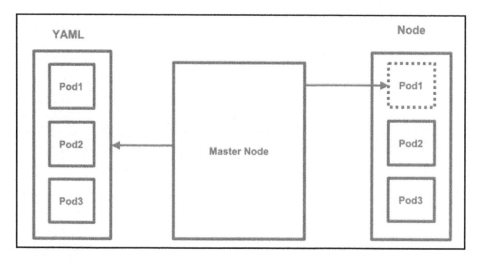

The master node runs multiple processes:

- **API server**: Exposes the Kubernetes API. It is the frontend of the control plane.
- **Controller manager**: Multiple controllers are responsible for the overall health of the cluster.
- **etcd**: A database that hosts the cluster state information.
- **Scheduler**: Responsible for placing the Pods across the nodes to balance resource consumption.

A cluster can run perfectly with just one master, but multiple nodes should be run for high availability and redundancy purposes. Without the master, the control plane is essentially down. All the cluster management operations you perform go through the master API. So, for production workloads, it is recommended that you have multiple master configurations.

Worker nodes

A worker node can be a virtual machine or even a physical server. In the case of GKE, it is a virtual machine instance. Worker nodes are responsible for running containerized applications. Worker nodes are managed by the master node. They run the following services:

- **Kubelet**: This reads the Pod specification and makes sure the right containers run in the Pods. It interacts directly with the master node.

- **Kube-proxy**: This is a network proxy running on each node. It enables the usage of services (we will learn about services shortly).
- **Container runtime**: This is responsible for running containers. Kubernetes supports multiple runtimes but in the case of GKE, Docker is used.

Kubernetes objects

Kubernetes objects are **records of intent** that are defined in YAML format. They are declarative in nature. Once created, Kubernetes will take care of keeping them in the state declared in the definition file. Some examples of the most important objects are as follows:

- Pods
- Replica sets
- Replication controllers
- Deployments
- Name spaces

It would take hundreds of pages to describe all the available Kubernetes objects, so for the purpose of the exam, we will concentrate on the preceding ones. Let's take a look at an example of a deployment object file. This deployment would basically deploy two Pods with containers using the nginx image:

```
apiVersion: apps/v1
kind: Deployment
metadata:
  name: nginx-deployment
  labels:
    app: nginx
spec:
  replicas: 3
  selector:
    matchLabels:
      app: nginx
  template:
    metadata:
      labels:
        app: nginx
    spec:
      containers:
      - name: nginx
        image: nginx:1.7.9
        ports:
        - containerPort: 80
```

No matter what kind of object we define, we need to have the following data in it:

- `apiVersion`: The version of the Kubernetes API we want to use
- `kind`: The kind of object to be created
- `metadata`: Data that helps uniquely identify the object, such as its name
- `spec`: The specification of the object, which is dependent on its type

To create or update an existing object, we can use the following command:

```
kubectl apply -f definition.yaml
```

Here, `definition.yaml` is the file with an object definition. To run our first deployment, we would save the preceding definition in the `definition.yaml` file and run the `kubectl` command.

There are multiple commands you can use to manage Kubernetes. `kubectl` is the most used as it allows us to create, delete, and update Kubernetes objects. Take a look at the following link to see what operations can be performed using `kubectl`: https://kubernetes.io/docs/reference/kubectl/overview/. Note that `kubectl` is installed in the GCP Cloud Shell console by default, but if you want to use it from any other machine, it needs to be installed.

Now, let's have a look at each object, starting with Pods.

Selectors and labels

You will notice that Kubernetes objects have parameters called **labels** and **selectors**.

Those parameters are used to associate different objects with each other. Say you want to associate a Pod with a namespace. In the Pod definition, you would use a property label such as `app: myapp` and in the namespace you would use a selector such as `app: myapp`.

Pods

A Pod is the atomic unit of deployment in Kubernetes. A Pod contains one or more containers and storage resources. Usually, there would be a single container within a Pod. Additional containers can be added to the Pod when we need small helper services. Each Pod has a unique IP address that is shared with the containers inside it. Pods are ephemeral by nature and are recreated when they need to be rescheduled. If they use no persistent volumes, the volume content vanishes when a Pod is recreated. To create a Pod, we use `kind` of `Pod` and define what image we want to use, like so:

```
apiVersion: v1
kind: Pod
metadata:
 name: my-pod
 labels:
 app: myapp
spec:
 containers:
 - name: my-container
 image: nginx:1.7.9
```

Here, we can see a definition of a Pod with a container that's been deployed from an `nginx` image.

Replica sets

A replica set object is used to manage the number of Pods that are running at a given time. A replica set monitors how many Pods are running and deploys new ones to reach the desired number of replicas. To define a replica set, use `kind` of `ReplicaSet`. The number of Pods to run is defined under the `replicas` parameter:

```
apiVersion: apps/v1
kind: ReplicaSet
metadata:
  name: frontend
  labels:
    app: guestbook
    tier: frontend
spec:
  # modify replicas according to your case
  replicas: 3
  selector:
    matchLabels:
      tier: frontend
  template:
```

```
metadata:
  labels:
    tier: frontend
spec:
  containers:
  - name: php-redis
    image: gcr.io/google_samples/gb-frontend:v3
```

Replica sets are successors of replication controller objects.

Deployments

Deployments are used to deploy, update, and control Pods. These deployments create replica sets without the need to define them separately. By stating how many replicas are needed, the appropriate replica set object will be created for you. By changing the image in the container, we can update the application to a new version. Deployment objects support both Canary and Blue/Green deployment methods.

 In **Canary** deployment, we deploy a new version of the application to a subset of users. Once we are sure that the new version works properly, the application is updated for all the users. In **Blue/Green** deployment, we use two environments, with only one active at a time. After updating the inactive one to a new version and testing it, we switch the traffic and make it the active one.

To create a deployment object, use `kind` of `Deployment`, like so:

```
apiVersion: apps/v1
kind: Deployment
metadata:
  name: deployment-demo
  labels:
    app: nginx
spec:
  replicas: 3
  selector:
    matchLabels:
      app: nginx
  template:
    metadata:
      labels:
        app: nginx
    spec:
      containers:
      - name: nginx
```

```
image: nginx:1.7.9
ports:
- containerPort: 80
```

In the preceding example, we created a deployment with three replicas from the `nginx:1.7.9` image. The deployment object will make sure that three replicas will be running at all times.

Namespaces

Namespaces are essentially virtual clusters within a Kubernetes cluster. In big environments, there can be multiple teams developing an application. By creating namespaces, users are allowed to reuse the names of resources. The names need to be unique within the namespaces but not across the cluster. By default, a Kubernetes cluster comes with three predefined namespaces:

- `default`: A default namespace for objects with no other namespace
- `kube-system`: Used for resources that are created by Kubernetes
- `kube-public`: Reserved for future use:

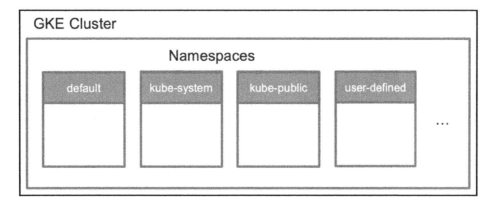

Additional namespaces can be created as needed by running the following command:

```
kubectl create namespace <namespace-name>
```

Here, `<namespace-name>` is the name of the new namespace.

To deploy to the new namespace, you should use the `--namespace` flag, for example:

```
kubectl --namespace=<namespace-name> run nginx --image=nginx
```

Alternatively, you can define the namespace attribute in the object definition.

Namespaces can be isolated from each other using network policies. To learn more about network policies, check the *Further reading* section of this chapter. You can also limit the resources that are available to a namespace by using resource quotas. The following quota requests/reserves a total of 1 CPU and 1 GB of memory. It also limits the CPU to 2 and the memory to 2 GB:

```
apiVersion: v1
kind: ResourceQuota
metadata:
  name: quota-demo
spec:
  hard:
    requests.cpu: "1"
    requests.memory: 1Gi
    limits.cpu: "2"
    limits.memory: 2Gi
```

As you can see, namespaces are a good way of separating your environment. Before you decide to deploy a new Kubernetes cluster, you might want to have a look at creating a new namespace instead.

Services

Services are used to group Pods into a single endpoint. As we know, Pods come and go. A service has a stable IP address, and so requests can be sent to it and forwarded to a Pod. What algorithm is used to perform the forwarding depends on the type of service. We will have a look at each type of service in the next section. Let's take a look at a simple definition of a service. Here, we are using a kind value of Service.

As we mentioned previously, you can use a selector in the service definition and a label in the Pod definition to assign the Pod to a service.

The following is a simple service definition:

```
apiVersion: v1
kind: Service
metadata:
  name: service-demo
spec:
  selector:
    app: myapp
  ports:
  - protocol: TCP
```

```
port: 80
targetPort: 9376
```

Let's take a look at the types of services.

Types of services

In this section, we will have a look at the most important service types. Services differ by how they handle traffic and whether they expose Pods externally or internally. The services we will discuss are as follows:

- ClusterIP
- NodePort
- LoadBalancer
- ExternalName

Let's discuss each service in detail:

- ClusterIP: This is a default service that uses an internal ClusterIP to expose Pods. This means that services are not available from outside of the cluster. The use case for ClusterIP is internal communication between microservices within the cluster:

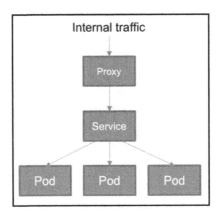

The following is a sample definition of a Service of the ClusterIP type:

```
apiVersion: v1
 kind: Service
 metadata:
   name: clusterip-demo
 spec:
```

```
selector:
  app: myapp
type: ClusterIP
ports:
- name: http
  port: 80
  targetPort: 80
  protocol: TCP
```

- NodePort: This simply exposes each node outside of the cluster. The Pods can be accessed using <NodeIP>:<NodePort>. If there are multiple nodes, then multiple IP addresses with the same port will be exposed:

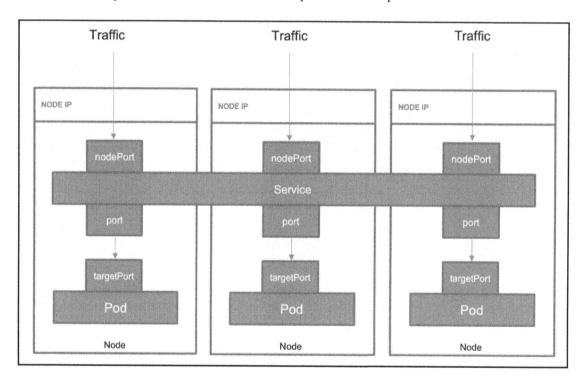

The following is a sample definition of a Service of the NodePort type:

```
apiVersion: v1
kind: Service
metadata:
  name: nodeport-demo
spec:
  selector:
```

```
    app: myapp
type: NodePort
ports:
- name: http
  port: 80
  targetPort: 80
  nodePort: 30080
  protocol: TCP
```

- LoadBalancer: This will dynamically create a provider load balancer. In the case of GCP, a network load balancer is created for you. Remember that it uses objects from outside of Kubernetes and generates additional costs:

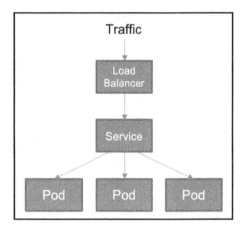

The following is a sample definition of a Service of the LoadBalancer type:

```
kind: Service
apiVersion: v1
metadata:
  name: loadbalancer-demo
spec:
  selector:
    app: myapp
  ports:
  - protocol: TCP
    port: 80
    targetPort: 9376
  clusterIP: 10.0.0.1
  loadBalancerIP: 70.10.10.19
  type: LoadBalancer
status:
  loadBalancer:
```

```
ingress:
- ip: 160.160.160.155
```

- **ExternalName**: This service is exposed using a DNS name specified in the `ExternalName` spec. The following is a sample definition of a `Service` of the `ExternalName` type:

```
kind: Service
apiVersion: v1
metadata:
  name: externalname-demo
  namespace: prod
spec:
  type: ExternalName
  externalName: my.app.example.com
```

- **Ingress**: This is an object that allows the routing of HTTP(S) traffic according to the defined rules (paths). It can be associated with one or more `Service` objects. The services are further associated with Pods. In the case of Google Cloud Platform, the ingress controller creates HTTP(S) load balancers. These load balancers are configured automatically using the definition in the `Ingress` object:

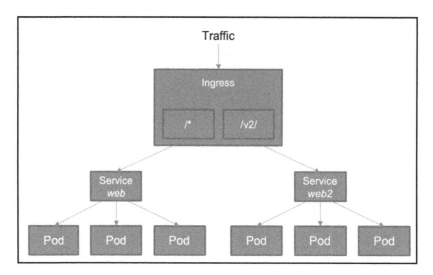

Let's have a look at the YAML definition. The ingress is defined with `kind` of `Ingress`. From here, you define rules. Depending on the path, you direct the traffic to the associated service. In the following example, `/*` traffic is directed to the web if `/v2/*` traffic is directed to the `web2` service:

```
ApiVersion: extensions/v1beta1
kind: Ingress
metadata:
  name: example-ingress
spec:
  rules:
  - http:
      paths:
      - path: /*
        backend:
          serviceName: web
          servicePort: 8080
      - path: /v2/*
        backend:
          serviceName: web2
          servicePort: 8080
```

This sums up the list of the most important Kubernetes objects. In the next section, we will have a closer look at GKE.

Google Kubernetes Engine

GKE is a fully managed service that allows us to provision Kubernetes clusters on demand. It offloads the burden of deploying clusters manually. It also comes with a number of benefits that manual deployment does not offer, such as the following:

- Automated cluster provisioning
- Automated cluster scaling
- Automated upgrades
- Auto-repair
- Integrated load balancing
- Node pools
- Integration with Stackdriver for monitoring and logging

A GKE cluster can be deployed in two modes: **zonal** or **regional**. In a zonal deployment, only one master node is deployed. In a regional deployment, three masters are deployed in different zones. This is shown in the following diagram:

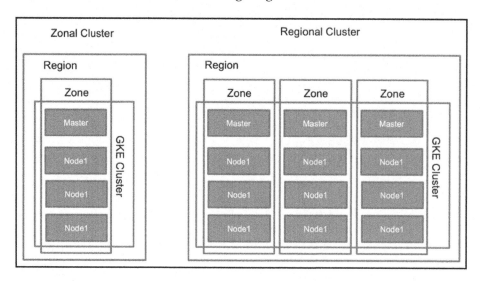

To have zero downtime when upgrading the management plane, you should deploy regional clusters. In this setup, the masters can be upgraded one by one so that the management plane is functional during the upgrade period.

Node pools

Node pools are used to put worker nodes into groups with the same configuration. When you create your first cluster, all the nodes are put into the default node pool. You might want to have multiple node pools if you want to have groups with specific characteristics, such as local SSDs, minimum CPU, a specific node image, or using a preemptible instance:

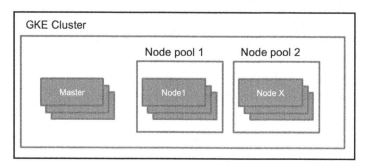

Node pools might be useful if your workloads have special resource requirements. You can use the concept of **node taints** to schedule your workload on a particular node pool. In the *Further reading* section, you will find a link to documentation on how to use node taints.

Node pools are managed with the `gcloud container node-pools` command.

We will have a look at how we can use this command to scale our nodes later, in the *Resizing the cluster* section.

Container-Optimized OS

By default, nodes in your Kubernetes Engine use Google's Container-Optimized OS. It is a locked-down version of Chromium OS, which has the purpose of running containerized applications. Images are maintained and updated by Google. Updates are downloaded automatically in the background. As it is stripped of unnecessary features, the attack surface is smaller than in the case of other Linux distributions.

Note that this OS is not good for running non-containerized applications or when you need enterprise support from a Linux provider. Use Container-Optimized OS for nodes unless you have a very good reason to use another Linux distribution.

Storage

The easiest way to use persistent storage in GKE is to use GCP services such as Cloud SQL, Datastore, or Cloud Storage. However, you can also expose storage directly to your Pods using Kubernetes abstraction layers. Storage is delivered to Pod containers using volumes. These volumes can be backed either by ephemeral or durable storage. While ephemeral storage is good for scratch space, to persist the state, durable storage is needed:

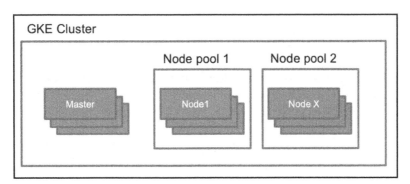

When a Pod crashes and is redeployed, the files that are stored on a local disk will be lost. To keep the state, you need to use external storage outside of the Pod. To do this, you can use **PersistentVolumes (PVs)** whose lifespans are not bound to the Pod's lifespan. In GKE, those volumes are usually backed by Google Cloud Computer Engine Persistent Disks and can be provisioned dynamically by using a **PersistentVolumeClaim (PVC)**. An example of a claim is shown here. Here, we are requesting a volume of 20 GB, with the access mode allowing us to attach it to one node:

```
apiVersion: v1
kind: PersistentVolumeClaim
metadata:
  name: claim-demo
spec:
  accessModes:
    - ReadWriteOnce
  resources:
    requests:
      storage: 20Gi
```

To use this claim as a volume for the Pod, you need to refer to the claim in the Pod definition:

```
apiVersion: v1
kind: Pod
metadata:
  name: mypod
spec:
  containers:
    - name: myfrontend
      image: nginx
      volumeMounts:
      - mountPath: "/var/www/html"
        name: myp
  volumes:
    - name: mypd
      persistentVolumeClaim:
        claimName: claim-demo
```

To learn more about PersistentVolumes, refer to the *Further reading* section.

GKE cluster management

We have finally gone through the theory that's needed to understand GKE. Now, let's have a look at some practical examples of managing a GKE cluster. We will start with the deployment of a cluster and then look at operations for scaling and upgrading.

There are a couple of tools you can use to manage a cluster, including the following:

- Google Cloud Console
- The gcloud command-line interface
- The REST API

For exam purposes, we will concentrate on the two first tools. Let's get to work!

Creating a GKE cluster

The simplest way to deploy a cluster is to use the Google Cloud Console. This is also a good way to see all the available options without having to read the command-line reference. Let's get started:

1. From the hamburger menu, choose **Kubernetes Engine | Clusters**. In the pop-up window, click on the **Create cluster** button, as shown in the following screenshot:

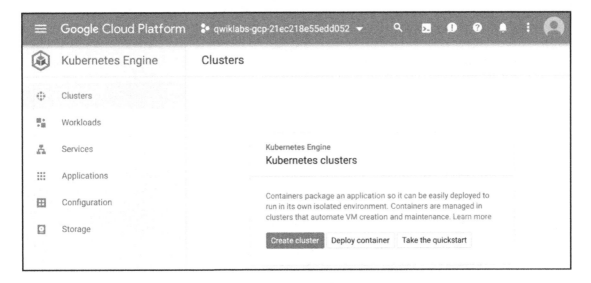

2. In the following pane, you can choose a template for your cluster, depending on the workload type. We will go with **Standard cluster** as we want to deploy a simple web application. On the right-hand side, we can choose more detailed settings for the cluster. Let's have a closer look at the available options:

3. First, choose the name of your cluster. Next, decide whether you want the cluster to be **Zonal** or **Regional**. If we choose **Zonal**, we will see that we are asked for the **Zone** to deploy to, as shown in the following screenshot:

4. If we choose **Regional**, we will have to choose a **Region**, as shown in the following screenshot:

5. No matter which **Location type** we select, we need to choose a **Master version**. By default, the most stable version is selected. We will keep the default value:

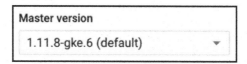

6. We can now define node pools. There can be one or more pools in a cluster. As we mentioned previously, pools group nodes with the same characteristics. If we choose a number of vCPUs, then the memory amount will be automatically filled in for us. If we click on **Customize**, we will have more granular choices:

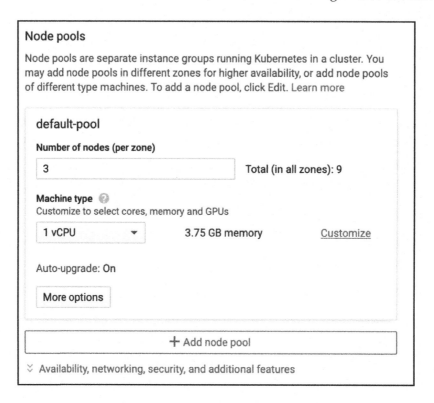

7. When we click on the **More options** button, we are presented with more settings. This includes disk size definitions, auto-repair, and auto-upgrade options. Note that the last two options are enabled by default:

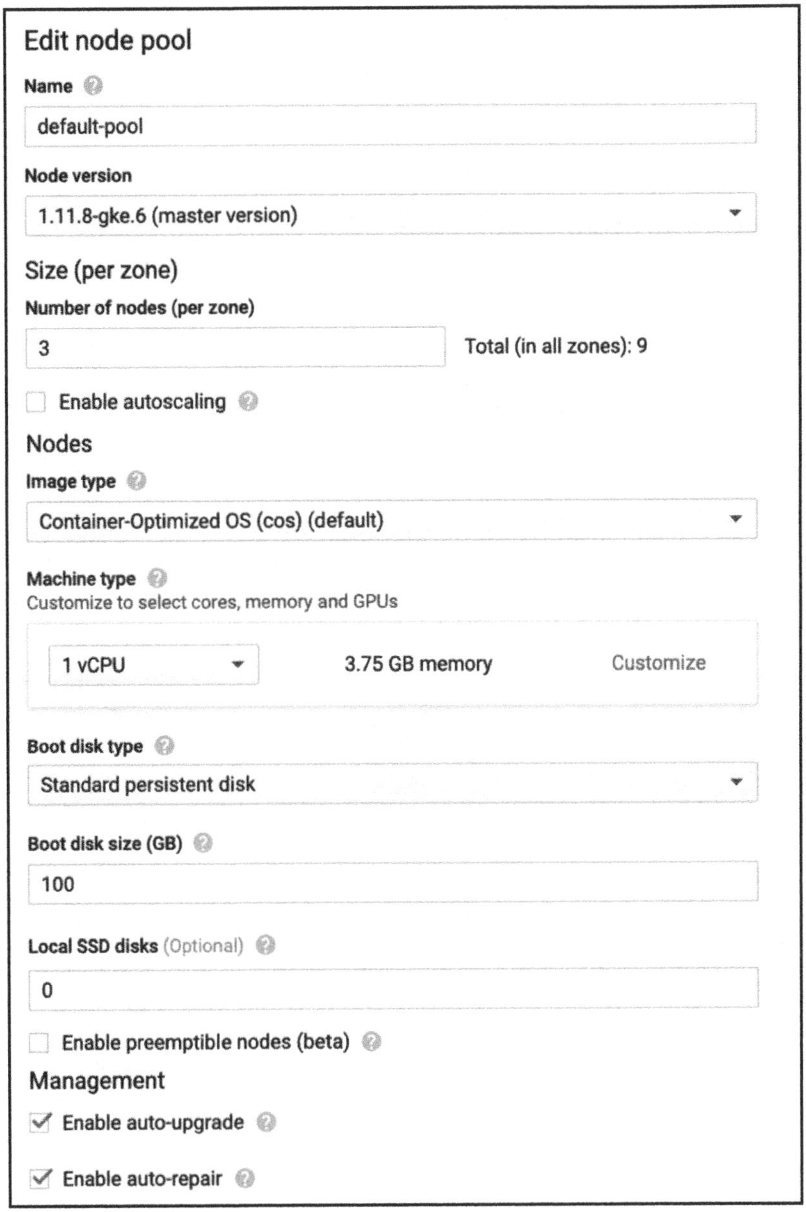

8. By scrolling down, we are presented with the **Security** section. We can see that the service account that's being used is the **Compute Engine default service account**. This is very similar to how the GCE security settings work. However, note that this account will be used by the workloads that have been deployed to the node pool. Remember to use the least privileges principle:

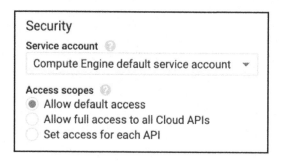

Now, let's have a look at advanced configuration.

Advanced configuration

If we click on the **Availability, networking, security, and additional features** link, we will see very granular settings that we would usually keep in the default states. Let's have a look at the most important ones:

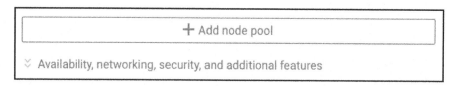

If we set **Location type** to **Zonal** in the **Availability** section, we can add additional zones to which an identical number of worker nodes will be deployed. This way, you can provide high availability in the case of zone failure. Obviously, this increases costs. Remember that you will still only deploy one master:

For regional clusters, you can manually select which zones you want to deploy to:

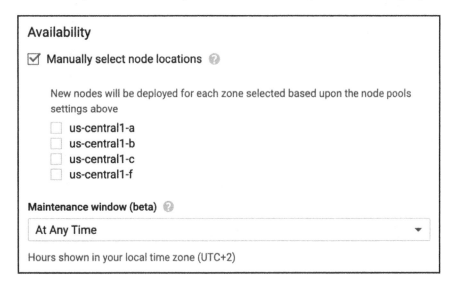

For both options, you can choose a **Maintenance window (beta)**. This is indicated when the automatic updates take place.

Networking

Let's go over the **Networking** section:

1. Here, we can choose the VPC and subnet, and define the Pod's IP address range, like so:

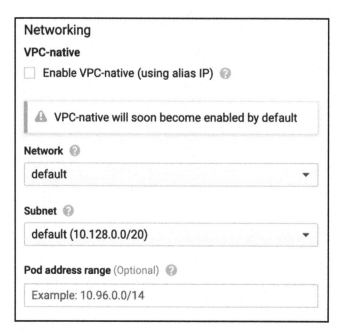

2. If we enable the **VPC-native** option, we will be able to use alias IP ranges. We can now define Pod and service ranges:

3. To be able to use ingress, we keep HTTP load balancing enabled:

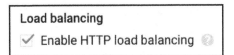

4. For VPC-native, we can enable a **Private cluster**. This allows us to restrict where the master can be connected to:

Now, we will have a look at the **Security** options.

Security

In the **Security** section, we have a couple of authentication authorization settings that are disabled by default:

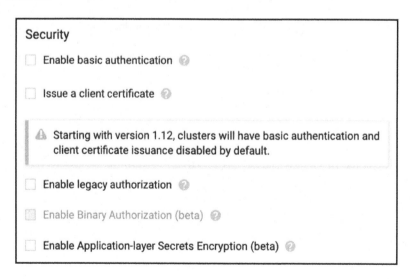

It is recommended to rely on IAM instead of those methods.

Stackdriver

In the **Stackdriver** section, we can enable new GKE monitoring that is available for Kubernetes version 1.12.7 and higher or use legacy monitoring and logging:

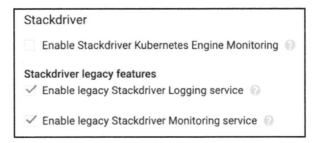

We leave the default settings as they are for legacy monitoring and logging.

Additional features

Finally, we are presented with a couple of additional features. Most of them are in their beta stage:

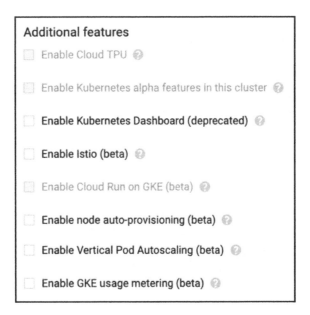

Exam tip: It might be worth remembering that we can do the following:

- **Enable Cloud TPU**: We will discuss this in `Chapter 12`, *Putting Machine Learning to Work*.
- **Enable Istio (beta)**: This is a service mesh product that allows us to control and observe network traffic.
- **Enable Kubernetes Dashboard (deprecated)**: A dashboard that helps us view and manage Kubernetes objects.

1. Now that we have all the settings populated, we can create the cluster by clicking on the **Create** button. Alternatively, we can generate a REST API call or command line by clicking on the respective hyperlinks:

2. Before clicking on **Create**, let's have a look at the command line. As usual, you can just copy this into Cloud Shell and execute it. In the following command, we can see that we used some features that are available in beta, such as the `gcloud beta container` command:

```
gcloud beta container --project " qwiklabs-
gcp-21ec218e55edd052" clusters create "standard-cluster-1" --
region "us-central1" --username "admin" --cluster-version
"1.11.8-gke.6" --machine-type "n1-standard-1" --image-type
"COS" --disk-type "pd-standard" --disk-size "100" --scopes
"https://www.googleapis.com/auth/devstorage.read_only","https:/
/www.googleapis.com/auth/logging.write","https://www.googleapis
.com/auth/monitoring","https://www.googleapis.com/auth/servicec
ontrol","https://www.googleapis.com/auth/service.management.rea
donly","https://www.googleapis.com/auth/trace.append" --num-
nodes "3" --enable-cloud-logging --enable-cloud-monitoring --
no-enable-ip-alias --network "projects/qwiklabs-
gcp-21ec218e55edd052/global/networks/default" --subnetwork
"projects/qwiklabs-gcp-21ec218e55edd052/regions/us-
central1/subnetworks/default" --addons
HorizontalPodAutoscaling,HttpLoadBalancing --enable-autoupgrade
--enable-autorepair
```

Notice that all the options/flags that we used in the GUI setup have been marked in bold in the code for your convenience.

3. Now, we can click on **Create** and wait until the cluster is created. Once it's done, we will see a green tick next to the cluster's name:

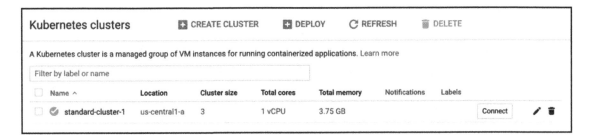

4. By clicking on **Connect**, we are presented with information regarding how to connect to the cluster:

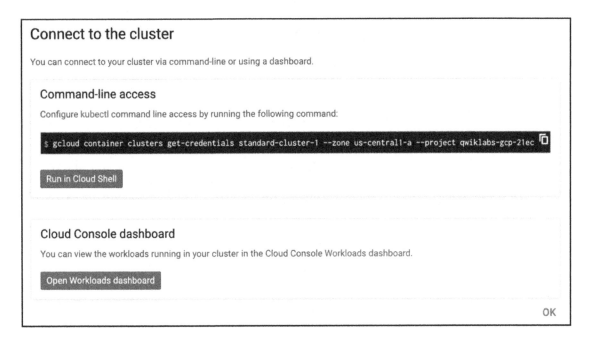

This information can be simply copied to Google Cloud Shell so that we can authenticate it against the newly created cluster. In the next section, we will use it and deploy our first application.

Deploying our first application

Now that we have created a cluster, we can deploy our first application. We will provision a simple NGINX web server using three Pods. For this purpose, we will use the Deployment object. Then, we will expose the application using the Service object.

To demonstrate different ways of creating Kubernetes objects, we will use both kubectl and the Google Cloud Console. Once they have been successfully deployed, we will check their connectivity. Let's get started:

 Exam tip: Expect to see questions on GKE and Kubernetes command-line tools. Remember that gcloud is used for managing the GKE cluster while kubectl is a Kubernetes native tool. So, as an example, if you want to scale a GKE cluster, you would use gcloud, while for scaling a deployment, you would use kubectl.

1. Let's open Cloud Shell and run the following command we copied from the Google Cloud Console:

   ```
   gcloud container clusters get-credentials standard-cluster-1 --
   zone us-central1-a --project qwiklabs-gcp-21ec218e55edd052
   ```

   This will configure the credentials for kubectl. Now, we can deploy Kubernetes resources to the cluster.

2. Now, let's open Cloud Shell in editor mode and create a deploy.yaml file with the Deployment definition. Save it and run the kubectl apply -f deploy.yaml file:

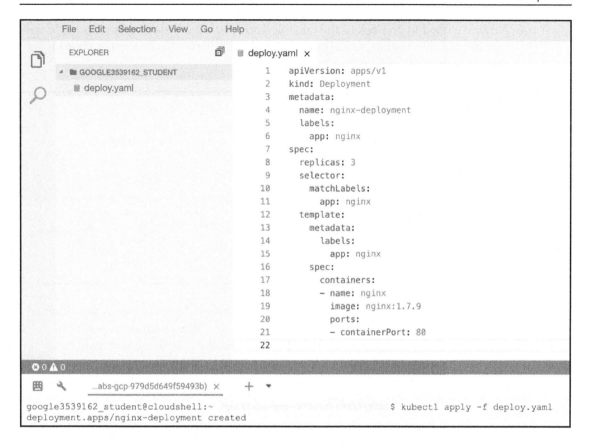

3. To verify that the Pods have been created, we can use the `kubectl get pods` command:

```
google3539162_student@cloudshell:~                              $ kubectl get pods
NAME                               READY   STATUS    RESTARTS   AGE
nginx-deployment-5c689d88bb-2d7pq  1/1     Running   0          2m33s
nginx-deployment-5c689d88bb-srtn8  1/1     Running   0          2m33s
nginx-deployment-5c689d88bb-z4mkp  1/1     Running   0          2m33s
```

4. Now, we need to go back to the console and check the **Workloads** menu. We will see that `nginx-deployment` is present. Click on **Name** to see details about it, as shown in the following screenshot:

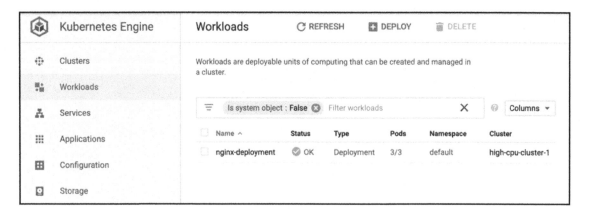

5. Click on the `nginx-deployment` link in the **Name** column to move to a detailed view. At the top of the detailed view, we are asked if we want to expose the service. Click on the **Expose** button, as shown in the following screenshot:

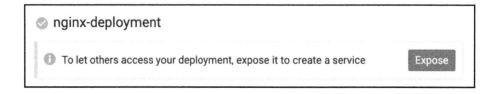

6. Now, we can choose a **Port** and a **Target port**, a **Protocol**, and the most important type of service. We will choose a **Load balancer**. If you click on **View YAML**, you will see a definition of the service. You could copy it and use `kubectl` to deploy it from the shell. Instead, we will click on the **Expose** button to see how this is done from the GUI:

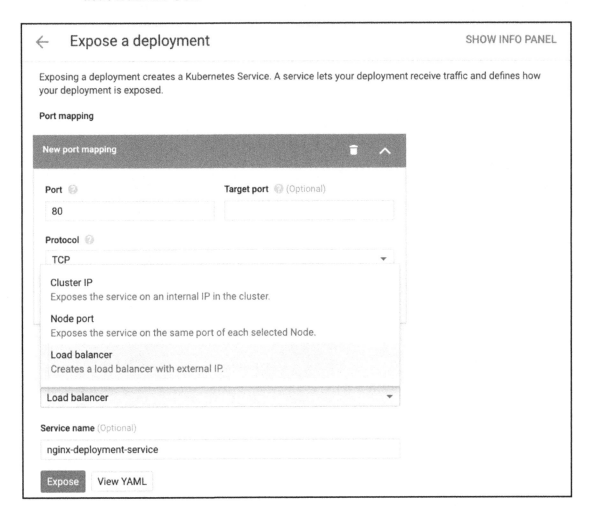

7. It will take a couple of seconds to deploy the service. Once deployed, it will be visible in **Services** under the **Kubernetes Engine** menu. Find the `nginx-deployment-services` service and click on its name to see the following details. Find the **Load balancer IP** value and copy it:

Cluster	high-cpu-cluster-1
Namespace	default
Labels	app : nginx
Stackdriver logs	Deployment: nginx-deployment
Type	LoadBalancer
External endpoints	35.194.21.47:80

LoadBalancer

Cluster IP	10.39.252.240
Load balancer IP	35.194.21.47
Load balancer	ac57afbda82f711e9b18142010a80008

Deployments

Name	Status	Pods
nginx-deployment	OK	3/3

Serving pods

Name	Status	Restarts	Created on ∧
nginx-deployment-5c689d88bb-2d7pq	Running	0	May 30, 2019, 6:20:12 PM
nginx-deployment-5c689d88bb-srtn8	Running	0	May 30, 2019, 6:20:12 PM
nginx-deployment-5c689d88bb-z4mkp	Running	0	May 30, 2019, 6:20:12 PM

Ports

Port	Node Port	Target Port	Protocol	
80	31871	80	TCP	Port forwarding

8. Paste the IP into your web browser. You will see the following NGINX welcome message:

We have successfully deployed our first application to a GKE cluster. As you have seen, you can do this by using either the GUI or the command line. The Google Cloud Console allows you to deploy Kubernetes objects without having to define the YAML files manually. It also visualizes the most useful ones and their relations. With the GUI, you can also perform some second-day operations. At this point, we encourage you to get some hands-on experience and play around with deploying your own application using either of these methods.

Cluster second-day operations

We have created the cluster and our first application has been deployed. Everything is up and running. Now, let's have a look at second-day operations such as upgrades and scaling. As you already know, these operations can be quite time-consuming if you deploy a cluster manually. When you use GKE, it takes care of automating those tasks for you. All you need to do is initiate this or even allow GKE to decide when the actions should be triggered. Let's start with upgrades.

Upgrading the cluster

Google Kubernetes allows us to simply upgrade cluster components without having to install anything manually. The master and the nodes are upgraded separately. Remember that masters can only work with nodes up to two minor versions older than their own version. Let's get started:

1. To check the current version of the master and nodes, use the following command:

```
gcloud container get-server-config
```

2. This will also show you the available versions. Google upgrades masters automatically but you can also trigger the upgrade of the master manually by running the following command:

```
gcloud container clusters upgrade $CLUSTER_NAME --master
```

3. Once your master has been upgraded, you can upgrade the nodes by running the following command:

```
gcloud container clusters upgrade $CLUSTER_NAME
```

GKE will attempt to reschedule the Pods from the node being upgraded. The node will be replaced with the new one with the desired version. When nodes register with the master, they are marked as schedulable.

 Although you can downgrade your node, Google does not recommend this. You can downgrade your nodes to one patch version lower than the master.

Auto-upgrades

Auto-upgrade is enabled by default for newly created clusters. The nodes are upgraded to keep up with the version of the master. The upgrade takes place during a chosen maintenance window. Only one node is upgraded at a time, and only within one node pool of the cluster. During the upgrade, the Pods residing in the node being upgraded are rescheduled. If it isn't possible to reschedule, the Pod goes into the pending mode. To enable auto-repair, use the --enable-autoupgrade flag when creating or updating your cluster.

Auto-repair

The auto-repair option allows you to keep the nodes of a cluster healthy. It monitors the state of the nodes' health and recreates them when needed. Recreation is triggered when the node reports NotReady or does not report at all for approximately 10 minutes. This will also trigger if the node is out of boot disk space for approximately 30 minutes. Before recreating, the node is drained. This might be unsuccessful if it is unresponsive. To enable auto-repair, use the --enable-autorepair flag when creating or updating your cluster.

Resizing the cluster

The GKE cluster can be resized by increasing or decreasing the number of nodes in a node pool. To perform a resize, use the following command:

```
gcloud container clusters resize $CLUSTER_NAME --node-pool $POOL_NAME --
size $SIZE
```

Here, we have the following options:

- $CLUSTER_NAME: The cluster's name
- $POOL_NAME: The name of the node pool to resize
- $SIZE: The number of nodes to run in the pool

When you increase the size of the cluster, new Pods might be scheduled on new nodes, but the old Pods will not be migrated. When you decrease the size of the cluster, the Pods hosted on the removed nodes will be deleted. They will only be recreated on other Pods if they are managed by the replication controller. To drain the nodes before removal, you can use the beta command:

```
gcloud beta container clusters resize $CLUSTER_NAME --node-pool $POOL_NAME
--size $SIZE
```

Autoscaling a cluster

You can also set your cluster to autoscale. The scaling event can be triggered by changes in workloads and resource usage. Autoscaling monitors your nodes and checks whether they should be increased or decreased. The maximum and minimum nodes to run in the cluster are defined in the following command:

```
gcloud container clusters create $CLUSTER_NAME --num-nodes $NUM --enable-
autoscaling --min-nodes $MIN_NODES --max-nodes $MAX_NODES --zone
$COMPUTE_ZONE
```

Here, we have the following options:

- $CLUSTER_NAME: The cluster's name
- $NUM: The initial number of nodes
- $MIN_NODES: The minimum number of nodes
- $MAX_NODES: The maximum number of nodes

You can also change the autoscaling settings using the following command:

```
gcloud container clusters update $CLUSTER_NAME --enable-autoscaling --min-
nodes $MIN_NODES --max-nodes $MAX_NODES --zone $COMPUTE_ZONE --node-pool
default-pool
```

Here, we have the following options:

- `$CLUSTER_NAME`: The cluster's name
- `$NUM`: The initial number of nodes
- `$MIN_NODES`: The minimum number of nodes
- `$MAX_NODES`: The maximum number of nodes

To disable autoscaling for a particular node, use the following command:

```
--no-enable-autoscaling flag
```

Rotating the master IP

The IP that's used by the master to server API calls is static and does not change unless it is initiated by the user. When you initiate IP rotation, the master uses both IPs temporarily until you confirm you want to finish the rotation.

To rotate the IP, use the following command:

```
gcloud container clusters update $CLUSTER_NAME]--start-ip-rotation
```

Here, `$CLUSTER_NAME` is the cluster's name.

The command will ask you whether you want to continue. When you continue, the old IP address will be deprecated.

IAM

Access to Google App Engine is secured with IAM. Let's have a look at a list of predefined roles, along with a short description of each:

- **Kubernetes Engine Admin**: Has the right to access the full management of clusters and their Kubernetes API objects
- **Kubernetes Engine Cluster Admin**: Has the right to access the management of clusters
- **Kubernetes Engine Cluster Viewer**: Has read-only access to clusters

- **Kubernetes Engine Developer**: Has full access to Kubernetes API objects inside clusters
- **Kubernetes Engine Host Service Agent User**: Has access to the GKE Host Service Agent
- **Kubernetes Engine Viewer**: Has read-only access to GKE resources

Kubernetes role-based access control

Native Kubernetes **role-based access control** (**RBAC**) can be used in combination with Cloud IAM. While Cloud IAM works on a project level. RBAC grants permissions to Kubernetes resources. Privileges are granted at the cluster or namespace level. The following is an example of a `Role` object that grants read access to all the Pods in a `mynamespace` namespace:

```
kind: Role
apiVersion: rbac.authorization.k8s.io/v1
metadata:
 namespace: mynamespace
 name: pod-reader
rules:
- apiGroups: [""] # "" indicates the core API group
 resources: ["pods"]
 verbs: ["get", "watch", "list"]
```

Container Registry

The container images that we use on application deployments to Kubernetes are stored in container repositories. Docker Hub (`hub.docker.com`) is a public Docker image repository. We can use it to pull public images. But what if we want a local repository where we want to store our own images? Google Cloud Platform comes with a service called Container Registry. This is essentially a single place where you can store, perform vulnerability scans on, and control access to your images. As it is hosted on GCP, it is also faster to use than Docker Hub. GKE clusters are able to access the registry that resides in the same project by default.

To run images that are stored in Container Registry, use the following command:

```
kubectl run $NAME --image=$HOSTNAME/$PROJECT-ID/$IMAGE:$TAG
```

Here, we have the following options:

- `$NAME`: Pod name
- `$HOSTNAME`: Depends on the location of the repository; for example, `gcr.io` (US), `eu.gcr.io` (European Union), or `asia.gcr.io` (Asia)
- `$PROJEC-ID`: ID of the GCP project
- `$IMAGE`: Image
- `$TAG`: Tag of the image

You can also use `HOSTNAME/$PROJECT-ID/$IMAGE:$TAG` in the Kubernetes YAML definition as the image parameter.

Cloud Build

Cloud Build is a service that originates from Container Builder. It was initially used for building container images. Google created this service with the intention of evolving it into a CI/CD service. Due to rebranding the service, additional functionalities were introduced. Cloud Build runs one or more build steps to produce artifacts. The build steps use so-called Cloud Builders, which are containers with a particular command-line tool installed on them. These include `git`, `docker`, `kubectl`, `maven`, `gcloud`, `gsutil`, and many others. The build steps are defined in YAML configuration files. The following YAML configuration file uses the Docker Cloud Builder to build a docker image and then push it to Container Registry:

```
steps:
- name: 'gcr.io/cloud-builders/docker'
  args: ['build', '-t', 'gcr.io/my-project/my-image', '.']
- name: 'gcr.io/cloud-builders/docker'
  args: ['push', 'gcr.io/my-project/my-image']
```

If standard builders are not enough, you can either search for a community cloud builder or create one of your own. This means that you can use whatever tools you need. To learn more about custom Cloud Builders, have a look at the *Further reading* section.

The build can be either run manually or triggered by a code repository. Cloud Build integrates with common code repositories such as Cloud Source Repository, GitHub, and Bitbucket.

Quotas and limits

Google Container Engine comes with the following limits:

- A maximum of 50 clusters per zone, plus 50 regional clusters per region
- A maximum of 5,000 nodes per cluster
- A maximum of 1,000 nodes per cluster if you use the GKE ingress controller
- 100 Pods per node
- 300,000 containers
- The GKE API limit is 10 requests per second

Note that GKE uses Compute Engine to host nodes, and so Compute Engine quotas also apply.

Additionally, there are resource quotas for the cluster itself. To view the quotas, use the `kubectl get resourcequota gke-resource-quotas -o yaml` command. Note that the quotas cannot be removed as they are there to protect the stability of the cluster.

Pricing

Under the hood, Kubernetes Engine uses Compute Engine services. You are billed for every virtual machine instance that is running as a node of the cluster. Because Kubernetes Engine abstracts master machines, you are not charged for them.

 Exam tip: Make sure you know the pricing model for the exam. Remember that you only pay for nodes.

Summary

In this chapter, we learned about GKE, as well as microservices and containers. We went through basic Kubernetes concepts and described the most important Kubernetes objects. We also looked at the advantages of using GKE, including auto-deployment, autoscaling, and auto-upgrades. We have deployed a cluster and looked at second-day operations. We also looked at how to connect to the cluster with the `kubectl` command. If you feel like doing some additional reading, have a look at the links that are provided in the *Further reading* section.

In the next chapter, we will talk about GCP's Platform as a Service offering, also known as App Engine.

Further reading

- **Kubernetes**: https://kubernetes.io
- **Microservices**: https://microservices.io/
- **Kubernetes tale**: https://www.youtube.com/watch?v=4ht22ReBjnot=31s
- **Kubectl**: https://kubernetes.io/docs/reference/kubectl/overview/
- **Network Overview**: https://cloud.google.com/kubernetes-engine/docs/concepts/network-overview
- **Services**: https://cloud.google.com/kubernetes-engine/docs/concepts/service
- **Ingress**: https://cloud.google.com/kubernetes-engine/docs/concepts/ingress
- **Node pools**: https://cloud.google.com/kubernetes-engine/docs/concepts/node-pools
- **Node taints**: https://cloud.google.com/kubernetes-engine/docs/how-to/node-taints
- **Autoscaler**: https://cloud.google.com/kubernetes-engine/docs/concepts/cluster-autoscaler
- **Upgrading a cluster**: https://cloud.google.com/kubernetes-engine/docs/how-to/upgrading-a-cluster
- **Persistent Volumes**: https://kubernetes.io/docs/concepts/storage/persistent-volumes/
- **Network Policies**: https://kubernetes.io/docs/concepts/services-networking/network-policies/
- **Quotas**: https://cloud.google.com/kubernetes-engine/quotas
- **Container Registry**: https://cloud.google.com/container-registry/docs/overview
- **Cloud Build**: https://cloud.google.com/cloud-build/docs/configuring-builds/create-basic-configuration
- **Cloud Builders**: https://cloud.google.com/cloud-build/docs/cloud-builders
- **Kubernetes RBAC**: https://kubernetes.io/docs/reference/access-authn-authz/rbac/

6
Exploring Google App Engine as a Compute Option

App Engine is a Platform as a Service offering. It is the fastest way to get your application running with Google Cloud. It is suitable for web, mobile, and IoT applications and takes away the overhead of managing the execution environment and scales quickly on demand. Multiple languages, such as Node.js, Java, Ruby, C#, Go, Python, and PHP, are supported. This way, the developer can concentrate on solely delivering the code. The applications are versioned and traffic can be directed to multiple versions, allowing us to perform A/B or canary tests. Applications in App Engine can be secured with firewalls, IAM roles, and SSL certificates, and can be scanned for common vulnerabilities using the Security Scanner service.

We will cover the following topics in this chapter:

- App Engine components
- Choosing the right location
- Working with App Engine
- Environment types
- Deploying an App Engine application
- Versions
- Splitting traffic
- Migrating traffic
- Firewall rules
- Settings
- Scaling

- Cron jobs
- Memcache
- IAM
- Quotas and limits
- Pricing

Exam tips: Expect a couple of questions on App Engine in the Cloud Architect exam. However, there is another (Cloud Developer) exam that tests your knowledge on App Engine in detail. For this exam, make sure you know about the following:

- How App Engine works
- The two types of App Engine environments, namely Standard and Flexible
- The two types of Memcache and use cases for them
- Versioning
- How to split migrate traffic
- What cron jobs are for
- Custom domains
- What SSL certificates can be used

Code in Action

Check out the following video to see the Code in Action:
http://bit.ly/31i6wpz

App Engine components

First, we need to understand that each project can host only one App Engine application.

The application can have multiple services with multiple versions, as shown in the following diagram:

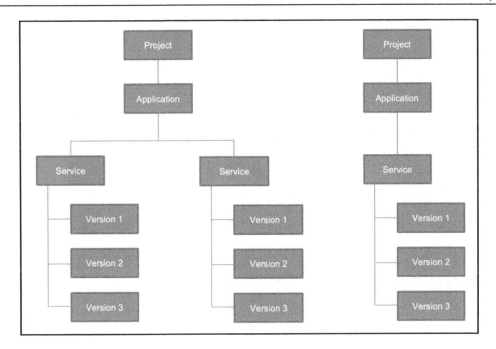

Which version is served to the end user is based on the network traffic configuration. We decide on the percentage of traffic that should be directed to a particular version. This means that it is very easy to make new rollouts and possibly even rollbacks.

Choosing the right location

Applications in App Engine are deployed regionally. This means that the infrastructure that's used to host it is spread across the zones within this region for high availability. The main consideration when it comes to choosing the region is where your end users will be connecting from. However, you should also remember that your app might use other GCP resources. This has an impact on delays as well as costs. At the time of writing, these are the available regions:

- northamerica-northeast1
- us-central
- us-west2
- us-east1
- us-east4
- southamerica-east1

- europe-west
- europe-west2
- europe-west3
- europe-west6
- asia-northeast1
- asia-northeast2
- asia-east2
- asia-south1
- australia-southeast1

Once the application has been deployed, you cannot change its region.

Working with App Engine

The deployment itself is fairly easy. We define an app.yaml file that defines the application and develop the code. With the use of gcloud app deploy, the application is deployed to App Engine:

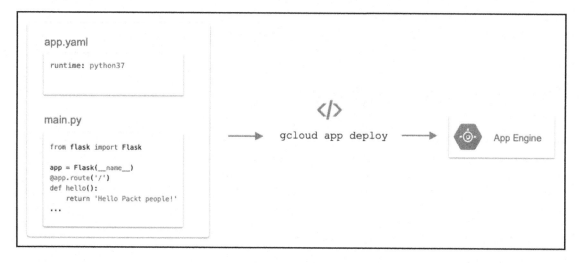

The preceding example is obviously very simple, and you can create far more sophisticated applications. The Cloud Architect exam does not require you to have deep knowledge of how to define the app.yaml file or how to write applications. However, we suggest that you have a look at the *Further reading* section as it might help you understand App Engine concepts better.

Environment types

App Engine comes with two types of environments, namely Standard and Flexible. If you don't have any special requirements, such as unsupported languages or need to customize the execution environment, always go for Standard. Let's have a look at these environment types.

App Engine Standard environment

The Standard environment uses **containers** running in GCP. These are standardized for each available execution environment. The traffic to your application is distributed using load balancing. The application can scale down to zero if it is not used and can be scaled up within seconds when the demand rises. The following execution environments are supported:

- Python 2.7 and 3.7
- Java 8 and 11
- Node.js 8 and 10
- PHP 5.5, 7.2, and 7.3
- Go 1.9, 1.11, and 1.12

 Exam tip: App Engine Standard is often also defined as a sandbox for developers.

Flexible environment

The Flexible environment uses GCE **virtual machine instances**. It also scales up and down automatically and distributes traffic using load balancing. However, it always requires at least a single instance to run. Starting the instances takes minutes, while in Standard environments, it takes seconds. The following execution environments are supported:

- Java 8
- Python 2.7 and 3.6
- Node.js
- Ruby
- PHP 5.6, 7.0, 7.1, and 7.2

- .NET core
- Go 1.9, 1.10, and 1.11
- Custom

Note that the runtimes can be customized. You can even create your own runtime. This is done by supplying a custom Docker image or Dockerfile.

Exam tip: As you may have noticed, the App Engine Standard environment can scale down to zero, while the Flexible environment will always run at least one instance. This obviously has an impact on the cost of running your application.

An App Engine Flexible environment service allows you to access root accounts on your instances via SSH. However, by default, this is disabled. Remember that the instances will be restarted on a weekly basis so that the necessary patches are applied.

Deploying an App Engine application

We have already seen how the applications are deployed to App Engine from a high level. Now, let's have a look at the actual steps we need to take. Here, we will provision a `Hello World` application. The application leverages the Python Flask web server. As you can probably imagine, the application will display static `Hello World` text on the website. Let's get started:

1. To start, go to the Google Cloud Console and switch to the project that your application will be deployed to. From the hamburger menu, choose **App Engine**. On the welcome screen, click the **Create Application** button:

2. In the **Create app** window, choose a region and click **Create app**, as shown in the following screenshot:

We have chosen `europe-west` as our region.

3. In the **Get started** window, choose the runtime language. We have selected **Python**:

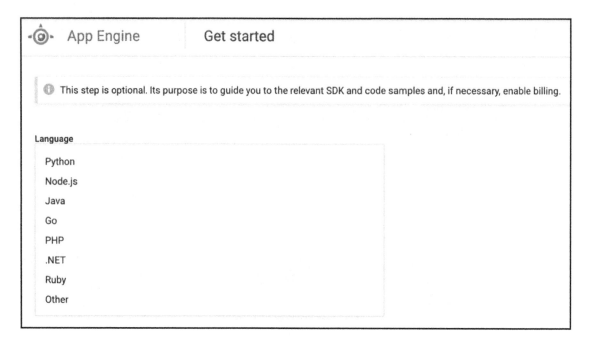

4. From the **Environment** dropdown, choose either **Standard** or **Flexible**. As we have no need for runtime customization, we have chosen the **Standard** environment. Click the **Next** button to continue:

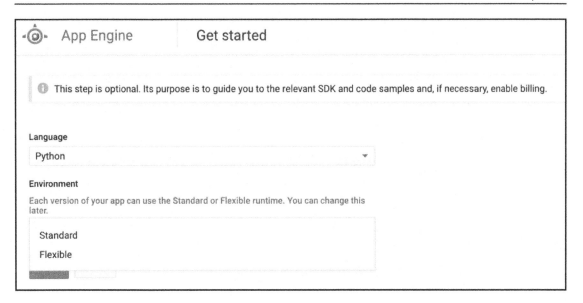

5. Now, we can either use the installation SDK on our own machine or use the Cloud Shell machine. To learn how to use both those tools, check out `Chapter 14`, *Google Cloud Management Options*.

   We will open the Cloud Shell as it comes with the SDK already installed and configured. Open the console and run the following command:

   ```
   gcloud config set project $PROJECT
   ```

   Here, `<project_id>` is the ID of the project you used in the Google Cloud Console.

6. Now, let's download a sample Python application that Google provides on GitHub:

   ```
   git clone
   https://github.com/GoogleCloudPlatform/python-docs-samples
   ```

7. Change directory to browse to the application:

   ```
   cd python-docs-samples/appengine/standard_python37/hello_world
   ```

8. Now, you can use any text editor to view the content of the `main.py` file, which contains our application code. You can see that the application is using the Flask web server and displays `Hello World` text on the `main` page:

```
main.py  ×
 1    # Copyright 2018 Google LLC
 2    #
 3    # Licensed under the Apache License, Version 2.0 (the "License");
 4    # you may not use this file except in compliance with the License.
 5    # You may obtain a copy of the License at
 6    #
 7    #       http://www.apache.org/licenses/LICENSE-2.0
 8    #
 9    # Unless required by applicable law or agreed to in writing, software
10    # distributed under the License is distributed on an "AS IS" BASIS,
11    # WITHOUT WARRANTIES OR CONDITIONS OF ANY KIND, either express or implied.
12    # See the License for the specific language governing permissions and
13    # limitations under the License.
14
15    # [START gae_python37_app]
16    from flask import Flask
17
18
19    # If `entrypoint` is not defined in app.yaml, App Engine will look for an app
20    # called `app` in `main.py`.
21    app = Flask(__name__)
22
23
24    @app.route('/')
25    def hello():
26        """Return a friendly HTTP greeting."""
27        return 'Hello World!'
28
29
30    if __name__ == '__main__':
31        # This is used when running locally only. When deploying to Google App
32        # Engine, a webserver process such as Gunicorn will serve the app. This
33        # can be configured by adding an `entrypoint` to app.yaml.
34        app.run(host='127.0.0.1', port=8080, debug=True)
35    # [END gae_python37_app]
```

9. If we have a look at that `app.yaml` file, we see that we only need to define the runtime type without any additional parameters:

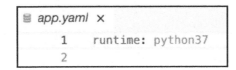

10. Finally, we will have a look at the `requirements.txt` file, which defines the modules that are used in our Python code:

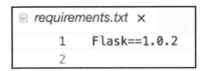

11. Now that we know what the configuration and code is, we can deploy the application to App Engine. Being in the folder where all the files are, run the following command:

```
gcloud app deploy app.yaml --project $PROJECT
```

It may take a minute or two to deploy.

12. Once the application has been deployed, we can check the URL that's assigned to the application by running the following command:

```
gcloud app browse
```

13. Copy the URL and paste into your browser. You will see that the application is already running in App Engine. Simple, isn't it?

Next, let's look at versions.

Versions

Now, let's imagine we want to update the application with new content:

1. Let's modify the welcome message to `Hello Packt people!`:

```
24    @app.route('/')
25    def hello():
26        """Return a friendly HTTP greeting."""
27        return 'Hello Packt people!'
```

2. We will save the changes and deploy the application again:

   gcloud app deploy app.yaml --project <project_id>

3. Now, if we switch to the Google Cloud Console and go to **App Engine |
   Versions**, we will see that a new version of the application has been deployed:

Note that all the traffic is still directed toward the old version.

Splitting traffic

Now, imagine that we want to test the changes that we've made on a small number of users. We can do that by clicking on **Split traffic**, which can be found in the top right corner. This will bring us to a window where we can choose how much traffic is directed to each version of the application. Choose an appropriate percentage and click the **Save** button:

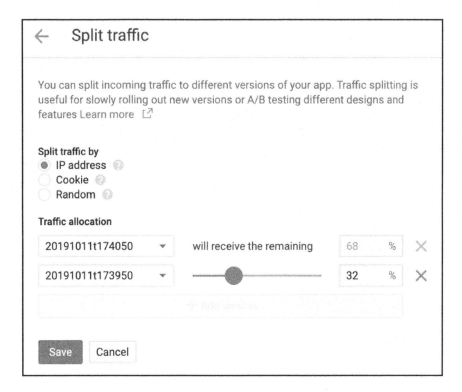

We can move 100% of the traffic to the new version if we wish.

Migrating traffic

Instead of splitting the traffic, we can also migrate the traffic at once. There are also gradual traffic migrating options as well so that we can gracefully change the version. Follow these steps to do so:

1. Select the checkbox next to the new version and click **MIGRATE TRAFFIC**, which can be found at top of the screen. On the popup window, click **MIGRATE**, as shown in the following screenshot:

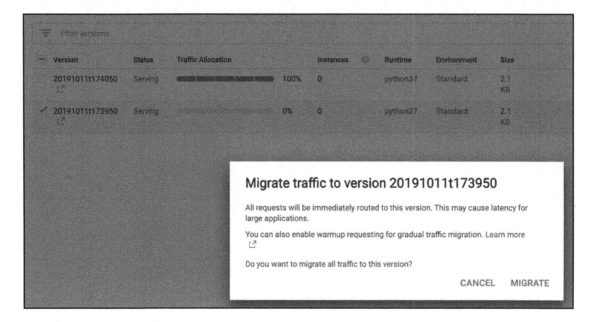

The traffic will now be migrated to the new version.

Exam tip: Pay special attention to how you switch traffic between different versions. This can be used for both rolling out the new version as well as rolling back to the last stable version.

2. Now, if we check the console, we will see that all the traffic is allocated to the new version:

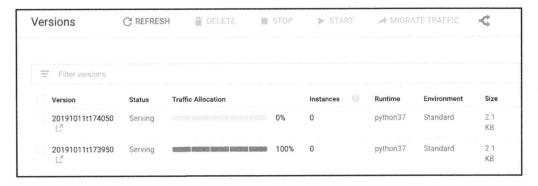

3. If we browse to the URL, we will see that the new version of the application is now being served:

We can see the updated message from the NGINX web server.

Firewall rules

The firewall for App Engine is pretty simple. It contains a list of rules for allowing or denying traffic to your application from a specific IP range. Note that the rules apply to all the resources of the application. The rules are ordered by priority, with a value of 1 being the most important and 2147483647 being the least important:

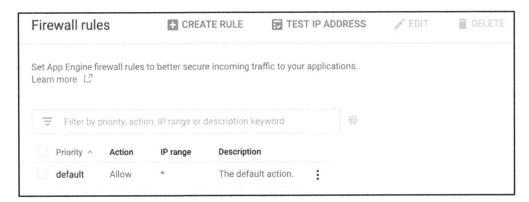

The default rule, which allows all traffic from all IP ranges, has the lowest priority and is always evaluated at the end.

Settings

From the hamburger menu, go to **App Engine** | **Settings**. Here, you will find two important settings: **Custom domain** and **SSL certificates**. Let's go over these now.

Custom domain

As you already know, when you deploy an application, you are assigned an URL in the form of `<project_id>.appspot.com`.

You can, however, add a custom domain or register a new domain. You do this from the **App Engine** | **Setting** | **Custom domains** menu:

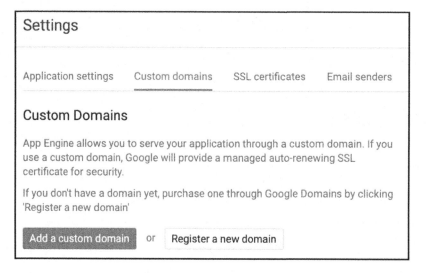

If you choose to register a new domain, you will be able to purchase it from the Google Domains service.

SSL certificates

Since the traffic in the App Engine is load balanced and uses SSL, GCP offers globally distributed SSL endpoints so that you can serve your application users. An application with a custom domain has a managed SSL certificate assigned to it by default. The certificate will be provisioned and renewed before expiration automatically. When you remove the custom domain, the certificate will be revoked:

If you wish to use your own certificate, you are responsible for managing its life cycle.

Scaling

One of the most important features of App Engine is its ability to scale a number of instances. We have a choice regarding the level of automation we want to use. App Engine offers three options, as follows:

- **Manual scaling**: In this setup, you specify the number of instances that will run, no matter what the load will be. Since the instances keep the memory state, it can be used for applications that depend on it.
- **Automatic scaling**: In this setup, a number of instances depend on the request rate, response latencies, and other application metrics. It also allows you to specify a number of instances that should always run independently of the load.
- **Basic scaling**: In this setup, an instance is created when a request is received by the application. The instance will be shut down when the application becomes idle. It can be used for apps that are driven by user activity.

Scaling is a very important topic for App Engine. We want to make sure that the application can handle the load, but we also want to control the cost. Remember that you pay for the time it takes to run the instances. You can control the scaling behavior using parameters in the YAML that defines your application. Check the *Further reading* section regarding App Engine scaling to find out more.

Cron jobs

With cron jobs, you can schedule tasks that run at a defined time or regular intervals. The use case for cron jobs includes administration tasks that need to reoccur; for example, you need to send out an email every day that includes a report about the environment.

For each language, the cron jobs are configured a little bit differently. See the *Further reading* section to see detailed configuration for various languages. The cron jobs are defined in YAML format and placed in the `cron.yaml` file.

The following is a YAML file that will run the task every 24 hours:

1. The actual task is to run it using the handler defined under the `url` parameter:

```
cron:
 - description: "daily summary job"
   url: /tasks/summary
   target: beta
   schedule: every 24 hours
```

2. To deploy the cron job, use the following command:

```
gcloud app deploy cron.yaml
```

3. Once deployed, the jobs are visible in the Google Cloud Console under **App Engine** | **Cron jobs**:

Cron jobs	C REFRESH				

A cron job is a scheduled task that runs at a specific time or at regular intervals.

Cron job ∧	Description	Frequency	Last run	Status	Log	
/tasks/summary	daily summary job	every 24 hours (GMT)		Has not run yet.	View	Run now

Exam tip: Remember that cron jobs are a way of triggering jobs periodically and are an alternative to using Compute Engine with native third-party tools.

Memcache

Caching is a common way of speeding up how we can access frequently accessed data. This includes session data, user preferences, or any other queries that don't change often. If there are multiple queries accessing the same data, it is a perfect candidate to be cached. Memcache is a service that's built in to App Engine. It allows you to keep key-value pairs in memory that can be accessed much faster than querying a database. There are two service levels for Memcache, as follows:

- **Shared**: This is the default and free version of Memcache. Note that this service is provided on best effort. The resources are shared with multiple applications within the App Engine platform.
- **Dedicated**: This is an optional and paid version of Memcache. It provides a fixed cache capacity dedicated to your application. It is paid per GB/hour. This should be used for applications that require predictable performance.

You can add values to be cached by accessing the **App Engine** | **Memcache** menu:

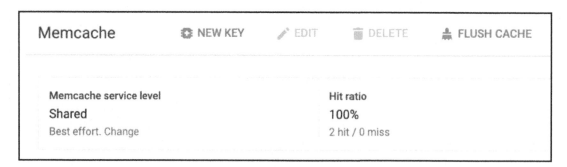

Exam tips: Make sure you understand that the standard cache is delivered on best effort and might not fit all use cases. If you want to have predictable performance, use a dedicated cache.

IAM

Access to Google App Engine is secured with IAM. Let's have a look at a list of predefined roles, along with a short description of each:

- **App Engine Admin**: Read/write/modify access to all application configuration and settings.
- **App Engine Service Admin**: Read-only access to application configuration and settings. Write access to service and version settings. Cannot deploy versions of apps.
- **App Engine Deployer**: Read-only access to application configuration and settings. Can deploy and create new versions and delete old ones. Cannot modify an existing version traffic configuration.
- **App Engine Viewer**: Read-only access to application configuration and settings.
- **App Engine Code Viewer**: Read-only access application configuration, settings, and deployed code.

For less granular access, you can also use primitive roles of **Owner**, **Editor**, and **Viewer.**

Quotas and limits

Google App Engine comes with predefined quotas. These default quotas can be changed via the hamburger menu, under **IAM & Admin** | **Quotas**. From this menu, we can review the current quotas and request an increase to these limits. You should be aware of the limits for each service as this can have an impact on your scalability.

For App Engine, we should be aware of the following quotas:

- **Free quotas**: For each application, you are allowed a certain amount of resources for free. This quota can be exceeded only for paid applications.
- **Spending limits**: This quota is used to control the limits you spend. It can be set by the **project owner** or **billing administrator**.
- **Safety limits**: This quota is set by Google to protect App Engine.

Pricing

The price of App Engine consists of multiple factors and differs for Standard and Flexible environments. For Standard environment instances, running in manual and basic scaling services are billed at hourly rates based on uptime. For Flexible environments, the applications are deployed into virtual machine instances that are billed on a per-second with a minimum of 1 minute usage.

On top of that, you need to include the cost of additional resources that are used by your application. To get the most recent prices, take a look at the following link: `https://cloud.google.com/appengine/pricing`.

Summary

In this chapter, we had a look at App Engine, which is a Platform as a Service offering. We have distinguished between two types of environments, namely Standard and Flexible. We have looked at how to deploy an App Engine application and how to update it to new versions. We also learned how to split and migrate traffic between the versions. Finally, we learned about cron jobs, which allow us to run scheduled jobs.

In the next chapter, we will have a look at Cloud Functions, which is a Function as a Service offering.

Further reading

To find out more about App Engine, check out the following links:

- **App.yaml reference**: https://cloud.google.com/appengine/docs/standard/python/config/appref
- **Environments**: https://cloud.google.com/appengine/docs/the-appengine-environments
- **Memcache**: https://cloud.google.com/appengine/docs/standard/python/memcache/
- **Firewall**: https://cloud.google.com/appengine/docs/standard/python/creating-firewalls
- **Cron Jobs for Python**: https://cloud.google.com/appengine/docs/standard/python/config/cron
- **Cron Jobs for Java**: https://cloud.google.com/appengine/docs/standard/java/config/cron
- **Cron Jobs for Go**: https://cloud.google.com/appengine/docs/standard/go/config/cron
- **Custom domains**: https://cloud.google.com/appengine/docs/standard/python/mapping-custom-domains
- **SSL certificates**: https://cloud.google.com/appengine/docs/standard/python/securing-custom-domains-with-ssl
- **App Engine scaling**: https://cloud.google.com/appengine/docs/standard/python/how-instances-are-managed

7

Running Serverless Functions with Google Cloud Functions

In this chapter, we will finally talk about fully serverless compute options, that is, Cloud Functions. This means no more servers and no more containers. Obviously, this service is leveraging them in the backend, but they aren't visible to the end user. All we need to care about now is the code. Cloud Functions is a **Function as a Service (FaaS)** offering. This means that you write a function in one of the languages supported by GCP and it can be triggered by an event or via HTTP. GCP takes care of provisioning and scaling the resources that are needed to run your functions.

How do Cloud Functions work in the backend? Again, you don't really need to bother about GCP's backend infrastructure, which runs the functions for you. However, being an engineer, I bet you will still search for answers on your own. Cloud Functions are actually using containers to set an isolated environment for your function. These are called Cloud Functions instances. If multiple functions are executed in parallel, multiple instances are created.

Exam tip: Expect Cloud Functions questions to appear in the Cloud Architect exam. You will need to understand what Cloud Functions are and what the most common use cases are. Being able to tell the difference between two types of functions, namely HTTP and backend functions, is also important. Knowing when you would use Cloud Functions rather than other compute options, as well as remembering what programming languages are supported, is crucial. Finally, be sure you can deploy the function both from the Google Cloud console and the command line.

In this chapter, we will go through the following topics:

- Main Cloud Functions characteristics
- Use cases
- Runtime environments
- Type of Cloud Functions
- Events and triggers
- Other considerations
- Deploying Cloud Functions
- IAM
- Quotas and limits
- Pricing
- Cloud run

Main Cloud Functions characteristics

The following are the key Cloud Functions characteristics:

- **Serverless**: Cloud Functions are completely serverless. The underlying infrastructure is abstracted from the end user.
- **Event-driven**: Cloud Functions are event-driven. There are triggered in response to an event or HTTP request. This means they are invoked only when needed and do not produce any cost when inactive.
- **Stateless**: Cloud Functions do not store state nor data. This allows them to work independently and scale as needed. It is very important to understand that each invocation has its own execution environment and does not share global variable memory or filesystems. To share state across function invocations, your function should use a service such as Cloud Datastore or Cloud Storage.
- **Autoscaling**: Cloud Functions scale from zero to the desired scale. Scaling is managed by GCP without any end user intervention. Autoscaling limits can be set to control the cost of execution. This is important as failures in the design might cause large spikes, resulting in your bill reaching the clouds.

Use cases

Now that we have a basic understanding of Cloud Functions, let's have a look at numerous use cases. Remember that, in each of these use cases, you can still use other compute options. However, it is a matter of delivering the solution fast, taking advantage of in-built autoscaling, and paying only for what we have actually used.

Application backends

Instead of using virtual machines for backend computing, you can simply use functions. Let's have a look at some example backends:

- **IoT backends**: In the IoT world, there's a large number of devices that send data to the backend. Cloud Functions allow you to process this data and auto-scale it when needed. This happens without any human intervention.
- **Mobile backends**: Cloud Functions can process data that's delivered by your mobile applications. They can interact with all GCP services to make use of big data, machine learning capabilities, and so on. There is no need to use any virtual machines and you can go completely serverless.
- **Third-party API integrations**: You can use functions to integrate with any third-party system that provides an API. This will allow you to extend your application with additional features that are delivered by other providers.

Real-time data processing systems

When it comes to event-driven data processing, Cloud Functions can be triggered whenever a predefined event occurs. When this happens, it can preprocess the data that's passed for analysis with GCP big data services:

- **Real-time stream processing**: When messages arrive in the Pub/Subs, Cloud Functions can be triggered to analyze or enrich the messages to prepare them for further data processing steps in the pipeline.
- **Real-time files processing**: When files are uploaded to your Cloud Storage bucket, they can be immediately processed. For example, thumbnails can be created or analyzed using GCP AI APIs.

Smart applications

Smart applications allow users to perform various tasks in a smarter way by using a data-driven experience. Some of these are as follows:

- **Chatbots and virtual assistants**: You can connect your text or voice platforms to Cloud Functions to integrate them with other GCP services, such as DialogFlow (see `Chapter 12`, *Putting Machine Learning to Work*), to give the user natural conversation experience. The conversation logic can be defined in DialogFlow without any programming skills. Integration with third-party applications can be created to provide services such as weather information or the purchase of goods.
- **Video and image analysis**: You can use Cloud Functions to interact with the various GCP AI building blocks, such as video and image AI. When a user uploads an image or video to your application, Cloud Functions can immediately trigger the related API and return the analysis. They may even perform actions depending on the results of that analysis.
- **Lightweight APIs and Webhooks**: Since Cloud Functions can be triggered using HTTP, you can expose your application to the external world for programmatic consumption. You don't need to build your API from scratch.

Runtime environments

Cloud Functions are executed in a fullymanaged environment. The infrastructure and software that's needed to run the function are handled for you. Each function is single-threaded and is run in an isolated environment with the intended context. You don't need to take care of any updates for that environment. They are auto-updated for you and scaled as needed.

Currently, there are a number of runtimes supported by Cloud Functions, namely the following:

- Node.js 6, 8, and 10
- Python 3.7
- Go 1.11

When you define a function, you can also define the requirements or dependencies file in which you state which modules or libraries your function is dependent on. Remember, however, that those libraries will be loaded when your function is executed. This causes delays in terms of execution. We will talk about this in more detail in the *Cold start* section of this chapter.

Types of Cloud Functions

There are two types of Cloud Functions: HTTP and background functions. They differ in the way they are triggered. Let's have a look at each of them.

HTTP functions

HTTP functions are invoked by HTTP(S) requests. The POST, PUT, GET, DELETE, and OPTIONS HTTP methods are accepted. Arguments can be provided to the function using the request body:

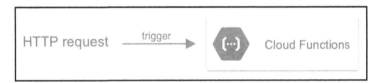

The invocation can be defined as synchronous as it can return a response that's been constructed within the function.

Interesting fact: Don't expect a question on this on the exam. However, it might be interesting to know that Cloud Functions handle HTTP requests using common frameworks. For Node.js, this is Express 4.16.3, for Python, this is Flask 1.0.2, and for Go, this is the standard http.HadlerFunc interface.

Background functions

Background functions are invoked by events such as changes in the Cloud Storage bucket, messages in the **Cloud Pub/Sup** topic, or one of the supported **Firebase** events:

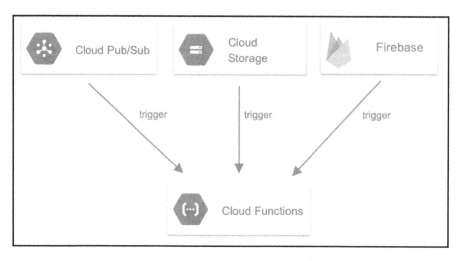

In the preceding diagram, we can see various triggers for **Cloud Functions**, that is, **Cloud Pub/Sub**, **Cloud Storage**, and **Firebase**.

Events

Events can be defined as **things** happening in or outside the GCP environment. When they occur, you might want certain actions to be triggered. An example of an event might be a file that's been added to Cloud Storage, a change that was made to your database table, and a new resource that has been provisioned to GCP, to name a few. These events can come from one of the following providers:

- Cloud Storage
- Cloud Pub/Sub
- Stackdriver Logging
- Cloud Firestore
- Firebase Realtime Database, Storage, Authentication

If you create a sink to forward the logs to Pub/Sub, then you can trigger Cloud Functions (for more details, check out Chapter 15, *Monitoring Your Infrastructure*).

Triggers

For your function to react to an event, a trigger needs to be configured. The actual binding of the trigger happens at deployment time. We will have a look at how to deploy functions with different kinds of triggers in the *Deploying Cloud Functions* section.

Other considerations

When using Cloud Functions, you should be aware of a couple of features and considerations. Let's have a look at each of them.

Cloud SQL connectivity

As we mentioned previously, Cloud Functions are stateless and the state needs to be saved on external storage or in a database. This can be done with external storage such as Cloud Storage or a database such as Cloud SQL. In general, any external storage can be used. We introduced Cloud SQL in `Chapter 3`, *Google Cloud Platform Core Services*. To remind you, it is a managed MySQL or Postgres database. With Cloud Functions, you can connect to Cloud SQL using a local socket interface that's provided in the Cloud Functions execution environment. It eliminates the need for exposing your database to a public network.

Connecting to internal resources in a VPC network

If your function needs to access services within a VPC, you can connect to it directly by passing a public network. To do this, you need to create a serverless VPC access connector from the network menu and refer to the connector when you deploy the function. Note that this does not work with Shared VPCs and legacy networks.

Environmental variables

Cloud Functions allow you to set environmental variables that are available during the runtime of the function. The variables are stored in the function's backend and follow the same life cycle as the function itself. The variables are set using the `--set-env-vars` flag, for example:

```
gcloud functions deploy env_vars --runtime python37 --set-env-vars FOO=bar
--trigger-http
```

Cold start

As we mentioned previously, Cloud Functions execute using function instances. These new instances are created in the following cases:

- The function is deployed
- Scale-up is required to handle the load
- When replacing an existing instance is triggered

Cold starts can impact the performance of your application. Google comes with a set of tips and tricks to help us reduce the impact of cold starts. Check out the *Further reading* section for a link to a detailed guide.

Local emulator

Deploying functions to GCP takes time. If you want to speed up tests, you can use a local simulator. This only works with Node.js and allows you to deploy, run, and debug your functions.

Deploying Cloud Functions

Cloud Functions can be deployed using a CLI, the Google Cloud Console, or with APIs. In this section, we will have a look at the first two methods since it's likely that you will be tested on them in the exam.

Deploying Cloud Functions with the Google Cloud Console

To deploy Cloud Functions from the Google Cloud Console, follow these steps:

1. Select **Cloud Functions** from the hamburger menu. You will see the **Cloud Functions** window. Click on **CREATE FUNCTION**:

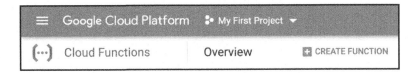

2. Fill in the name of your function and choose the memory you wish to allocate under **Memory allocated**:

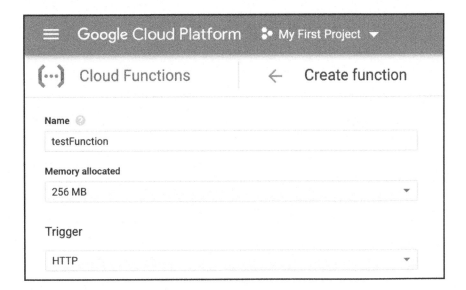

3. Choose the trigger type from the drop-down menu:

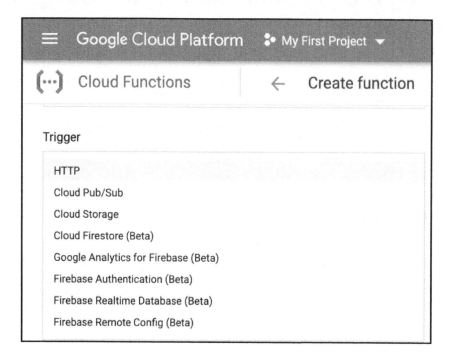

If you have chosen to use an HTTP trigger, the URL to call your function will be generated for you in the **URL** section, like so:

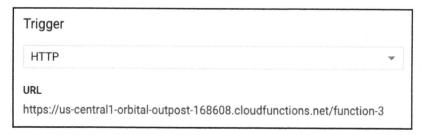

4. Next, select how you will provide your code. You can either use the **Inline editor**, upload it from your local machine (**ZIP upload**) or **ZIP from Cloud Storage**, or even use **Cloud Source repository**:

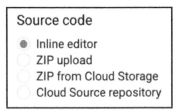

5. From the **Runtime** dropdown, choose the programming language you will use to write your functions. For this example, we decided to use the inline editor for Python 3.7. Therefore, we need to provide two files: `main.py`, where we define the function, and `requirements.txt`, with dependencies:

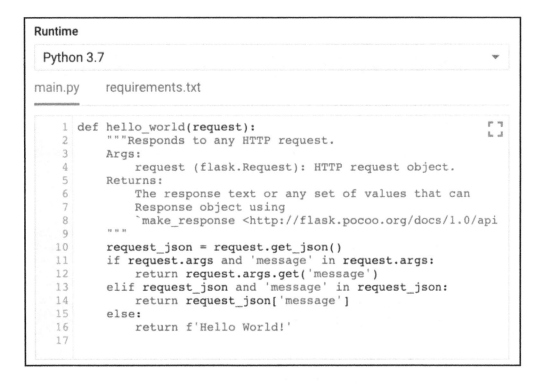

6. Click on the `requirements.txt` hyperlink. As an example, to be able to make REST API calls, we need to define that the `requests` module needs to be loaded:

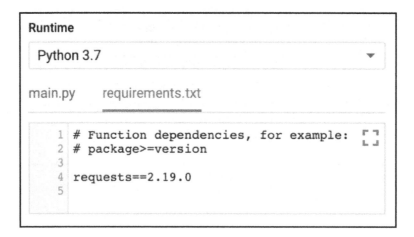

7. In the **Function to execute** field, we define the name of the function, for example, `hello_world`:

8. Now, we can simply deploy the function or continue with the **Advanced** options.

Let's have a look at them:

- **Region**: Defines which region the Function will be executed in.
- **VPC connector**: Allows you to choose a predefined VPC connector.
- **Timeout**: Defines the time after which the function will time out.
- **Maximum function instances**: Defines how many functions can be executed in parallel.
- **Service account**: Allows you to choose a service account the Function will use. By default, the App Engine service account will be used.

- **Environmental variables**: Allows you to define environmental variables:

9. Now that we have everything configured, we can click on **Create** to deploy the function:

10. Once your function has been deployed, you will be able to see it in the **Cloud Functions** list:

Your function is ready to execute.

Deploying functions with the gcloud command

Now that we have seen how to deploy the function using Google Cloud Console it will be easier to explain the parameters and flags for the `gcloud` command.

To deploy Cloud Functions, we will use the following command:

```
gcloud deploy cloud functions $FUNCTION_NAME \
--region=$REGION \
--entry-point=$ENTRY_POINT \
--memory=$MEMORY \
--runtime=$RUNTIME \
--service-account=$SERVICE_ACCOUNT\
--source=$SOURCE \
--stage-bucket=$STAGE_BUCKET \
--timeout=$TIMEOUT \
--retry
```

Here, we have the following options:

- `$REGION`: Region for the function.
- `$ENTRY_POINT`: Name of the functions (as defined in the source code).
- `$MEMORY`: Limit on the amount of memory. The allowed values are 128 MB, 256 MB, 512 MB, 1,024 MB, and 2,048 MB.
- `$SERVICE_ACCOUNT`: IAM service account associated with the function.
- `$SOURCE`: Source code location. Can be either Cloud Storage, source repository, or the local filesystem.

- `$STAGE_BUCKET`: If a function is deployed from a local directory, it defines the name of the Cloud Storage bucket in which the source code will be stored.
- `$TIMEOUT`: The function's execution timeout.
- `--retry`: Applies only to background functions. If present, it defines that the function should retry running if it's not executed successfully.

Triggers

After defining the necessary parameters, you can define the following triggers, depending on how you want your function to be initiated.

To define an HTTP trigger, use the following command:

```
--trigger-http
```

An endpoint will be assigned to the function.

To trigger a function on changes to a Cloud Storage bucket, use the following command:

```
--trigger-bucket=$TRIGGER_BUCKET
```

Here, we have the following option:

- `$TRIGGER_BUCKET`: Google Cloud Storage bucket name. Every change that's made to the files in this bucket will trigger function execution.

To trigger a function on messages that are arriving in a Pub/Sub queue, use the following command:

```
--trigger-topic=$TRIGGER_TOPIC
```

Here, we have the following option:

- `$TRIGGER_TOPIC`: Name of Pub/Sub topic. Messages arriving in the queue will trigger the function. The message content will be passed to the function.

For other sources, such as Firebase, use the following command:

```
--trigger-event=$EVENT_TYPE
--trigger-resource=$RESOURCE
```

Here, we have the following options:

- `$EVENT_TYPE`: Action that should trigger the function
- `$RESOURCE`: A resource from which the event occurs

Let's have a look at an example of configuring a trigger from Pub/Sub:

```
gcloud functions deploy hello_pubsub --runtime python37 --trigger-topic
mytopic
```

This will deploy a function called `help_pubsub`, where there will be a message arriving to the `mytopic` Pub/Sub topic.

 You may be interested in looking at some more advanced triggers, for example, using Firebase authentication. Check out `https://cloud.google.com/functions/docs/calling/` for examples for every possible trigger.

IAM

Access to Google App Engine is secured with IAM. Let's have a look at the list of predefined roles, along with a short description for each:

- **Cloud Functions Developer**: Has the right to create, update, and delete functions, as well as view source code. Cannot set IAM policies.
- **Cloud Functions Viewer**: Has the right to view functions. Cannot get IAM policies nor view the source code.

Note that, for the Cloud Functions Developer role to work, you must also assign the user the IAM Service Account User role on the Cloud Functions runtime service account.

Quotas and limits

Google Cloud Functions come with predefined quotas. These default quotas can be changed via the hamburger menu via **IAM & Admin** I **Quotas**. From this menu, we can review the current quotas and request an increase to these limits. We recommend that you become familiar with the limits for each service as this can have an impact on your scalability. For Cloud Functions, we should be aware of the following three types of quotas:

- **Resource limits**: Defines the total amount of resources your functions can consume
- **Time limits**: Defines how long things can run
- **Rate limits**: Defines the rate at which you can call the Cloud Functions API

The list of values is quite extensive. Check out the *Further reading* section if you wish to see a detailed list.

Pricing

The price of Cloud Functions consists of multiple factors. These include the number of **Invocations**, **Compute time**, and network rate (**Networking**). These are shown in the following diagram:

Remember that there is a monthly free usage tier you can play around with without generating any cost. At the time of writing this book, it consists of 2 million invocations, 1 million seconds of compute time, and 5 GB of egress network traffic. Enjoy it!

Cloud Run

Cloud Run is a new service that was recently announced at Google Next. It probably won't appear in the exam, but it might be an interesting alternative to Cloud Functions if you want to use a language that is not supported by Cloud Function. With Cloud Run, you can define containers that can be hosted natively on Cloud Run or on a GKE cluster. The container's number can scale to zero and can be triggered using HTTP requests.

Summary

In this chapter, we have talked about Cloud Functions and a number of use cases where they work perfectly. We talked about two types of functions, namely HTTP and background functions, and also understood that functions can be executed via a particular event or via an HTTP request. Finally, we looked at how a function can be deployed both with the Google Cloud Console and with the `gcloud` command.

With this chapter, we have concluded Google Compute options. In the next chapter, we will have a look at networking.

Further reading

- **Cloud Functions behind the scenes**: https://cloud.google.com/functions/docs/concepts/exec
- **Cloud Functions and VPC**: https://cloud.google.com/functions/docs/connecting-vpc
- **Local Emulator**: https://cloud.google.com/functions/docs/emulator
- **Cold Starts**: https://cloud.google.com/functions/docs/bestpractices/tips
- **Quotas**: https://cloud.google.com/functions/quotas
- **Pricing**: https://cloud.google.com/functions/pricing-summary/
- **The gcloud command**: https://cloud.google.com/sdk/gcloud/reference/functions/deploy
- **Cloud Run**: https://cloud.google.com/run/

Networking Options in GCP 8

We already know that compute is the most fundamental cloud feature. But even if we are able to do the computation without connecting to our resources, we get no value. Networking covers many types of connections. We need to be able to connect to the Google Cloud Console and the GCP API. We may want to connect our on-premise datacenter to GCP either through a **Virtual Private Network** (**VPN**) or through a high bandwidth interconnect. Finally, we might need to have load-balanced connectivity to virtual machine instances. GCP networking will help us with all of that.

In this chapter, we will go through all the theory that we need to know so that we understand how workloads communicate internally and externally to GCP. We will also have a look at all the basic networking services.

We will cover the following topics:

- Exploring GCP
- Understanding Virtual Private Cloud
- Load balancing
- **Network Address Translation** (**NAT**)
- Hybrid connectivity
- DNS
- Firewall rules
- Private access

Exploring GCP networking

Google Network is something that differs from other clouds. To understand the huge amount of investment Google has made in networking, we should have a look at the following map (`https://cloud.google.com/about/locations/#network-tab`). This map shows hundreds of thousands of fiber optic cables running between 61 zones and 134 **point-of-presence** (PoP). Keep in mind that this view is from September 2019 and that it is still growing:

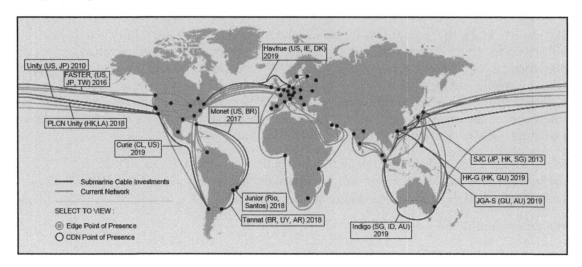

Source: https://cloud.google.com/about/locations/#network-tab
License: https://creativecommons.org/licenses/by/4.0/legalcode

Having such a massive network infrastructure allows you to connect GCP very closely to your ISP. In fact, GCP offers two service tiers, as follows:

- **Premium**: The premium tier provides high-performance routing. On top of that, it offers global load balancing and a **Content Delivery Network (CDN)** service. It is aimed at use cases where global presence is required and has the best user experience in mind. This tier comes with **Service Level Agreements (SLAs)**.

- **Standard**: The standard tier is a lower performance network with no SLAs attached. The CDN service is not available and load balancers are regional. It is aimed at use cases where cost is the main deciding factor. The GCP networking that's exposed to the user is based on a **Software-Defined Network (SDN)** called **Andromeda**. This platform is an orchestration point for all network services in GCP. Fortunately, this is abstracted from the user and there is no need to understand how Andromeda works itself.

Exam tip: Interestingly enough, networking is not the key topic of the exam; however, there is a GCP Certified Network Engineer exam that will test your GCP network knowledge thoroughly. It is impossible to understand other GCP services without understanding the basics of networking. Therefore, in this chapter, you will learn about Google's global network and the GCP network services.

Understanding Virtual Private Cloud

The fundamental concept of the GCP network is VPC, which is also simply called a **network**. As you learned in `Chapter 2`, *Getting Started with Google Cloud Platform*, GCP can be divided into projects that logically isolate Google Cloud. Within a project, you can create multiple VPCs.

By default, up to five networks can be created per project (the quota can be extended by contacting support). Multiple VPCs make it possible to separate GCP resources such as VM, containers, and so on at a network level. VPC has a **global** scope and it can span through all GCP regions. To allow connectivity between VMs residing in different VPCs, you have two options: you can create a shared VPC or peer the VPCs. We will have a look at each option in detail later in this chapter.

Furthermore, the VPCs are divided into regional subnetworks, also known as **subnets**, that have associated IP ranges that are used to assign addresses to resources.

When you create a new project, a default network is created for you. Subnets are created for each region and have allocated non-overlapping CIDR blocks.

Classless Inter-Domain Routing (**CIDR**) is an IP addressing schema that replaces the classful A, B, C system. It is based on variable-length subnet masks. In the case of CIDR, the prefixes of the subnet can be defined as an arbitrary number, making the network mask length more flexible. This means that organizations can make more efficient utilization of the IP address schemas.

Also, default firewall rules are created to allow us to ingress ICMP, RDP, and SSH from anywhere. Any traffic within the default network is also allowed:

Name	Region	Subnets	Mode	IP addresses ranges	Gateways	Firewall Rules
default		11	Auto ▾			11
	us-central1	default		10.128.0.0/20	10.128.0.1	
	europe-west1	default		10.132.0.0/20	10.132.0.1	
	us-west1	default		10.138.0.0/20	10.138.0.1	
	asia-east1	default		10.140.0.0/20	10.140.0.1	
	us-east1	default		10.142.0.0/20	10.142.0.1	
	asia-northeast1	default		10.146.0.0/20	10.146.0.1	
	asia-southeast1	default		10.148.0.0/20	10.148.0.1	
	us-east4	default		10.150.0.0/20	10.150.0.1	
	australia-southeast1	default		10.152.0.0/20	10.152.0.1	
	europe-west2	default		10.154.0.0/20	10.154.0.1	
	europe-west3	default		10.156.0.0/20	10.156.0.1	

VPC networks   CREATE VPC NETWORK   REFRESH

If you create a new VPC, you have two modes to choose from:

- **Auto mode**: Automatically creates one subnet per region with predefined IP ranges with the /20 mask from the 10.128.0.0/9 CIDR block. Each subnet is expandable to the /16 mask.
- **Custom mode**: It does not create subnets automatically and delegates complete control to the user. You decide how many subnets should be created and in which regions.

When creating a subnet, you must define one primary range and can also define up to five secondary ranges (though this is optional):

- **Primary IP address range**: For this range, addresses can be assigned from RFC 1918 CIDR address spaces and should not overlap in the same network. These can be assigned to a VM primary internal IP addresses, VM alias IP addresses, and the IP addresses of internal load balancers. Note that there are always four addresses reserved in this range.
- **Secondary IP address range**: For this range, addresses can be assigned from the RFC 1918 CIDR address space and can only be used for alias IP addresses. There are no addresses reserved in those ranges.

 Alias IP addresses can be assigned to a VM if there are multiple services running on it. You can map them to the Alias IP that's assigned to that VM. It is also used in the Google Kubernetes Engine Pods. For more information, refer to the *Further reading* section of this chapter.

It is possible to convert an auto mode network in a custom mode network, but not the other way round. Remember to not use IP ranges that overlap between VPCs or on-premise if you will be connecting those networks either through VPC peering or VPNs.

Connectivity

It is time to understand how the connectivity between the virtual machine instances works in VPC. We have already stated that networks are global and that subnets are regional. Now, let's have a look at virtual machine networking. We should note that VMs can have two types of IP addresses:

- **Internal IP address**: Assigned within the virtual machine operating system
- **External IP address (optional)**: Assigned to a virtual machine but not visible in the operating system

The internal IP will be always assigned to the VMs. The external IP can be either created automatically for you or you can create an IP address yourself. If you don't want to use this type of address, you need to set the address to **None** when you request the virtual machine. Note that the external IP address is not visible to the VM itself. Which IP address will be used to initiate a connection depends on the following scenarios:

- VMs with the same network can communicate using the internal IP, even if they are in a different region.
- VMs in a different network can communicate using external IPs, even if they are in the same regions.

Let's have a look at the following diagram:

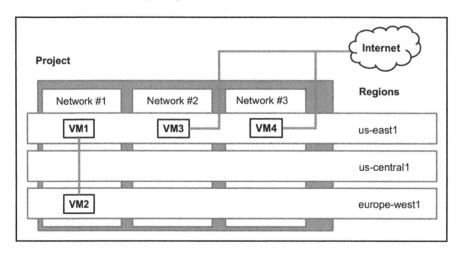

In this scenario, **VM1** and **VM2** can communicate using internal IPs. **VM3** and **VM4** need to communicate using external IPs. Note that the traffic between **VM3** and **VM4** does not need to traverse the internet but is routed through the Google Edge router.

Cost

It is very important to understand how network traffic flows work as it can impact your billing. The general rule of thumb is that the following traffic is free:

- Ingress traffic
- Egress within the same zones using internal IPs
- Egress to a different GCP service within the same region using an external IP address or an internal IP address

This free traffic does not include a number of services that haven't mentioned in this book yet: Cloud Memorystore for Redis, Cloud Filestore, and Cloud SQL.

The following traffic is charged for:

- Egress between zones within the regions
- Egress between regions
- Internet egress

For current pricing, please refer to `https://cloud.google.com/compute/pricing`.

VPC Flow Logs

VPC Flow Logs allow you to record network flows to and from virtual machine instances. The flows are recorded in 5-second intervals. Note that only the flows are recorded rather than the full network packets capture. The logs contain information regarding the source and destination VPC and the instance start and end time. VPC Flow Logs are enabled at the subnet level.

Cross-VPC connectivity

In some cases, you might need to provide connectivity between two VPCs. As an example, departments in your organization are merging and now they need connectivity to services residing in their respective VPCs.

To do this, there are currently two options:

- Shared VPC
- VPC peering

Let's have a look at both these options.

Shared VPC

In this model, we have a single VPC that is shared between different projects. The project where the shared VPC is created is called the **host project**. The projects that can use the VPC are called **service projects**. In the following diagram, **Recommendation**, **Personalization**, and **Analytics** are service projects:

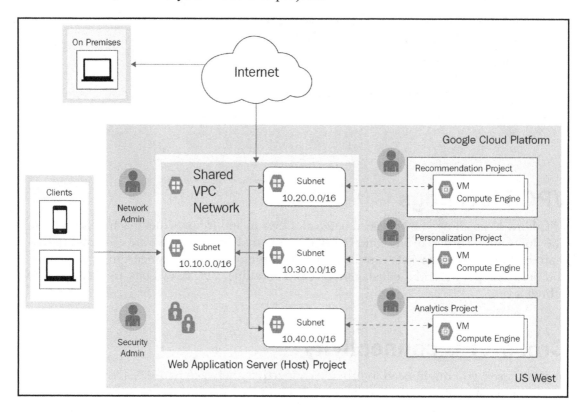

To create a shared project, a shared VPC admin role is required
(`roles/compute.xpnAdmin`). The shared VPC admin can further delegate the permissions
to the following:

- **Network Admin**: Full control over networks, excluding firewall rules and SSL
  certificates
- **Security Admin**: Control over firewall and SSL certificates

Users in the service project can provision virtual machines that are shared VPC. To be able
to do so, they need to have a Network User role assigned. Note that it can be assigned
either at a project or subnet level.

VPC peering

With VPC peering, you can connect two existing VPCs, regardless of whether they belong
to the same project or organization. In this scenario, the administration of each VPC stays
separated.

Each site of the peering is set up independently and peering is only established once both
sides are configured. Project Owner/Editor and Network Admin roles are allowed to
perform the configuration. It is important to remember that the CIDR prefixes cannot
overlap between peering VPCs subnets. Once peering has been established, every internal
IP becomes accessible across peered networks. Multiple peers can be created per VPC, but
transitive peering is not supported. This means that only connectivity between directly
peered VPCs is allowed. You cannot bridge the traffic between two VPCs via another
VPC. To understand this better, take a look at the following diagram:

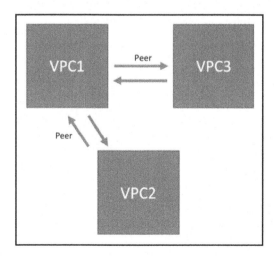

In this scenario, **VPC1** is peered with **VPC2** and **VPC3**. There is no communication between **VPC2** and **VPC3** until peering between those two is configured. Note that peering can be also established with a shared VPC.

Choosing between shared VPC and VPC peering

There are two main factors that will allow you to choose between a shared VPC and VPC peering, as follows:

- If VPCs exist in different organizations, choose VPC peering.
- If you need a shared governance model, choose a shared VPC.

 In real-life scenarios, you might have more detailed requirements for your cross VPC communication, so we encourage you to do further reading on the subject.

Load balancing

Load balancing is one of the most important features of GCP networking. It allows you to distribute a workload between your scaling resources. It works with GCE, GAE, and GKE.

Load balancing in GCP is one of those topics that can be difficult to comprehend at the beginning. There are many types of load balancers, and the Google documentation makes it slightly difficult to map them to what you can see in the console. When we go to the GCP console (https://console.cloud.google.com) and navigate to **Network Services** | **Load Balancing**, will get the following configuration options:

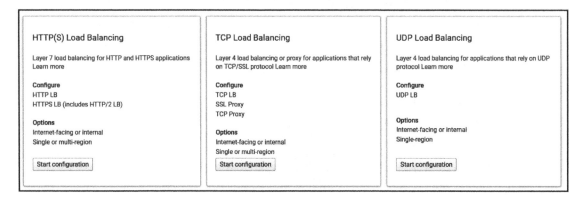

When you look at the documentation, it distinguishes between the following load balancing options. We will look at these in more detail in the *Load balancer types* section:

- HTTP(S) load balancing
- SSL proxy load balancing
- TCP proxy load balancing
- Network load balancing
- Internal TCP/UDP load balancing

You can clearly see that this does not match the GUI options. Note that to configure an internal TCP/UDP load balancer, you need to choose either **TCP Load Balancing** or **UDP Load Balancing** and then choose the **Only between my VMs** option:

Internet facing or internal only

Do you want to load balance traffic from the Internet to your VMs or only between VMs in your network?

○ From Internet to my VMs
◉ Only between my VMs

Thankfully, the exam does not require you to know how to exactly configure each load balancing method and instead concentrates on differences. However, you will need it when you put your knowledge into practice.

 Refer to the how-to guide. All the options are described step by step: `https://cloud.google.com/load-balancing/docs/how-to`.

You might need to perform a couple of labs (such as `Qwiklabs.com`) to feel comfortable with load balancing configuration. For our discussion, we will stick to the documentation definitions as they are also in line with the exam guidelines.

Global versus regional load balancing

Load balancing can be delivered on a regional or global level. This means that for regional load balancing, the balanced resources will reside within one region, whereas in global load balancing, the resources can reside in many regions. The feature that distinguishes GCP from other cloud providers is that some of the load balancing options are available globally. You don't really need to worry about placing the load balancer in the right region:

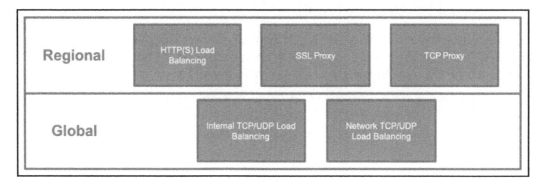

As shown in the preceding diagram, the internal and network load balancers are regional only.

External versus internal

We can also distinguish between load balancers in terms of whether they are external or internal. In most scenarios, you would like to expose an application to the internet. This would be the perfect use case for an external load balancer. However, you may also want to load balance traffic in the backend of your application for high availability scenarios. In this case, you would use an internal load balancer, which does not allow connectivity from outside of the VPC.

Proxy versus load balancer

There is an important difference between a proxy and a load balancer in terms of the source IP reaching your backend VM. In the case of a proxy, the source IP is swapped to the proxies IP as the connection is terminated at the proxy. In the case of a load balancer, the source IP is preserved. Keep this in mind when you configure your firewall rules using the source IP.

Load balancer types

Keeping in mind the key differences we mentioned previously, let's have a look at each load balancing type:

- **HTTP(s) load balancing**: One of the load balancers that requires special attention is the HTTP(S) load balancer. It is global and allows external connectivity. It supports both IPv4 and IPv6. It can be only used for HTTP and HTTPS traffic but offers a couple of additional features, such as the following:
  - CDN caching
  - Integrates with Cloud Armor
  - Supports URL maps
  - Host SSL certificates
  - Supports Cloud Storage
  - Supports session affinity
  - Supports **Quick UDP Internet Connections** (**QUIC**) protocol

 Session affinity sticks the client session to one virtual machine instance as long as the instance is healthy.

- **SSL proxy load balancing**: The SSL proxy terminates the user's SSL (TLS connections) and is intended for non-HTTP(s) traffic. It is global and allows external connectivity that supports both IPv4 and IPv6. The traffic from the proxy to the machines can use either TCP or SSL protocols.
- **TCP proxy load balancing**: The TCP proxy terminates non-HTTP traffic that does not require SSL. It is global and allows external connectivity that supports both IPv4 and IPv6.
- **Network TCP/UDP load balancing**: Network load balancing is a non-proxied load balancer that distributes traffic-based inbound IP protocol data such as address, port, and protocol type. It is regional and external with support for IPv4 only. The network load balancer collects virtual machines to be load balanced into a logical group called **target pools**.
- **Internal TCP/UDP load balancing**: Internal load balancing is a non-proxied form of load balancing. It is regional and internal with support for IPv4 only. As an example, it can be used for three-tier applications where web services need to load balance an internal connection to the application tier.

Comparison

Now that we have learned about each load balancer, let's have a look at a table that will help us put the most important features into one area:

Load balancer	Traffic type	Global/Regional	External/Internal	External Ports for Load Balancing
HTTP(S)	HTTP or HTTPS	Global	External	HTTP on 80 or 8080; HTTPS on 443
SSL Proxy	TCP with SSL offload	Global	External	25, 43, 110, 143, 195, 443, 465, 587, 700, 993, 995, 1883, and 5222
TCP Proxy	TCP without SSL offload. Does not preserve client IP addresses	Global	External	25, 43, 110, 143, 195, 443, 465, 587, 700, 993, 995, 1883, 5222
Network TCP/UDP	TCP/UDP without SSL offload. Preserves client IP addresses.	Regional	External	Any
Internal TCP/UDP	TCP or UDP	Regional	Internal	Any

Source: https://cloud.google.com/load-balancing/docs/choosing-load-balancer
License: https://creativecommons.org/licenses/by/4.0/legalcode

Looking at the preceding table, think about the use cases for each of the balancers. A good example could be a three-tier application. Which load balancer would you use to balance each tier?

Choosing the right load balancer

To choose the right load balancer, let's have look at the following diagram, which has been provided by Google:

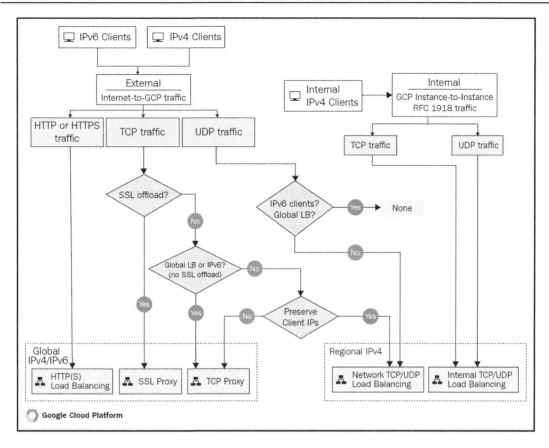

Source: https://cloud.google.com/load-balancing/docs/choosing-load-balancer
License: https://creativecommons.org/licenses/by/4.0/legalcode

Let's go through the preceding diagram step by step:

1. First, we need to choose whether we want the load balancer to be accessible externally or internally. For external exposure, we choose what traffic we want to balance.

2. For HTTP and HTTPS traffic, we use an HTTP(S) load balancer.

3. For TCP traffic with an SSL offload, we would go for the SSL proxy. If we don't need the offload SSL but need IPv6 or global scope support, we would choose the TCP proxy.

4. Then, we need to check whether we need to preserve client IPs. If yes, we go for the network load balancer; if not, we stay with the TCP proxy. The network load balancer can be also used for UDP traffic that does not need IPv6 or global scope.

5. For internal load balancing, use an internal TCP/UDP load balancer.

As you can see, choosing the appropriate load balancer can be quite an intimidating task. However, if you follow the preceding flow chart, you should be able to choose the best option.

Now that we have understood how load balancing works, we will look at NAT.

NAT

NAT is a service that translates source and/or destination addresses when traffic passes through a routing device. In the case of GCP, NAT allows us to hide the original IP address of our virtual machine when communicating with external networks. In the case of GCP, it allows VMs with internal addresses to access the internet.

There are currently two options for NAT, as follows:

- NAT gateway
- Cloud NAT

Google recommends using Cloud NAT over NAT gateway. If you are still using NAT gateway, Google recommends that you migrate it to Cloud NAT as it is a managed and self-scaling service.

NAT gateway

Google allows us to provision a virtual machine that will act as a NAT gateway. This way, you are exposing only one VM to the internet. The gateway machine needs to be configured with the `--can-ip-forward` parameter, which allows traffic forwarding. You will also need to create default routes for the subnets that should be using the gateway. As you can see, this solution does not look scalable and introduces the concept of single point of failure.

To eliminate this problem, you can create multiple gateways and put them in managed instance groups. Next, you configure the routing rule to the NAT gateways with the same priority. In this case, GCP uses the **equal-cost multi-path** (**ECPM**) to distribute the traffic between the NAT gateways.

 To learn more about ECMP, check out `https://en.wikipedia.org/wiki/Equal-cost_multi-path_routing`. To find out how to create highly available NAT gateways, complete the *Building High Availability and High Bandwidth NAT Gateways* lab at `https://www.qwiklabs.com/focuses/612?parent=catalog`.

If this sounds complicated, fortunately, there is an easier solution. Yes, you guessed right! Cloud NAT.

Cloud NAT

Cloud NAT is a regional self-scaling service that's fully managed by Google. It allows VMs to access the internet without the need for an external IP address. It does not, however, allow inbound internet traffic to the VMs. This service is provided by Google SDN, so there are no gateway instances to manage. In fact, under the hood, there are no actual proxy VMs.

In terms of bandwidth, each VM gets exactly the same bandwidth it would get if it had an external IP.

Hybrid connectivity

By hybrid connectivity, we mean connectivity between GCP and your on-premise datacenter. It is important if you want to connect through a secure channel to GCP and not simply traverse the internet. There are a number of ways this connectivity can be achieved. The method you choose will depend on your bandwidth and latency requirements.

Now, let's have a look at some possible hybrid connectivity options, that is, VPN interconnect and peering.

VPN

Cloud VPN is a regional service that will securely connect your on-premise network to GCP VPC using an IPSec tunnel. All traffic traversing the internet through the tunnel is encrypted. Both **IKEv1** and **IKEv2** ciphers are supported. The VPN connection requires a Cloud VPN gateway, an on-premise VPN gateway, and two VPN tunnels that are set up from the perspective of each gateway. A connection is established when both tunnels are created. The on-premise gateway can be either a hardware or software device. There is a special requirement that the MTU of your on-premise gateway should not be higher than 1,460 bytes. VPN supports both static and dynamic routes. Dynamic routing requires a Cloud Router to be configured.

The Cloud VPN offers bandwidth between 1.5-3 GBps per tunnel. Multiple tunnels can be created to scale the capacity. It also provides an SLA of 99.9%.

Interconnects

Interconnect is a layer 2 connectivity method that incurs a monthly cost. You would use it when you need low latency and highly available connectivity between GCP and your on-premise network and you are planning for large data transfers.

It comes in two flavors, as follows:

- **Dedicated Interconnect**: Connection established with Google Edge
- **Partner Interconnect**: Connection established with the Google Partner network

The connections can be scaled by introducing multiple connections. For a dedicated interconnect, each connection delivers 10 Gbps. Up to eight connections can be created, giving us a maximum of 80 Gbps total per interconnect. With Partner Interconnect connections, bandwidth ranges from 50 Mbps to 10 Gbps. Interconnect comes with an uptime **SLA of either 99.9% or 99.99%**. This depends on your configuration and number of connections.

Peering

Peering is a layer 3 connectivity method. It provides connectivity to services such as G Suite, YouTube, and Google APIs with public IP addresses. It allows us to establish connectivity with higher availability and latency. Note that those connections exist outside of GCP. Peering has no maintenance costs and also comes in two flavors, as follows:

- **Direct Peering**: Connection established with Google Edge
- **Carrier Peering**: Connection established with Google Edge

Direct peering offers 10 GBps connections per link established with GCP PoP, which are points where Google Networks connects with the rest of the internet. Carrier peering bandwidth depends on the provider. Note that peering provides no SLA.

Choosing the right connectivity method

In general, Google's recommendation is to start the connectivity with Cloud VPN and move to interconnect if needed. Again, Google comes with a nice flow diagram that will help you make the right choice when it comes to the best connectivity method for your situation:

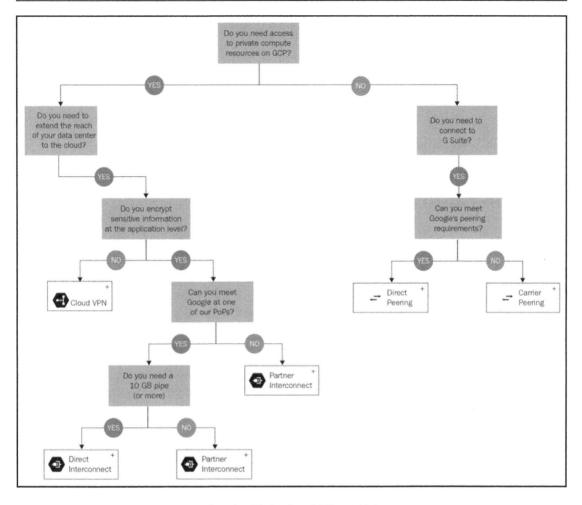

Source: https://cloud.google.com/hybrid-connectivity/

This concludes the hybrid connectivity section. Again, think twice before you go for interconnect connectivity. Unless you have high bandwidth and low latency requirements, start with VPN and only move to interconnect if you aren't getting the right results. In the next section, we will look at the **Domain Name System (DNS)**, which is critical for proper hostnames and URL resolution.

DNS

DNS allows the resolution of domain names into IP addresses. There are a couple of concepts you need to understand when it comes to DNS in GCP, such as the following:

- DNS resolution
- Cloud DNS
- **DNS Security (DNSSEC)**

DNS resolution

VPC comes with internal DNS services. Machines get their internal names registered automatically within an internal zone. This allows VMs within the same network to access each other using the internal DNS names. The DNS record follows the life cycle of the VM. It's created when the VM is created and is deleted when the VM is deleted. This means that names are created when the instance is deployed and are removed when the instance is deleted. Note that the records are only created for the internal IPs (not external and alias IPs). The resolution only works for VMs within the same VPC.

As you probably know, there are many types of DNS records (A, MX, SRV, CNAME, and so on). The actual records that are created in this case are so-called **A** records. These are records that translate the hostname into an IP address. They are created using the following pattern:

```
<INSTANCE_NAME>.c.<PROJECT_ID>.internal
```

Here, INSTANCE_NAME is the hostname that is auto-generated by GCP and PROJECT_ID is the ID of the project in which the VM is deployed.

When a virtual machine is provisioned, the TCP/IP settings are configured automatically. The VMs DNS server setting is also configured and is pointing to its metadata server. For public name resolutions, queries are forwarded to Google's public DNS servers. For external IPs, the records are not registered automatically. They can be registered in external DNS servers or in a DNS zone hosted in the Cloud DNS service.

Cloud DNS

Cloud DNS is a managed service that allows you to host millions of DNS records without the need to manage any servers or software. As this is hosted on the same infrastructure on which Google is hosted, it provides an up time SLA of 100%.

Cloud DNS allows us to create managed zones that will contain multiple records. To migrate from your current provider, you can export the zones and then import them into Cloud DNS. The records can be managed using APIs and the `gcloud` command.

DNSSEC

DNSSEC is a DNS extension that allows the authentication of domain lookup responses. It protects the requester from the manipulation and poisoning of DNS request responses. In GCP, DNSSEC can be enabled per DNS zone. Note that it also needs to be configured at your domain registrar. On top of that, the requester needs to make sure that the resolver on their workstation validates signatures for DNSSEC-signed domains.

For more details, refer to `https://cloud.google.com/dns/docs/dnssec`.

Firewall rules

A firewall is either a hardware or software device that filters network traffic that's passing through it. This filtering can be done based on many conditions, such as source, target IPs, protocol, or ports. It allows you to secure your network from unwanted access.

The firewall rules allow you to control traffic flow to and from VM-based instances. Firewall rules work independent of the VM operating system and are always enforced if put in an enabled state. VPC acts as a distributed firewall that leverages micro-segmentation. This means that the firewall rules are enforced per virtual machine, even if the machines reside in the same network. The firewall rules are constructed of the following components:

- **Ingress (inbound) firewall rules**:
    - **Priority 0**: 65545 with a default value of `1000`
    - **Action**: `allow` or `deny`
    - **Enforcement**: `enabled` or `disabled`
    - **Target (destination)**: All instances in the network, tag, and service account
    - **Source**: Address range, subnet, service account, and network tag
    - **Protocol and ports**: Protocol or protocol and a port

- **Egress (outbound) firewall**:
    - **Priority 0**: 65545 with a default value of 1000
    - **Action**: allow or deny
    - **Enforcement**: enabled or disabled
    - **Target (source)**: All instances in the network, tag, and service account
    - **Destination**: Address range and subnet
    - **Protocol and ports**: Protocol or protocol and a port

We can further divide these firewall rules as follows:

- Default firewall rules
- Implied rules
- Always allowed traffic rules
- Always allowed rules
- User-defined rules

The preceding rules are the actual rules that you would defined once you have an understanding of what traffic you need for your infrastructure and application to communicate. The former are defined by Google to provide the basic protection and basic functionality that's needed so that you can manage your environment. Now, let's have a closer look at each of them.

Default rules

There are a number of allow ingress firewall rules with a priority of 65534 that are created for the default network, as follows:

- default-allow-internal: Ingress connections for all protocols and ports between instances in the VPC
- default-allow-ssh: Ingress connections on TCP port 22 from any source to any instance in the VPC
- default-allow-rdp: Ingress connections on TCP port 3389 from any source to any instance in the VPC
- default-allow-icmp: Ingress ICMP traffic from any source to any instance in the VPC:

Name	Type	Targets	Filters	Protocols/ports	Action	Priority	Network ^
default-allow-http	Ingress	http-server	IP ranges: 0.0.0.0/0	tcp:80	Allow	1000	default
default-allow-https	Ingress	https-server	IP ranges: 0.0.0.0/0	tcp:443	Allow	1000	default
default-allow-icmp	Ingress	Apply to all	IP ranges: 0.0.0.0/0	icmp	Allow	65534	default
default-allow-internal	Ingress	Apply to all	IP ranges: 10.128.0.0/9	tcp:0-65535 udp:0-65535 icmp	Allow	65534	default
default-allow-rdp	Ingress	Apply to all	IP ranges: 0.0.0.0/0	tcp:3389	Allow	65534	default
default-allow-ssh	Ingress	Apply to all	IP ranges: 0.0.0.0/0	tcp:22	Allow	65534	default

There are also predefined rules for HTTP and HTTPS traffic. The targets for those rules are tags. You can assign those tags to your VMs to allow this type of traffic from any source.

Implied rules

There are two implied firewall rules with the lowest possible priority (65535), as follows:

- **Deny ingress rule** with source 0.0.0.0/0
- **Allow egress rule** with destination 0.0.0.0/0

The rules cannot be removed but can be overridden by any rules that have higher priority.

Always allowed traffic rules

There are certain types of traffic that are always allowed from a VM, as follows:

- Traffic to a metadata server
- DHCP traffic
- DNS traffic
- NTP traffic

Always denied rules

There are also types of traffic that are always blocked, as follows:

- GRE traffic
- Protocols other than TCP, UDP, ICMP, and IPIP
- Egress SMTP traffic on TCP port 25

User-defined rules

Finally, user-defined rules are the rules that you would define to allow communication that's needed for your application that do not match the default, always allowed, or implied rules:

These rules can be created by going to the **Navigation** menu, **VPC network** I **Firewall rules**, and clicking **CREATE FIREWALL RULE**.

Firewall logging

Firewall logging allows you to verify whether your firewall rules are functioning correctly. It can be enabled for new and existing firewall rules. The logs are injected into the stack driver.

Private access

VMs with only internal IP addresses can access a Google API's external IP addresses using Private Google Access. This access is enabled per subnet. This setting does not affect the VMs with external IP addresses. It is also possible to allow private access for your on-premises VMs. This requires a VPN to be configured. Note that not all services are available for private access.

 For more details, check out the Google documentation at `https://cloud.google.com/vpc/docs/private-access-options`.

Summary

In this chapter, we have gone through basic networking concepts in GCP. We have learned about VPC, load balancing, firewall, DNS, and hybrid connectivity. Make sure that you understand how you connect virtual machines to the GCP network, as well as how to protect and load balance them. Now that you have an understanding of different ways to connect to your on-premises datacenter, we suggest that you get some hands-on experience. Set up your first VPC, create firewall rules, and deploy and manage a virtual machine instance group with a load balancer of your choice. If you have any problems doing this, return to this book and check this chapter or `Chapter 4`, *Working with Google Compute Engine*.

In `Chapter 9`, *Exploring Storage Options in GCP – Part 1*, and `Chapter 10`, *Exploring Storage Options in GCP – Part 2*, we will see how we can store data. This is essential for stateful workloads.

Further reading

The overview of networking services that we provided in this chapter should be good enough for the exam. If you still feel like you need a deeper knowledge of GCP networking, check out the following links:

- **VPC**: https://cloud.google.com/vpc/docs/
- **Firewalls**: https://cloud.google.com/vpc/docs/firewalls
- **Load balancing**: https://cloud.google.com/load-balancing/docs/
- **Interconnects**: https://cloud.google.com/interconnect/docs/
- **VPN**: https://cloud.google.com/vpn/docs/
- **DNS**: https://cloud.google.com/dns/docs/
- **NAT**: https://cloud.google.com/nat/docs/
- **Alias IP addresses:** https://cloud.google.com/vpc/docs/alias-ip

9
Exploring Storage Options in GCP - Part 1

In the previous two chapters, we learned about important topics in networking and compute services. We will continue now with another fundamental offering by GCP—**storage**. Every application needs to store data, but not all data is the same. Data could be structured, unstructured, relational, or transactional, and GCP offers services to meet these requirements. Your application may even require the use of multiple storage services to achieve your needs.

In this chapter, we will look at the different types of storage offered by Google and explain what should be considered before selecting a particular service. Google provides numerous storage options, and covering all of these in a single chapter may make the facts difficult for you to digest. Therefore, we have divided this chapter into two parts.

In part one, we will consider which storage option we should choose and look into the following topics:

- Choosing the right storage option
- Understanding Cloud Storage
- Understanding Cloud Datastore
- Understanding Cloud SQL

In part two, we will look at the following services:

- Cloud Spanner
- Bigtable

Although BigQuery can be considered a storage option, we will specifically look at that product in `Chapter 11`, *Analyzing Big Data Options*.

 Exam tip: Understanding the options is critical. You may be presented with a scenario where relational databases are needed over nonrelational databases, or where you need to select an option that is suitable for structured data. You also need to understand the limits of storage; as an example, let's say you are told that you need to assess a service that offers a NoSQL database and can scale to terabytes of data. After reading this chapter, you should be able to map this scenario to a service.

OK, so let's start this chapter with a look at when we would select a specific storage service. After that, we will look at each service individually, concentrating on exam topics.

Code in Action

Check out the following video to see the Code in Action:
`http://bit.ly/31i6wpz`

Choosing the right storage option

As we mentioned at the start of this chapter, there are various storage services offered by Google. You must understand what the correct storage to use is for your requirements. Google provides a nice flow chart that we can walk through. It is easy to follow and shows how requirements will dictate which storage option to select. Take some time to look at the following decision tree. The diagram works through key questions to make sure that the storage service we select will fulfill the requirements:

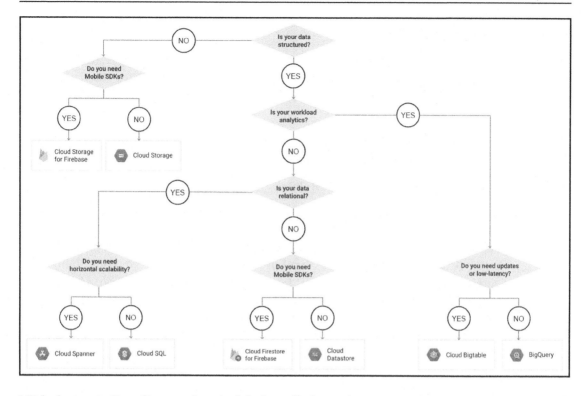

With the preceding diagram in mind, let's walk through an example:

1. First, we need to understand whether our data will be structured. Different services will be recommended depending on this answer.
2. If our data is structured, then we should check whether our workload is for analytics.
3. If our data is not for analytics, then we should check whether our data is relational.
4. If our data is relational, then we finally need to know whether we require horizontal scaling.
5. If we do, then we should select Cloud Spanner. If not, we should select Cloud SQL.

As you can see from the preceding diagram, there are various outcomes depending on our requirements. There are a lot of storage services offered by GCP, but if we follow this flow chart, we should be able to choose the best option.

In the next section, we will discuss data consistency.

Data consistency

Data consistency refers to how the storage service handles transactions and how data is written to a database. As you go through this chapter, make sure you review the consistency of each service, as this is one of the main design factors when choosing a product or service.

We will also take this chance to explain ACID. This is a key term in data consistency, and we will refer to this several times throughout this chapter.

ACID is an acronym for the following attributes:

- **Atomicity**: This is where a transaction involves two or more pieces of information, then all pieces are committed or none at all. For example, when performing a bank transfer, the debit and credit of the funds would be treated as a single transaction. If either the debit or credit failed, then both would fail.
- **Consistency**: If the aforementioned failure occurs, then all data would be returned to the state before the transaction began.
- **Isolation**: The bank transfer would be isolated from any other transaction. In our example, this means that we would not debit from the bank until the transfer was complete.
- **Durability**: Even in the event of failure, the data would be available in its correct state.

 Exam tip: It's also important for you to be able to identify storage services that support structured data, low latency, or horizontal scaling. Likewise, you should be able to identify storage services that offer strong consistency or support ACID properties.

Let's now look more closely at each of these services. We will begin with Cloud Storage.

Understanding Cloud Storage

Cloud Storage is fully managed and can scale dynamically. It is commonly used for object storage, video transcoding, video streaming, static web pages, and backup. It is designed to provide secure and durable storage while also offering optimal pricing and performance for your requirements through different storage classes.

Cloud Storage uses the concept of buckets; you may be familiar with this term if you have used AWS S3 storage. A bucket is the basic container where your data will reside and is attached to a GCP project, such as other GCP services. Each bucket name is globally unique and once created you cannot change it. There is no minimum or maximum storage size, and we only pay for what we actually use. Access to our buckets can be controlled in several ways. We will speak more on security in `Chapter 13`, *Security and Compliance*, but as an overview, we have the following main methods:

- **Cloud Identity and Access Management (IAM)**: We speak about IAM more in `Chapter 13`, *Security and Compliance*. IAM will grant access to buckets and the objects inside it. This gives a centralized way to manage permissions rather than providing fine-grained control over individual objects. IAM policies are used throughout GCP and permissions are applied to all objects in a bucket.
- **Access Control Lists (ACLs)**: ACLs are used only by Cloud Storage. This allows us to grant read or write access for individual objects. It is not recommended that you use this method, but there may be occasions when it is required. For example, you may wish to customize access to individual objects inside a bucket.
- **Signed URLs**: This gives time-limited read or write access to an object inside your bucket through a dedicated URL. Anyone who receives this URL can access the object for the period of time that was specified when the URL was generated.

We also mention encryption in `Chapter 13`, *Security and Compliance*. By default, Cloud Storage will always encrypt your data on the server side before it is written to disk. There are three options available for server-side encryption:

- **Google-Managed Encryption Keys**: This is where Cloud Storage will manage encryption keys on behalf of the customer, with no need for further setup.
- **Customer-Supplied Encryption Keys (CSEKs)**: This is where the customer creates and manages their own encryption keys.
- **Customer-Managed Encryption Keys (CMEKs)**: This is where the customer generates and manages their encryption keys using GCP's **Key Management Service (KMS)**.

There is also the **client-side encryption** option where encryption occurs before data is sent to Cloud Storage and additional encryption takes place at the server side.

Storage classes

We previously mentioned storage classes, and we should make it clear that it's vital to understand the different offerings to be successful in this exam. Let's take a look at these in more detail now:

- **Regional**: Use a Regional storage class for data that is used in a single region. This allows us to store data at a lower cost but with a reduced availability SLA of 99.9%. This SLA is dependent on whether the data is stored in a specific regional location. You would commonly use this class to store data near a GCE instance for better performance. There is no cost for retrieving this data.

- **Multi-Regional**: Use the Multi-Regional storage class for data that requires global distribution or has no regional restrictions. This allows for greater availability as data is stored in at least two locations separated by 100 miles. Data will only ever be stored in regions, such as the U.S., the European Union, or Asia; there will not be any option to specify a particular zone, such as US-Central1. This allows GCP to offer a higher 99.95% availability SLA, which is the highest available for any storage class. This class is ideal for data that is accessed frequently, such as a static web page or other supporting data for mobile applications. Like the Regional data class, there is no cost for retrieving the data.

- **Nearline**: Use the Nearline storage class for data that will be read or modified no more than once per month—for example, backup data. Nearline offers two kinds of SLA for availability, depending on whether you are Regional (which grants you a 99.0% availability SLA) or Multi-Regional (which grants you a 99.9% availability SLA). Nearline has very low cost-per-GB storage, but it does come with a retrieval cost. There is a 30-day minimum storage duration.

- **Coldline**: Use the Coldline storage class for data that is accessed no more than once per year—for example, archived data. Coldline also offers two kinds of SLA for availability, depending on whether you are Regional (which grants you a 99.0% availability SLA) or Multi-Regional (which grants you a 99.9% availability SLA). This class offers the lowest cost-per-GB storage but again comes with a retrieval cost. Interestingly, for this type of archival storage, the data is available in milliseconds rather than hours or days, as it is with other vendors. There is a 90-day minimum storage duration.

These different classes are summarized in the following screenshot:

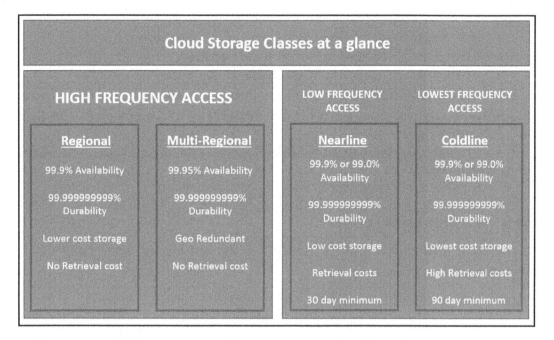

Buckets get a default storage class upon their creation, and any objects inside this will inherit this class unless otherwise specified. We can change the default storage class of our bucket, but it will only apply to new objects after the change; the existing objects will remain in the original class. We can also change bucket types after creation, with one important caveat: you cannot change between Regional and Multi-Regional buckets. It is therefore important to think ahead when you are creating your buckets:

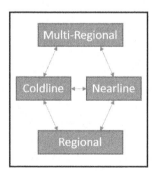

The preceding diagram shows which bucket types can be changed after creation. Let's look at this in more detail:

- **Multi-Regional** can be changed to **Nearline** and **Coldline**.
- **Regional** can be changed to **Nearline** and **Coldline**.
- **Nearline** can be changed to **Multi-Regional**, **Regional**, and **Coldline**.
- **Coldline** can be changed to **Multi-Regional**, **Regional**, and **Nearline**.
- **Multi-Regional** *cannot* be changed to **Regional** even if you change to **Coldline** or **Nearline** first.
- **Regional** *cannot* be changed to **Multi-Regional** even if you change to **Coldline** or **Nearline** first.

Data consistency

Cloud Storage will provide both strong consistency and eventual consistency under certain circumstances.

Strong consistency can be expected in the following circumstances:

- When uploading data into Cloud Storage, meaning the data will always be available to read after a write or update operation.
- After we delete data successfully, the files will be instantly unavailable.

Eventual consistency can be expected in the following circumstance:

- When access to resources is revoked. It will typically take around one minute for the revocation of access to take effect, and in some cases, this may take even longer.

Cloud Storage FUSE

Cloud Storage cannot be mounted to a Google Compute Engine instance. However, if this is something that you would like to explore, GCP currently offers third-party integration using an open source FUSE adapter that will allow you to mount a storage bucket as a filesystem on Linux. This is available free of charge and is not officially supported; however, normal Cloud Storage charges are applicable.

Creating and using a bucket

Now that we have a good understanding of storage classes, let's take a look at how to actually create a bucket. We will also learn how to copy files into our bucket and change the storage policy of an object.

We have two options to create a bucket—either through a console or using `gsutil`. We will learn more about `gsutil` in `Chapter 11`, *Google Cloud Management Options*, but for the context of this chapter, it's enough for you to know that it is a dedicated command-line tool that will make RESTful API calls to your Cloud Storage service. Let's look at how to create a bucket from the console by going through the following steps:

1. Browse to **STORAGE** from the navigation menu select **Storage** | **Browser**:

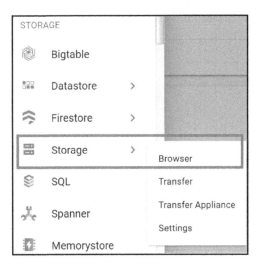

2. Click on **Create bucket**, as shown in the following screenshot:

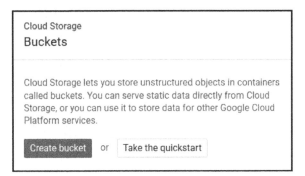

3. Give the bucket a name. Remember that this must be globally unique:

4. Select a storage class that fits your needs. Select a location. You will notice that the location will either be a zone or a region, depending on whether your selection is Multi-Regional or Regional. Bear in mind that your selection will have an impact on the cost:

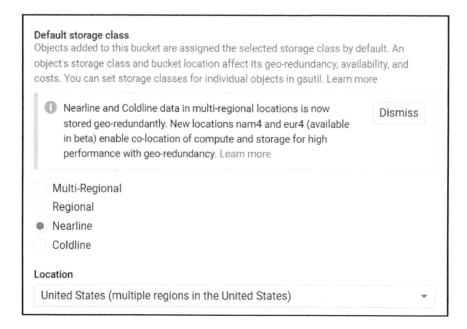

5. Select either an ACL or IAM access control model:

Access control model
Choose how you'll control access to this bucket's objects. Learn more

○ Set permissions uniformly at bucket-level (Bucket Policy Only)
Enforces the bucket's IAM policy without object ACLs. May help prevent unintended access. If selected, this option becomes permanent after 90 days.
● Set object-level and bucket-level permissions
Enforces the IAM policy and object ACLs for more granular control of object access.

6. We can also set more advanced settings that will show the encryption and retention policies. By default, Google will manage our keys. A retention policy can also be set. This will offer a minimum duration in which objects in the bucket will be protected from deletion:

Encryption
Data is encrypted automatically. Select an encryption key management solution.

● Google-managed key
No configuration required
○ Customer-managed key
Manage via Google Cloud Key Management Service

Retention policy
Set a retention policy to specify the minimum duration that this bucket's objects must be protected from deletion or modification after they're uploaded. You might set a policy to address industry-specific retention challenges. Learn more

☐ Set a retention policy

7. Simply click **Create** and we are done.

As you can see, this is a pretty simple process. Let's make it even simpler by creating it from our dedicated command-line tool, `gsutil`, which we can access from Cloud Shell:

1. In Cloud Shell, we can run the following command:

```
gsutil mb -c <storage class> -l <location> gs://<bucket name>
```

Let's look at the code in a little more detail:

- `<storage class>` is the class we would like to apply to our bucket.
- `<location>` is the region we want to create our bucket in.
- `<bucket name>` is the unique name we want to assign to our bucket.

2. Let's create a new bucket called `cloudarchitect001` in the `us-east1` region and apply the `regional` storage class:

```
gsutil mb -c regional -l us-east1 gs://cloudarchitect001
```

3. Now we have a bucket with no data inside. Let's use `gsutil` and move some objects into our bucket with the following syntax:

```
gsutil cp <filename> gs://<bucketname>
```

Let's look at the code in a little more detail:

- `<filename>` is the name of the file you wish to copy.
- `<bucketname>` is the destination bucket.

4. In this example, let's copy over a file called `conf.yaml` to our new bucket, called `cloudarchitect001`:

```
gsutil cp conf.yaml gs://cloudarchitect001
```

5. Let's look at how to change the storage class of a file. The storage class of an individual object inside a bucket can only be achieved from `gsutil`. We should use the following syntax:

```
gsutil rewrite -s <storage class> gs://<bucket name>/<file name>
```

6. Let's change our file, `conf.yaml`, so that it uses Coldline storage:

```
gsutil rewrite -s coldline gs://cloudarchitect001/conf.yaml
```

Great! So we now know how to manage our buckets. In the next section, we will take a look at some key features of Cloud Storage.

Versioning and lifecycle management

Let's now take a look at versioning and lifecycle management. These are important features offered by Cloud Storage and are of particular significance for the exam.

Exam tip: Cloud Storage offers an array of features. To succeed in your exam, you must understand the versioning and lifecycle management features of Cloud Storage. Like the storage classes, you should review these and make sure you are comfortable before moving onto future sections of this chapter.

Versioning

Versioning can be enabled to support the retrieval of objects that we have deleted or overwritten. We should note, at this point, that this will increase storage costs, but this may be worth it for you to be able to roll back to previous versions of important files. The additional costs come from the archived versions of each object that are created each time we overwrite or delete the live version of an object. The archived version of the file will retain the original name but will also be appended by a generation number to identify it. Let's go through the process of versioning:

1. To enable versioning, we should use the `gsutil` command:

    gsutil versioning set on gs://<bucket name>

    Here, `<bucket name>` is the bucket that we want to enable versioning on.

    Let's look at the following screenshot, which shows how this looks. In this example, we are enabling versioning on our `cloudarchitect` bucket and then confirming that versioning is indeed enabled:

    ```
    google3339831_student@cloudshell:~                              $ gsutil versioning set on gs://cloudarchitect
    Enabling versioning for gs://cloudarchitect/...
    google3339831_student@cloudshell:~                              $ gsutil versioning get gs://cloudarchitect
    gs://cloudarchitect: Enabled
    ```

2. Let's now copy a file called `vm.yaml` to our bucket. We can use the `-v` switch to version it:

    ```
    google3339831_student@cloudshell:~                              $ gsutil cp -v vm.yaml gs://cloudarchitect
    Copying file://vm.yaml [Content-Type=application/octet-stream]...
    Created: gs://cloudarchitect/vm.yaml#1557763393469362

    Operation completed over 1 objects/492.0 B.
    ```

3. If we modify this file, we can list the available versions by running the command with the following syntax:

    gsutil ls -a gs://<bucket name>/<filename>

Let's run this command on our file, named `vm.yaml`, which resides in our `cloudarchitect` bucket. We can see that we have several archived versions now available:

```
google3339831_student@cloudshell:~ (qwiklabs-gcp-o7f0f69cdda1b280)$ gsutil ls -a gs://cloudarchitect/vm.yaml
gs://cloudarchitect/vm.yaml#1557760768160333
gs://cloudarchitect/vm.yaml#1557763393469362
gs://cloudarchitect/vm.yaml#1557763527069403
```

We can turn versioning on and off whenever we want. Any available archived versions will remain when we turn it off, but we should remember that we will not have any archived versions until we enable it.

Lifecycle management

It's clear that archived files could quickly get out of hand and impact our billing unnecessarily. To avoid this, we can utilize lifecycle management policies. Lifecycle management configurations can be assigned to a bucket. These files are a set of rules that can be applied to current or future objects in the bucket. When any of the objects meet the guidelines of the configuration, Cloud Storage can perform actions automatically.

One of the most common use cases for using lifecycle management policies is when we want to downgrade the storage class of objects after a set period of time. For example, there may be a scenario where data needs to be accessed frequently up to 30 days after it is moved to Cloud Storage, and after that, it will only be accessed once a year. It makes no sense to keep this data in Regional or Multi-Regional storage, so we can use lifecycle management to move this to Coldline storage after the 30 days. Perhaps objects are not needed at all after one year, in which case we can use a policy to delete these objects. This helps to keep costs down. Let's learn how we can apply a policy to a bucket.

The first thing we need to do is create a lifecycle configuration file. As we mentioned, these files contain a set of rules that we want to apply to our bucket. If the policy contains more than one rule, then an object has to match all of the conditions before the action will be taken. It might be possible that a single object could be subject to multiple actions; in this case, Cloud Storage will perform only one of the actions before re-evaluating any additional actions.

We should also note that a `Delete` action will take precedence over a `SetStorageClass` action. Additionally, if an object has two rules applied to it to move the object to Nearline and Coldine, then the object will always move to the Coldline storage class if both rules use the exact same condition. A configuration file can be created in JSON or XML.

In the following example, we will create a simple configuration file in JSON format that will delete files after 60 days. We will also delete archived files after 30 days. Let's save this as `lifecycle.json`:

```json
{
    "lifecycle": {
        "rule": [{
            "action": {
                "type": "Delete"
            },
            "condition": {
                "age": 60,
                "isLive": true
            }
        }, {
            "action": {
                "type": "Delete"
            },
            "condition": {
                "age": 30,
                "isLive": false
            }
        }]
    }
}
```

Exam tip: If the value of `isLive` is `true`, then this `lifecycle` condition will match only live objects; however, if the value is set to `false`, the `lifecycle` condition will match only archived objects. We should also note that objects in non-versioned buckets are considered live.

We can once more use `gsutil` to enable this policy on our buckets using the following syntax:

```
gsutil lifecycle set <lifecycle policy name> gs://<bucket name>
```

Here, `<lifecycle policy name>` is the file we have created with our policy and `<bucket name>` is the unique bucket name we want to apply the policy to. The following code shows how to apply our `lifecycle.json` file to our `cloudarchitect` bucket:

```
gsutil lifecycle set lifecycle.json gs://cloudarchitect
```

We mentioned earlier that a common use case for `lifecycle` would be to move objects to a cheaper storage class after a set period of time. Let's look at an example that would map to a common scenario. Suppose we have objects in our `cloudarchitect` bucket that we want to access frequently for one year. After a year, we only need to access the data monthly. Finally, after two years, we will only access the data on a yearly basis. We can translate these requirements into storage classes and create the following policy that will help keep our costs to a minimum.

Let's break this down a little, as we now have a policy with two rules that each have two conditions. Any storage object with an age greater than `90` days and that has the `REGIONAL` storage class applied to it will be moved to `NEARLINE` storage. Any object with an age greater than `180` days and that has the `NEARLINE` storage class applied to it will be moved to `COLDLINE` storage:

```json
{
    "lifecycle": {
        "rule": [{
            "action": {
                "type": "SetStorageClass",
                "storageClass": "NEARLINE"
            },
            "condition": {
                "age": 90,
                "matchesStorageClass": ["REGIONAL"]
            }
        },
        {
            "action": {
                "type": "SetStorageClass",
                "storageClass": "COLDLINE"
            },
            "condition": {
                "age": 180,
                "matchesStorageClass": ["NEARLINE"]
            }
        }
        ]
    }
}
```

Exam tip: At least one condition is required. If you enter an incorrect action or condition, then you will receive a 400 bad request error response.

Transferring data

There will obviously be cases where we want to transfer files to a bucket from on-premises or other cloud-based storage, and Google offers many ways to do so. There are some considerations that we should bear in mind to make sure that we select the right option. The size of data and the available bandwidth will be the deciding factors. Let's take a quick look at a chart to show how long it would take to transfer some set data sizes over a specific bandwidth:

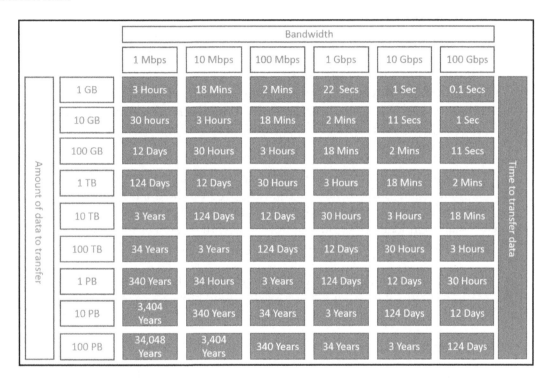

Amount of data to transfer	Bandwidth						Time to transfer data
	1 Mbps	10 Mbps	100 Mbps	1 Gbps	10 Gbps	100 Gbps	
1 GB	3 Hours	18 Mins	2 Mins	22 Secs	1 Sec	0.1 Secs	
10 GB	30 hours	3 Hours	18 Mins	2 Mins	11 Secs	1 Sec	
100 GB	12 Days	30 Hours	3 Hours	18 Mins	2 Mins	11 Secs	
1 TB	124 Days	12 Days	30 Hours	3 Hours	18 Mins	2 Mins	
10 TB	3 Years	124 Days	12 Days	30 Hours	3 Hours	18 Mins	
100 TB	34 Years	3 Years	124 Days	12 Days	30 Hours	3 Hours	
1 PB	340 Years	34 Hours	3 Years	124 Days	12 Days	30 Hours	
10 PB	3,404 Years	340 Years	34 Years	3 Years	124 Days	12 Days	
100 PB	34,048 Years	3,404 Years	340 Years	34 Years	3 Years	124 Days	

Some of these timelines are as follows:

- Cloud Storage Transfer Service
- Google Transfer Appliance

Cloud Storage Transfer Service

Cloud Storage Transfer Service allows us to transfer our data from online sources to a data sink. Let's say, for example, that we want to move data from our AWS S3 bucket into our Cloud Storage bucket. S3 would be our source and the destination Cloud Storage bucket would be our data sink. We can also use Cloud Storage Transfer Service to move data from an HTTP/HTTP(s) source or even another Cloud Storage bucket. To make these data migrations or synchronizations easier, Cloud Storage Transfer Service offers several options:

- We can schedule a one-time transfer operation or a recurring operation.
- We can delete existing objects in the destination data sink if they don't have any corresponding objects in the source.
- We can delete source objects after we have transferred them.
- We can schedule periodic synchronizations between the source and destination using folders based on file creation dates, filenames, or even the time of day you wish to import data.

Exam tip: You can also use `gsutil` to transfer data between Cloud Storage and other locations. You can speed up the transfer of files on premises by using the `-m` option to enable multi-threaded copy. If you plan to upload larger files, `gsutil` will split these files into several smaller chunks and upload these in parallel.

It is recommended that you use Cloud Storage Transfer Service when transferring data from Amazon S3 to Cloud Storage.

Google Transfer Appliance

If we look at the preceding chart, we can see that there are some pretty large transfer times. If we have petabytes of storage to transfer, then we should use Transfer Appliance. This is a hardware storage device that allows secure offline data migration. It can be set up in our data center and is rack mountable. We simply fill it with data and then ship it to an ingest location where Google will uploaded it to Cloud Storage.

Google offers 100 TB or 480 TB of raw capacity per appliance. The following is a quote from `https://cloud.google.com/transfer-appliance/`:

"Once the transfer is complete, Google will erase the appliance, meeting NIST-800-88 standards."

A common use case for Transfer Appliance is to move large amounts of existing backups from on premises into cheaper Cloud Storage using the Coldline storage class.

We will now have a look at IAM in the next section.

Understanding IAM

Access to Google Cloud Storage is secured with IAM. Let's have a look at the following list of predefined roles and their details:

- **Storage Object Creator**: Has rights to create objects but does not give permissions to view, delete, or overwrite objects
- **Storage Object Viewer**: Has rights to view objects and their metadata, but not the ACL, and has rights to list the objects in a bucket
- **Storage Object Admin**: Has full control over objects and can create, view, and delete objects
- **Storage Admin**: Has full control over buckets and objects

Cloud Storage also offers security via ACLs. Let's have a look at the permissions available and their details:

- **Reader**: This can be applied to a bucket or an object. It has rights to list a bucket's contents and read bucket metadata. It also has rights to download an object's data.
- **Writer**: This can be applied to a bucket only and has rights to list, create, overwrite, and delete objects in a bucket.
- **Owner**: This can be applied to a bucket or an object. It grants reader and writer permissions to the bucket and grants reader access to an object.

Quotas and limits

Google Cloud Storage comes with predefined quotas. These default quotas can be changed via the **Navigation** menu, under the **IAM & Admin | Quotas** sections. From this menu, we can review the current quotas and request an increase to these limits. We recommend that you familiarize yourself with the limits of each service, as this can have an impact on your scalability. For Cloud Storage, we should be aware of the following limits:

- Individual objects are limited to a maximum size of 5 TB.
- Updates to an individual object are limited to one per second.

- There is an initial limit of 1,000 writes per second per bucket.
- There is an initial limit of 5,000 reads per second per bucket.
- There is a limit of 100 ACL entries per object.
- There is a limit of 1 bucket creation operation every 2 seconds.
- There is a limit of 1 bucket deletion operation every 2 seconds.

Pricing

Pricing for Google Cloud Storage is based on four components:

- **Data storage**: This applies to at-rest data that is stored in Cloud Storage, is charged per GB per month, and cost depends on the location and class of the storage.
- **Network usage**: This applies when object data or metadata is read from our buckets. It is divided into four categories called egress within GCP, especially, network services, and general network usage.
- **Operations usage**: This applies when you perform actions within Cloud Storage that make changes or retrieve information about buckets and their objects. Cost depends on the class of the storage.
- **Retrieval and early deletion fees**: This applies when accessing data on Nearline and Coldline storage classes. Retrieval costs will apply when we read, copy, or rewrite data or metadata. Minimum storage duration applies to data stored in Nearline or Coldline storage. You will still be charged for the duration of an object even if the file is deleted before the minimal period.

Understanding Cloud Datastore

Google Cloud Datastore is a NoSQL database that is built to ease application development. It uses a distributed architecture that is highly scalable, and because it is serverless, we do not have to worry about the underlying infrastructure. Cloud Datastore distributes our data over several machines and uses a masterless, synchronous replication over a wide geographical area.

 Exam tip: Datastore can scale up to terabytes in size and, importantly, down to zero, which can result in large savings.

It's wise to note early on in this section that Google has released a newer major version of Datastore called **Cloud Firestore**. At the time of writing, the exam still refers to Cloud Datastore; however, we recommend that you familiarize yourself with Firestore and the relationship between the two products. We will discuss this later in this section.

Before we go any further into the details of Cloud Datastore, we don't want to make any assumptions that every reader knows what a NoSQL database is. SQL databases are far more well known by non-database administrators in the industry. A SQL database is primarily a relational database that is based on tables consisting of several rows of data that have predefined schemas.

Compare that to the concept of a NoSQL database, which is a non-relational database based around key-value pairs that do not have to adhere to any schema definitions. Ultimately, this allows us to scale efficiently; therefore, we can see how it becomes a lot easier to add or remove resources as we need to. This elasticity makes Cloud Datastore perfect for transactional information, such as real-time inventories, ACID transactions that will always provide data that is valid, or for providing user profiles to keep a record of user experience based on past activities or preferences.

OK, so now that we know what a NoSQL database is, let's look at what makes up a Datastore database, as relationships between data objects are addressed differently than other databases that you may be familiar with. A traditional SQL database would be made up of tables, rows, and columns. In Cloud Datastore, an entity is the equivalent of a row and a kind is the equivalent of a table. Entities are data objects that can have one or more named properties.

Each entity has a key that identifies it. Let's look at the following table to compare the terminology that is used with SQL databases and Cloud Datastore:

Concept	SQL Database	Cloud Datastore
Category of object	Table	Kind
One object	Row	Entity
Individual data for an object	Column	Property
Unique ID for an object	Primary Key	Key

Exam tip: Data objects in Datastore are known as entities.

Data consistency

Cloud Datastore offers ways to achieve both strong and eventual consistency. Non-relational databases are built on the concept of eventual consistency; however, Cloud Datastore offers two APIs that provide strong consistency for reading entity values and indexes:

- Lookup by key method (for values only)
- Ancestor query

If either of these APIs is called, then Cloud Datastore will flush all pending updates for one of its replicas and index tables, then execute the lookup or ancestor query to provide the latest updates. If we have strong consistency requirements along with our filtering requirements, then we can only use the ancestor query.

Creating and using Cloud Datastore

Let's now look at how to create a Datastore database and run some queries on the entities that we create. Before we do so, let's remind ourselves that Datastore is a managed service. You will notice as we go through this process that we are directly creating our entities without provisioning any underlying infrastructure first. You should also note that, like all storage services from GCP, Cloud Datastore automatically encrypts all data before it's written to the disk. Follow these steps to create a Datastore database:

1. From our GCP console, browse to **STORAGE** | **Datastore** | **Entities**:

2. We are now required to choose an operational mode. **Native mode** is the official Firestore mode, which is the next major version of Cloud Datastore and offers new features, such as real-time updates and mobile and web client libraries. Datastore mode uses traditional Cloud Datastore system behavior. In our example, we will use **Datastore mode**:

	Native mode	Datastore mode
	Enable all of Cloud Firestore's features, with offline support and real-time synchronization.	Leverage Cloud Datastore's system behavior on top of Cloud Firestore's powerful storage layer.
	SELECT NATIVE MODE	SELECT DATASTORE MODE
API	Firestore	Datastore
Scalability	Automatically scales to millions of concurrent clients	Automatically scales to millions of writes per second
App engine support	Not supported in the App Engine standard Python 2.7 and PHP 5.5 runtimes	All runtimes
Max writes per second	10,000	No limit
Real-time updates	✓	✗
Mobile/web client libraries with offline data persistence	✓	✗
Query consistency	Strong	Strong
Data model	Documents / collections	Entities / kinds
Web console	Firestore page in Google Cloud Platform and Firebase	Datastore page in Google Cloud Platform

3. Select a location for your Datastore database and click **CREATE DATABASE**:

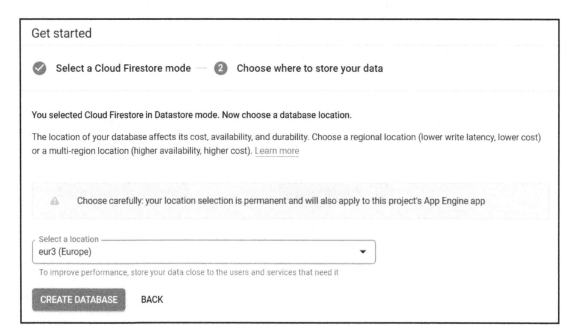

4. Once the database is ready, we will be directed to the **Entities** menu. Click **CREATE ENTITY** to create our first Datastore entity:

5. We can now give our entity a namespace, a **Kind** (a table, in SQL terminology), and a key identifier, which will be auto generated. Let's leave our namespace as the default and create a new kind called exam:

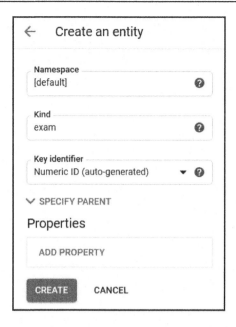

6. Click **ADD PROPERTY** to specify a name—in this case, `title`. We can also
    select from several types, but in this example, we want to use **String**. Finally, we
    will give it a value of `Professional Cloud Architect`. Click **DONE** to add
    the property:

7. We can repeat *step 6* to add another property. This time we can use `cost` as the name, **Integer** as the type, and `200` as the value. When we have added all of the properties we want in our entity, click **CREATE**. Let's also create two new entities with the `exam` kinds for the `Associate Cloud Engineer` exam and for the `Professional Cloud Developer` exam:

8. We can now filter our entities to a query based on cost or title. Let's look for information on the `Professional Cloud Developer` exam:

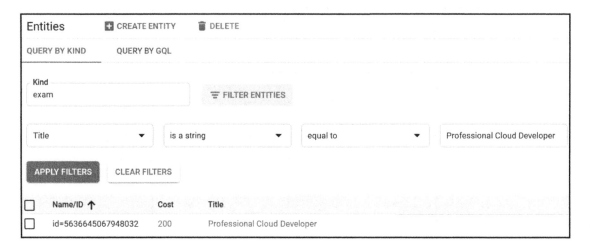

9. We can also use **QUERY BY GQL** and enter a SQL-like query to get the same results:

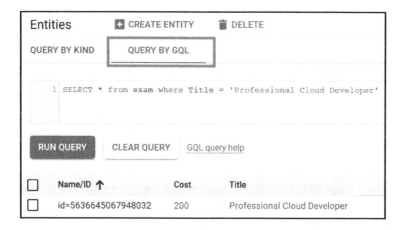

We can now see how easy it is to create a Datastore database and query the entities we create. Let's move on now to look at some of the differences between Datastore and Firestore.

Datastore versus Firestore

We mentioned at the beginning of this section that Firestore is the latest release of Datastore. While the exam will still refer to Datastore, it is important that we mention Firestore. You will have noticed in the previous section that, when selecting **Datastore mode**, we can choose between **Native mode** and **Datastore mode**.

Cloud Firestore in native mode is the complete re-branded product. It takes the best of Cloud Datastore and the Firebase real-time database to offer the same conceptual NoSQL database as Datastore, but as Firebase is built for low-latency mobile applications, it also includes the following new features:

- New strongly consistent storage layer
- Collect and document data model
- Real-time updates
- Mobile and web-client libraries

Cloud Firestore in Datastore mode uses the same Datastore system behavior, but will access the Firestore storage layer, which will remove some limitations, such as the following:

- No longer limited eventual consistency, as all queries become strongly consistent
- No longer limited to 25 entity group limit
- No longer limited to 1 write per second to an entity group

IAM

Access to Google Cloud Datastore is secured with IAM. Let's have a look at the list of predefined roles and their details:

- **Datastore owner with appengine app admin**: Has full access to Datastore mode.
- **Datastore owner without appengine app admin**: Has access to Datastore mode but cannot enable admin access, check whether Datastore mode admin is enabled, disable Datastore mode writes, or check whether Datastore mode writes are disabled.
- **Datastore user**: Has read/write access to data in a Datastore mode database. Mainly used by developers or service accounts.
- **Datastore viewer**: Has rights to read all Datastore mode resources.
- **Datastore import export admin**: Has full access to manage imports and exports.
- **Datastore index admin**: Has full access to manage index definitions.

Quotas and limits

Google Cloud Datastore comes with predefined quotas. These default quotas can be changed by going to the **Navigation** menu and **IAM & Admin | Quotas**. From this menu, we can review the current quotas and request an increase to these limits. We recommend that you familiarize yourself with the limits for each service as this can have an impact on your scalability. For Cloud Datastore, we should be aware of the following limits:

- There is a maximum API request size (outside of its use with App Engine) of 10 MiB.
- There is a maximum transaction size of 10 MiB.
- There is a maximum entity size of 1,048,572 bytes.
- There is a maximum depth of 20 nested entity values.
- There is a maximum write rate to an entity of 1 per second.
- There is a maximum number of entities that can be passed to a commit operation in the API of 500.
- There is a maximum number of keys allowed for an `allocateIds` operation in the Cloud Datastore API of 500.
- There is a maximum number of keys allowed for a `lookup` operation in the Cloud Datastore API of 1,000.

- There is a maximum size of an indexed string property's UTF-8 encoding of 1,500 bytes.
- There is a maximum size of an unindexed property of 1,048,572 bytes.
- There is a maximum sum of the sizes of an entity's composite index entries of 2 MiB.
- There is a maximum number of composite indexes for a project of 200.
- There is a maximum sum of indexed property values for an entity of 20,000.
- There is a maximum sum of composite index entries for an entity of 20,000.
- There is a maximum of 20 import and export requests for a project allowed per minute.
- There is a maximum of 50 concurrent exports and imports.

Pricing

Pricing for Google Cloud Datastore offers a free quota to get us started. The free limit per day is set as follows:

- 1 GB of stored data
- 50,000 entity reads
- 20,000 entity writes
- 20,000 entity deletes
- 50,000 small operations

If these limits are exceeded, there will be a charge that will fluctuate depending on the location of your data. Storage will be charged per GB per month. Entity reads, writes, and deletes will be charged per 100,000 entities and small operations will continue to be free. Small operations are defined as calls to allocate IDs, key-only queries, or projection queries that don't use the `DISTINCT ON` clause.

Understanding Cloud SQL

Given the name, it won't be a major surprise to hear that Cloud SQL is a database service that makes it easy to set up, maintain, and manage your relational PostgreSQL or MySQL database on Google Cloud. Cloud SQL announced plans to release support for Microsoft SQL Server during 2019, but at the time of writing, it is not yet generally available.

When selecting MySQL, we can choose first-or second-generation instances. Although we are provisioning the underlying instances, it is a fully managed service that is capable of handling up to 10 TB of storage. Cloud SQL databases are relational, which means that they are organized into tables, rows, and columns. As an alternative, we can also install the SQL Server application image onto a Compute Engine instance, but Cloud SQL offers many benefits that come from being fully managed by Google—for example, scalability, patching, and updates are applied automatically, automated backups are provided, and it offers high availability out of the box.

 Exam tip: Cloud SQL can accommodate up to 10 TB of storage. If you need to handle larger amounts of data, then you should look at alternative services, such as Cloud Spanner.

Let's look at some of the features offered by Cloud SQL. We should note that any first generation MySQL instances will be automatically upgraded in 2020. It is best to select second generation whenever you are creating a new MySQL instance.

Cloud SQL for MySQL offers us the following:

- The first generation offers support for MySQL 5.5 or 5.6 and can provide up to 16 GB of RAM and 500 GB of storage. The default option is to create a second generation version.
- The second generation offers support for MySQL 5.6 or 5.7 and can provide up to 416 GB of RAM and 10 TB of storage.
- There's data replication between availability zones.
- There's automatic failover.
- There's point-in-time recovery.
- There's instance cloning.
- It offers integration with GCPs monitoring and logging solutions—Stackdriver.

Cloud SQL for PostgreSQL offers us the following:

- A fully managed database that is based on the Cloud SQL second generation instances
- Up to 10 TB of storage, which can be increased if needed; we also have the ability to enable automatic storage increases
- Custom machine types with up to 416 GB RAM and 64 CPUs

- Instance cloning
- On-demand backups
- Integration with GCPs monitoring and logging solutions—Stackdriver

Now that we know the main features, let's look at some of the things to bear in mind when we create a new instance:

- **Selecting an instance**: Similar to other GCP services, we have the option to select a location for our instances. It makes sense to locate our database instance close to the services that depend on it. We should understand our database requirements and have a baseline of active connections, memory, and CPU usage to allow us to select the correct machine type. If we over-spec, this will have an impact on our cost, and likewise, if we under-spec, we may impact our performance or availability if resources are exhausted.
- **Selecting storage**: When creating an instance, we can select different storage tiers. Depending on our requirements, we may wish to select an SSD for lower latency and higher throughput; however, we can also select HDD if our requirements are not for such a high-performing disk.

 We cannot select a storage tier on first-generation MySQL instances.

Selecting the correct capacity to fit your database size is also extremely important, as after you have created your instance, you cannot decrease the capacity. If we over-spec our storage, then we will be paying for unused space.

If we under-spec our storage, then we can cause issues with availability. One method to avoid this is through the automatic storage increase setting. If this is enabled, your storage is checked every 30 seconds to ensure that the storage has not fallen below a set threshold size. If it has, then additional storage will be automatically added to your instance. A threshold size depends on the amount of storage your instance currently has provisioned, and it cannot be larger than 25 GB. This sounds great, but we should also be mindful that if we have spikes in demand, then we will suffer a permanent increase in storage cost.

- **Selecting an IP address**: We can select from a public or a private IP address. The default is to use a public IP address, which will block all IP addresses. We, therefore, have to add specific IP addresses or ranges to open our instances up too. In order to use a private IP address, we must first enable the Google's Service Networking API. This is required for each project. If we wish to use a private IP address, we also need to ensure that we have VPC peering set up between the Google service VPC network where our instance resides and our VPC network. This is shown in the following diagram:

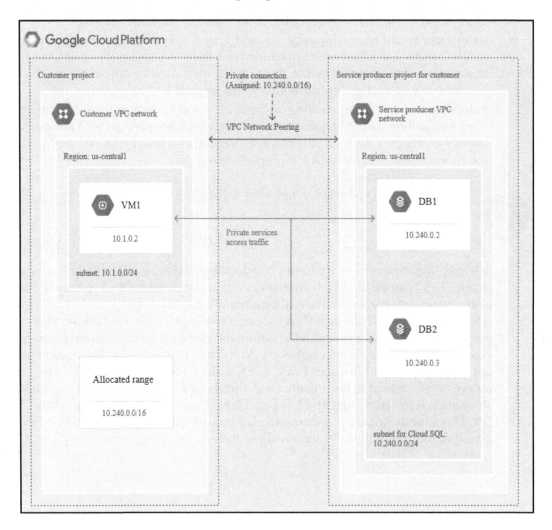

We discussed VPC peering in more detail in `Chapter 8`, *Networking Options in GCP*. Using a private IP will help lower network latency and improve security as traffic will never be exposed to the internet; however, we should also note that to access a Cloud SQL instance on its private IP address from other GCP resources, the resource must be in the same region.

It is recommended that you use a private IP address if you wish to access a Cloud SQL instance from an application that is running in Google's container service—Google Kubernetes Engine.

We cannot select a private IP address from first generation MySQL instances.

Exam tip: Cloud SQL instances will reside on their own VPC network and not a VPC network that we have created manually.

- **Automatic backups**: Enabling automatic backups will have a small impact on performance; however, we should be willing to accept this to take advantage of features such as read replicas, cloning, or point-in-time recovery.
- **Maintenance windows**: When working with this offering, we should also specify a maintenance window. We can choose a specific day and one-hour time slot when updates can be applied. GCP will not initiate any update to that instance without this specified window. Please note that, if no window is specified, then potentially disruptive updates can happen at any time.

Data consistency

Cloud SQL is a relational database that offers strong consistency and support for ACID transactions.

Creating and managing Cloud SQL

Now that we have an understanding of the concepts, let's look at how to create a new MySQL instance:

1. Go to the navigation menu and then go to **STORAGE** | **SQL**:

2. Click on **Create an instance.**
3. Select the database engine you require. In our example, we will select **MySQL**. By default, this is second generation:

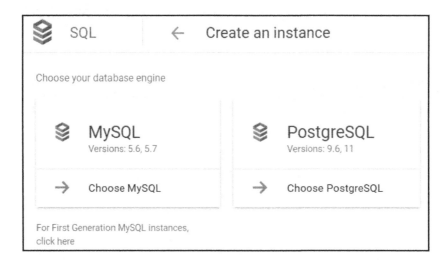

4. Give the instance a name and a password. You can either enter your own password or click **Generate** to receive a random password. Additionally, you can select a location and database version. We will leave the defaults in this example:

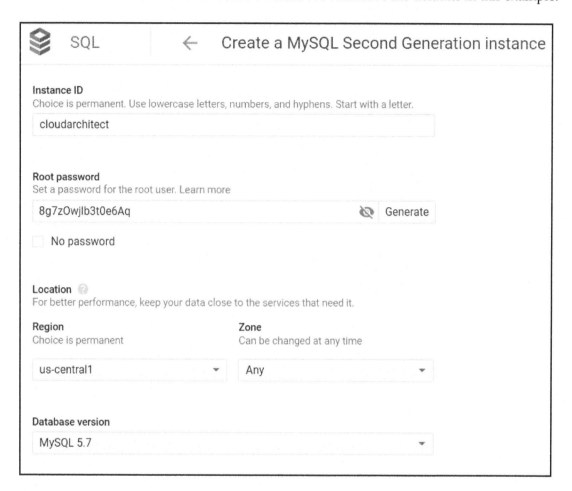

5. Let's now look at the advanced configurations. First, we can select whether we want a public or private IP address:

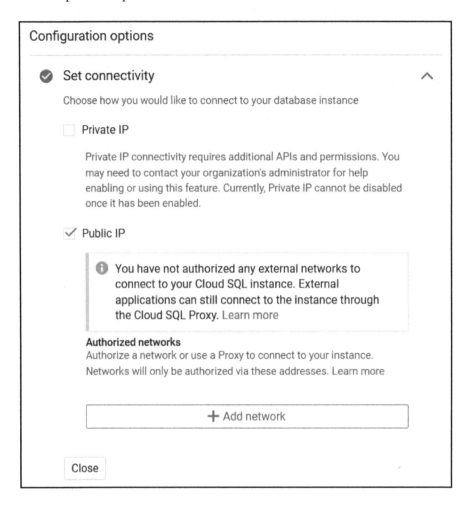

6. We can now select the machine type and storage tier to ensure that they meet our requirements. When the storage capacity is increased, then the disk throughput and IOPS will improve:

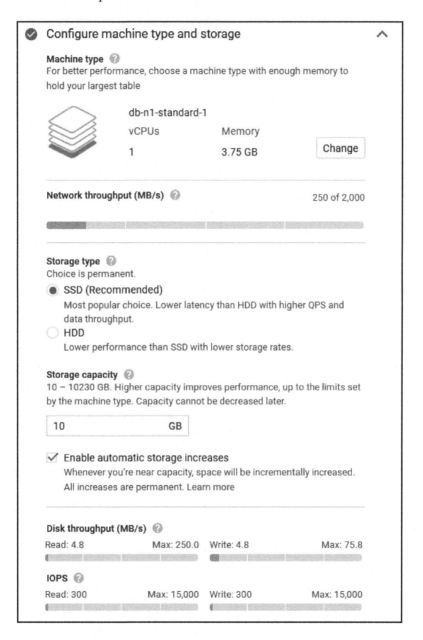

7. Provide a four-hour time period for a backup. Also, ensure that you check the **Create failover replica** option if required:

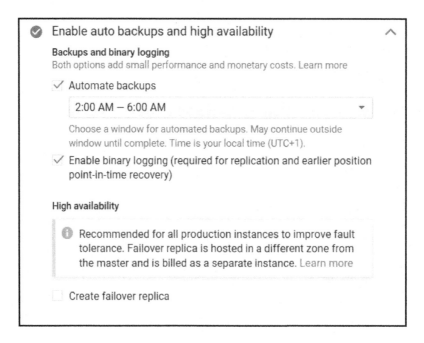

8. Set a maintenance schedule by selecting a day and one-hour time slot:

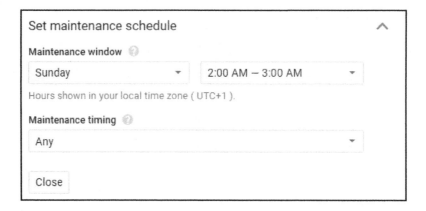

9. At this point, we can also add any tags we require. Finally, click **CREATE**.

Like other services, we can create an instance by using the command-line tools available to us. In earlier sections, we have touched on some command-line tools, and likewise, we can use `gcloud` to create a new instance. We can run the following syntax to create a new database:

```
gcloud sql instance create <instance name> --database-version=<DATABASE
version> --cpu=<cpu size> --memory=<RAM size> --region=<region name>
```

Let's look at the code in a little more detail:

- `<instance name>` is the name of our database instance.
- `<DATABASE version>` is the name of the specific version of MySQL or PostgreSQL you wish to create.
- `<cpu size>` and `<RAM size>` are the sizes of the resources we wish to create.
- `<region name>` is the region we wish to deploy our instance into.

Let's create a new PostgreSQL DB with version 9.6 called `cloudarchitect001` and allocate 4 CPU and 1,024 MiB of RAM. We will deploy this instance in the `us-central` region:

```
gcloud sql instances create cloudarchitect001 --database-
version=POSTGRES_9_6  --cpu=1 --memory=3840MiB --region=us-central
```

 Exam tip: You can directly map your on-premises MySQL, SQL, or PostgreSQL database onto Cloud SQL without having to convert it into a different format. This makes it one of the common options for companies looking to experiment in public cloud services.

Now that we have created a new instance by console and command line, let's look deeper at some important features—Read Replicas and Failover Replicas.

Read Replicas

Cloud SQL offers the ability to replicate our master instance to one or more Read Replicas. This is essentially a copy of the master that will register changes to the master instance in almost real time. We should highlight here that Read Replicas do not provide high availability, and we cannot fail over to a Read Replica from a master. They also do not fall in line with any maintenance window that we may have specified when creating the master instance. There a number of scenarios that Cloud SQL offers for read replication:

- **Read Replica**: This offers additional read capacity and an analytics target to optimize performance on the master.

- **External Read Replica**: This replicates to a MySQL instance that is external to Cloud SQL. It can help to reduce latency if you are connecting from an on-premise network.
- **Replication from an external server**: This is where an external MySQL instance is the master and is being replicated into Cloud SQL.

Enabling Read Replicas is a simple process. Let's learn how to do this from our GCP console:

1. Browse once more to **Storage | SQL**. Let's add a replica to our existing `cloudarchitect` instance. We simply need to open up our options and select **Create read replica**:

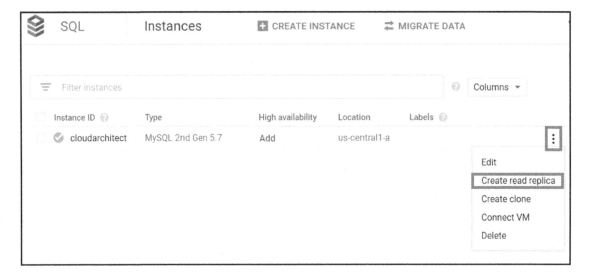

Exam tip: Before we can create a read replica, the following requirements must be met:

- Binary logging must be enabled.
- At least one backup must have been created since binary logging was enabled.

Note that we cannot change the region, but we can select a different zone.

2. Simply give the instance a name and click **Create**. We will have configuration options similar to those we used when we created a master instance:

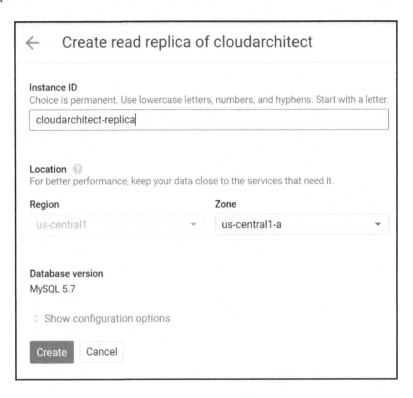

3. Once the Read Replica is created, we can see this in our normal instance view:

In the next section, we will look at Failover Replicas.

Failover Replica

To achieve high availability, we need to create a cluster that is made up of a primary instance and a Failover Replica in a secondary zone. When we make changes to the primary instance's data, it is copied onto the failover instance. This, of course, reduces any downtime caused by instance failure. We can see from the following diagram that replication between the primary and replica is semi-synchronous:

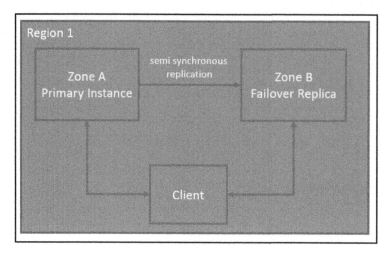

Our Failover Replica is configured in the same way as the primary instance, which means that all users, passwords, authorized applications, networking, and databases are the same.

A failover will occur when an instance becomes unresponsive, at which point Cloud SQL will automatically switch to serving data from the Failover Replica. The primary instance will write a heartbeat signal to the database every second. An instance is classed as unresponsive if it misses multiple heartbeats totaling 60 seconds. A failover will also occur if there is an outage in the primary instance's zone. Cloud SQL will wait for the Failover Replica to catch up to the primary instance's state and then promote the Failover Replica to the primary instance role.

The original primary instance's name and IP address will move to the old Failover Replica, allowing clients to reconnect without any issue. Of course, for the failover to be successful, the Failover Replica must be in a healthy state itself and not be in a stopped state or undergoing any maintenance. If a failure to the primary instance occurs while the Failover Replica is not in a healthy state, then we will experience an outage.

We can enable a Failover Replica when we create a new instance; however, it is a simple process to enable it on an existing instance. We can do this from our GCP console or by using the `gcloud` command-line tool:

1. To do this, we would use the following syntax:

   ```
   gcloud sql instances create <replica name> --master-instance-
   name=<master instance> --replica-type=<replica type>
   ```

   Let's look at the code in a little more detail:

   - `<replica name>` is the name we wish to assign to our Failover Replica.
   - `<master instance>` is the master instance we wish to configure for failover.
   - `<replica type>` is one of the types of replication we spoke about earlier in this chapter.

2. Let's look at how to enable this on our `cloudarchitect` instance for replication. The call is `cloudarchitect-failover`:

   ```
   gcloud sql instances create cloudarchitect-failover --master-
   instance-name=cloudarchitect --replica-type=FAILOVER
   ```

3. When the failover node is created, we can view this on our **SQL** instance page. Note that the instance is now enabled for high availability:

Instance ID	Type	High availability
cloudarchitect	MySQL 2nd Gen 5.7	Enabled
cloudarchitect-failover	MySQL 2nd Gen failover	—

Exam tip: The replication type is case sensitive—for example, FAILOVER not failover.

Backup and recovery

We have mentioned backup and recovery previously when we created a new instance. We can create a backup schedule and trigger an on-demand backup from our console or command line whenever required. If we want to edit our instance, we have to check the backup schedule that we have configured or change the backup time if necessary:

Backups are, obviously, a way to restore our data from a certain period of time in the event of corruption or data loss. Cloud SQL gives us the option to restore data back to the original instance or to a different instance. Both methods will overwrite all of the current data on the target instance.

Let's look at how we can restore from the console:

1. From our MySQL deployment, we can click on the **BACKUPS** tab and then the **Restore** option for the specific backup we would like to restore:

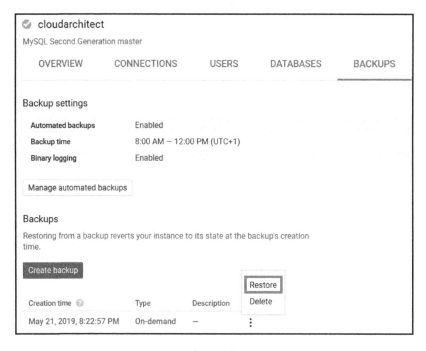

Note that if we are trying to restore a backup from an instance that has a replica created, we are forced to delete this first:

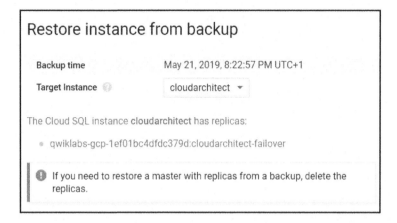

2. If we don't have any replicas, or indeed if we have deleted them, then we can proceed. You will notice that we can restore directly back to the source instance or select another instance:

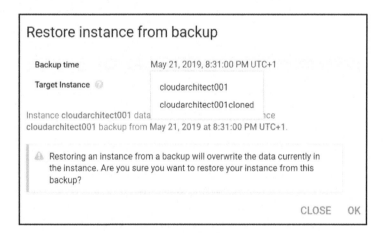

In the next section, we will look at how to migrate data.

Migrating data

If we wish to migrate the master copy of our MySQL data into the cloud, then it is best practice to create a replica managed by Cloud SQL and then promote this replica to a standalone instance. To get our data onto Cloud SQL, we should go through the following process:

1. Create a Cloud Storage bucket for your data.
2. Export your data to the Cloud Storage bucket.
3. Set up the replication configuration.
4. Configure the source database server to accept connections from the replica.
5. Restrict access to the MySQL replication user.
6. Finalize the replica configuration.
7. Confirm the replication status.
8. Clean up your storage.

If we wish to import a SQL dump file, then the process is similar to the preceding steps:

1. We should create our dump file and upload it to a Cloud Storage bucket.
2. From our instance page, we can click on the **Import** option and point it toward our Cloud Storage bucket.
3. Similarly, we can click on the **Export** option and move our Cloud SQL dump file to a Cloud Storage bucket.

More information on this process is available in the *Further reading* section.

Instance cloning

We have previously mentioned that we can clone our instances. This will create a copy of our source instance, but it will be completely independent. This does not mean that we have a cluster or read-only replica in place. Once the cloning is complete, any changes to the source instance will not be reflected in the new cloned instance and vice versa. Instance IP addresses and replicas are not copied to the new cloned instance and must be configured again on the cloned instance. Similarly, any backups taken from the source instance are not replicated to the cloned instance.

This can be done from our GCP console or by using our `gcloud` command-line tool:

1. Let's look at the syntax that we would use to perform this:

```
gcloud sql instances clone <instance source name> <target
instance name>
```

Let's look at the code in a little more detail:

- `<instance source name>` is the name of the instance you wish to clone.
- `<target instance name>` is the name you wish to assign to the cloned instance.

2. Let's look at how to clone our `cloudarchitect001` instance:

```
gcloud sql instances clone cloudarchitect001
cloudarchitect001cloned
```

We will call the cloned instance `cloudarchitect001cloned`.

IAM

Access to Google Cloud SQL is secured with IAM. Let's have a look at the list of predefined roles and their details:

- **Owner**: Has full access and control for all GCP resources
- **Writer**: Has read/write access to all GCP and Cloud SQL resources
- **Reader**: Has read-only access to all GCP resources, including Cloud SQL resources
- **Cloud SQL Admin**: Has full control over all Cloud SQL resources
- **Cloud SQL Editor**: Has rights to manage specific instances; can't see or modify permissions or modify users for SSL certificates; cannot import data or restore from a backup nor clone, delete, or promote instances; and cannot stop or start replicas or delete databases, replicas, or backups
- **Cloud SQL Viewer:** Has read-only rights to all Cloud SQL resources
- **Cloud SQL Client**: Has access to cloud SQL instances from App Engine and Cloud SQL Proxy

Quotas and limits

Google Cloud SQL comes with predefined quotas. These default quotas can be changed via the **Navigation** menu and **IAM & Admin** | **Quotas**. From this menu, we can review the current quotas and request an increase to these limits. We recommend that you familiarize yourself with the limits for each service, as this can have an impact on your scalability. For Cloud SQL, we should be aware of the following important limit.

Exam tip: MySQL (second generation) and PostgreSQL have a storage limit of 10 TB.

Other limits to be aware of include the following:

- There is a limit of 250 GB storage for MySQL first-generation instances.
- There is a limit of 40 instances per project.
- There is a limit of 250 maximum concurrent connections for `db-f1-micro` machines for MySQL second generation.
- There is a limit of 1,000 maximum concurrent connections for `db-g1-small` machines for MySQL second generation.
- There is a limit of 400 maximum concurrent connections for all other machines for MySQL second generation.
- For Cloud SQL for PostgreSQL, there is a maximum concurrent connection limit of 25 for 0.6 GiB RAM.
- For Cloud SQL for PostgreSQL, there is a maximum concurrent connection limit of 50 for 1.76 GiB RAM.
- For Cloud SQL for PostgreSQL, there is a maximum concurrent connection limit of 100 for 3.75–6 GiB RAM.
- For Cloud SQL for PostgreSQL, there is a maximum concurrent connection limit of 200 for 6–7.5 GiB RAM.
- For Cloud SQL for PostgreSQL, there is a maximum concurrent connection limit of 400 for 7.5–15 GiB RAM.
- For Cloud SQL for PostgreSQL, there is a maximum concurrent connection limit of 500 for 15–30 GiB RAM.
- For Cloud SQL for PostgreSQL, there is a maximum concurrent connection limit of 600 for 30–60 GiB RAM.
- For Cloud SQL for PostgreSQL, there is a maximum concurrent connection limit of 800 for 60–120 GiB RAM.

- For Cloud SQL for PostgreSQL, there is a maximum concurrent connection limit of 1000 for 120+ GiB RAM.
- There is a limit of 250 maximum concurrent connections for Tier D0–D2 for MySQL first generation.
- There is a limit of 500 maximum concurrent connections for Tier D4 for MySQL first generation.
- There is a limit of 1,000 maximum concurrent connections for Tier D82 for MySQL first generation.
- There is a limit of 2,000 maximum concurrent connections for Tier D16 for MySQL first generation.
- There is a limit of 4,000 maximum concurrent connections for Tier D32 for MySQL first generation.

Pricing

Pricing for Cloud SQL is based on a charge for every minute that the instance is running. The price will fluctuate depending on the location and the machine type we select. Read Replicas and Failover Replicas are charged at the same rate as standalone instances. There is also a charge for storage, again depending on the location in which our instance is stored. Network egress traffic is also chargeable depending on the destination of the traffic and whether a partner is involved. More information on pricing is available in the *Further reading* section.

Summary

In this chapter, we covered the storage options available to us, looking at which ones were most appropriate for common requirements. We also learned about Google Cloud Storage, Cloud Datastore, and Cloud SQL.

With Google Cloud Storage, we looked at use cases, storage classes, and some main features of the service. We also covered some considerations to bear in mind when transferring data. It's clear that Cloud Storage offers a lot of flexibility, but when we need to store more structured data, we need to look at alternatives.

With Cloud Datastore, we learned that this service is a NoSQL database and is ideal for your situation should your application rely on highly available and structured data. Also, Cloud Datastore can scale from zero up to terabytes of data with ease and is ideal for ACID transactions. We also learned that it offers eventual or strong consistency; however, if we have different requirements and a need for a relational database that has full SQL support for **Online Transaction Processing (OLTP)**, then we should consider Cloud SQL.

For Cloud SQL, we learned that we have two offerings—MySQL and PostgreSQL. We reviewed how to create and manage our instances, how to create replicas, and how to restore our instances.

In part two, we will continue looking at GCP storage options with Cloud Spanner and Bigtable.

Further reading

Read the following articles for more information:

- **Cloud Storage:** https://cloud.google.com/storage/docs/
- **Cloud Datastore:** https://cloud.google.com/datastore/docs/
- **Cloud SQL:** https://cloud.google.com/sql/docs/
- **Cloud SQL pricing:** https://cloud.google.com/sql/pricing
- **Importing data into Cloud SQL:** https://cloud.google.com/sql/docs/mysql/import-export/importing
- **Exporting data from Cloud SQL:** https://cloud.google.com/sql/docs/mysql/import-export/exporting

10
Exploring Storage Options in GCP - Part 2

In the first part of our storage exploration, we looked at several services. Now we will continue our focus on the remaining core options. In this chapter, we will look at the remaining topics/storage options:

- Cloud Spanner
- Bigtable

The concepts of these databases may sound familiar to the services we discussed in the previous chapter. For example, Cloud Spanner has similarities to Cloud SQL, while Bigtable may have you thinking about Cloud Datastore. In this chapter, we will not only look at the services but show you how they differ and why you may need to select these over the other offerings.

Cloud Spanner

There may be situations where you require horizontal scaling and Cloud SQL will not fit these requirements. Enter Cloud Spanner. Cloud Spanner is a cloud-native, fully managed offering that is designed specifically to combine relational database features such as support for ACID transactions and SQL queries with the horizontal scaling of a non-relational database. We should look to use Cloud Spanner when we require storage capacity requirements above 10 TB, as well as if we have requirements for high queries per second or to deliver over multiple regions. Unlike most databases, Cloud Spanner is globally distributed and provides a strongly consistent database service with high performance.

Exam tip: Cloud Spanner is strongly consistent.

It also offers an availability SLA of 99.999% when you're using a multi-regional instance and is capable of providing up to 10,000 queries per second of reads or 2,000 queries per second of writes. It is important to understand that Cloud Spanner is SQL-like and has a schema; however, because of its high availability, it is ideal for mission-critical workloads. Its key use cases are from the financial and retail industries.

Exam tip: With capacity for petabytes of storage, Cloud Spanner can meet requirements of over 10 TB of data, which Cloud SQL cannot achieve. With horizontal scalability, it will also support applications hosting across multiple regions. Remember that Cloud Spanner is ideal for workloads that require strong consistency.

Let's look at the configurations of Cloud Spanner. We must create a Cloud Spanner instance inside our GCP project to do this.

Instances configuration

When we create a new instance, we should select an instance configuration. This will determine where our instance will reside and the replication of the databases in the instance. We can select between the following:

- **Multi-regional**: By using this instance, we will gain a higher availability of SLA 99.999% – or downtime of approximately 5 minutes per year – but it will be more costly. Multi-regional configuration will replicate data between multiple zones within a single region. We should be mindful of this architecture and ensure that it fits our requirements. It may not be optimal to select this if we write our workloads and they come from a different location than our reads. Multi-region configurations allow us to replicate our data between multiple zones across multiple regions, allowing us to read data with low latency from locations. However, because replicas will be spread across more than one region, our applications will see a small increase in write latency.

- **Regional**: This will result in a 99.99% SLA, which is still very high and equivalent to approximately only 52 minutes of downtime per year. Regional instances should be selected if users and services are within the same region. This will offer the lowest latency. As you can see, the requirements will dictate the best option. We cannot change the instance's configuration after creation. Regional configurations will contain three read/write replicas that allow us to meet any governance requirements regarding where our data is located.

Node count

We are also required to select the number of nodes to allocate to our instance. This will determine the amount of CPU/RAM and storage resources that are available to our instance. Each node will provide up to 2 TiB of storage, and it is recommended that a minimum of three nodes are used for production environments. We can change the number of nodes after creation in order to scale up or down.

Replication

We mentioned replicas previously, and it's important to take a closer look at replication within Cloud Spanner. The underlying distributed filesystem that Cloud Spanner is built on will automatically replicate at the byte level. However, to provide additional data availability and geographic locality, Cloud Spanner will also replicate data by creating copies (replicas) of the rows that Cloud Spanner organized data into. These copies are then stored in a different geographic area. One of these replicas is elected to act as the leader and will be responsible for handling writes. Cloud Spanner has three types of replicas:

- **Read/Write**: This type of replication will maintain a full copy of our data and is eligible to become a leader. This is the only type of replication that's available to regional instances.
- **Read-Only**: This type of replication will only support reads and cannot become a leader. It will maintain a full copy of our data, which has been replicated from our read/write replica. Read-Only is only available in multi-regional configurations.
- **Witness**: This type of replication doesn't support reads, nor does it maintain a full copy of our data. Witness replication makes it easier for us to achieve quorums for writes without the compute resources that are required by a read/write replica. Witness is only available in multi-regional configurations.

TrueTime

TrueTime is a globally distributed clock built on GPS and atomic clocks. It returns a time interval that is guaranteed to contain the clock's actual time. TrueTime is provided to applications on Google Servers, which allows applications to generate monotonically increasing timestamps. Cloud Spanner uses TrueTime to assign timestamps to transactions whenever Cloud Spanner deems the transaction to have taken place.

Data consistency

If you are looking for guaranteed strong consistency, then Cloud Spanner is the storage offering for you! This is all down to the fact it is designed for the cloud and, therefore, will negate a lot of the constraints of other storage offerings. In fact, we should note that Cloud Spanner actually provides external consistency, which is a stronger property than strong consistency. This is the strictest consistency property for transaction-processing systems.

When we speak about data consistency with regard to Cloud Spanner, it is wise to raise awareness of the concept of the CAP theorem. This theorem says that a database can only have two out of three of the following properties:

- **C**: **Consistency**. This implies a single value for shared data.
- **A**: **Availability**. 100% for both read and updates.
- **P**: **Partitions**. Tolerance to network partitions.

This means that systems can be made up of CA, CP, and AP. The theorem is about 100% availability, but we know that systems will not offer 100% availability; therefore, the developers of systems are forced to think seriously about the trade-off. If we believe that some network partitions are inevitable at some point in a system's life cycle, then a distributed system should be designed to forfeit consistency or availability – but only during a partition. Cloud Spanner, in times of a partition, will forfeit availability to ensure consistency. Given that Spanner offers 99.999% availability, which equates to less than 5.26 minutes per year, this is deemed to be high enough that we don't need to worry about availability trade-offs.

Creating a Cloud Spanner instance

Let's look at actually creating a Cloud Spanner instance. We will also create a database, that is, a table, and run a query on it:

1. Browse to **STORAGE** | **Spanner**, as shown in the following screenshot:

2. Choose to create an instance, and then enter an instance name. The ID will be auto-populated based on our name, but this can be modified if needed. We can also select our regional configuration and the number of nodes. Remember that the recommended number for production is 3:

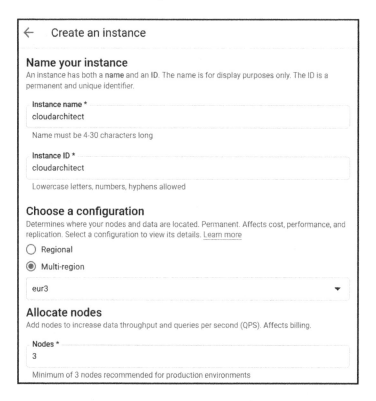

3. Once our instance has been created, click on **Create database**:

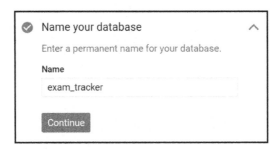

4. Now we can create a table. Let's create a table
   called `ProfessionalCloudArchitect`. Our table will keep track of how
   employees did while sitting the Google Professional Cloud Architect Exam:

5. Now we can populate it with values by browsing to **DATA** and then
   clicking **Insert**:

6. Let's fill in our table data:

7. Let's add more data to our tables to reflect our team members:

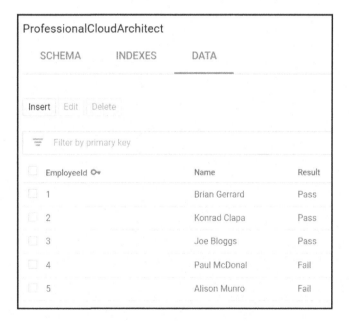

8. Now, let's perform a query on our information to see who has passed the exam:

9. Let's view our results, as follows:

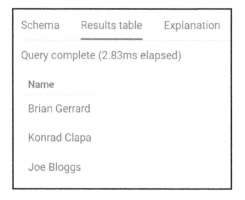

By doing this, we get a list of team members who passed the exam.

IAM

Access to Google Cloud Spanner is secured with IAM. The following is a list of predefined roles, along with a short description for each one:

- **Spanner Admin**: This has complete rights to all Cloud Spanner resources in a project.
- **Spanner Database Admin**: This has the right to list all Cloud Spanner instances and create/list/drop databases in the instances it was created in. It can grant and revoke access to a database in the project, and it can also read and write to all Cloud Spanner databases in the project.
- **Spanner Database Reader**: This has the right to read from the Cloud Spanner database, execute queries on the database, and view the schema for the database.

- **Spanner Database User**: This has the right to read and write to a Cloud Spanner database, execute SQL queries on the database, and view and update the schema for the database.
- **Spanner Viewer**: This has the right to view all Cloud Spanner instances and view all Cloud Spanner databases.

Quotas and limits

Google Cloud Spanner comes with predefined quotas. These default quotas can be changed via the **Navigation** menu and via **IAM & Admin** | **Quotas**. From this menu, we can review the current quotas and request an increase for these limits. We recommend that you are aware of the limits for each service as this can have an impact on your scalability. For Cloud Spanner, we should be aware of the following limits:

- There is a limit of 2 to 64 characters on the instance ID length
- There is a limit of 100 databases per instance
- There is a limit of 2 to 30 characters on the database ID length
- There is a limit of 2 TB storage per node
- There is a limit of 10 MB schema size
- There is a limit of 10 MB schema change size
- There is a limit of 2,048 tables per database
- There is a limit of 1 to 128 characters for the table name length
- There is a limit of 1,024 columns per table
- There is a limit of 1 to 128 characters for the column name length
- There is a limit of 10 MB data per column
- There is a limit of 16 columns in a table key
- There is a limit of 4,096 indexes per database
- There is a limit of 32 indexes per table
- There is a limit of 16 columns in an index key
- There is a limit of 1,000 function calls
- There is a limit of 25 nodes per project, per instance configuration

Pricing

Cloud Spanner charges for the number of nodes and the amount of storage and network bandwidth that's used. We will be charged for the following:

- For the maximum number of nodes that exist over an hour. This number is then charged by the hourly rate. These prices will fluctuate, depending on the location of our instances.
- The average amount of data in our tables over a one-month period. This is also multiplied by the monthly rate. These prices will fluctuate, depending on the location of our instances.
- Egress network traffic for some types of traffic. There is, however, no charge for replication or ingress traffic.

Exam tip: An important point to remember about Cloud Spanner is that it offers ACID transactions. If an atomic transaction involves two or more pieces of information, then all of the pieces are committed; otherwise, none are.

Bigtable

There is a clue in the name, but Bigtable is GCP's big data NoSQL database service. Bigtable is low latency and can scale to billions of rows and thousands of columns. It's also the database that powers many of Google's core services, such as Search, Analytics, Maps, and Gmail. This makes Bigtable a great choice for analytics and real-time workloads as it's designed to handle massive workloads at low latency and high throughput.

Exam tip: Bigtable can support petabytes of data and is suitable for real-time access and analytics workloads. It's a great choice for **Internet of Things (IoT)** applications that require frequent data ingestion or high-speed transactions.

Given Bigtable's massive scalability, we will cover the storage model and architecture. When we discuss Bigtable, we will make references to **HBase**. HBase is effectively an open source implementation of the Bigtable architecture and follows the same design philosophies. Bigtable stores its data in tables, which are stored in a key/value map. Each table is comprised of rows, which will describe a single entity.

Tables are also comprised of columns, which contain individual values for each row. Rows will be indexed by a row key, and columns that are related to one another are grouped into a column family. Bigtable only offers basic operations such as create, read, update, and delete. This means it has some good use cases while also not being great for others. Bigtable should not be used for transaction support as it will only offer row-level ACID guarantees. As we mentioned previously, CloudSQL or Spanner would be better suited for OLTP.

The following diagram shows the architecture of Bigtable:

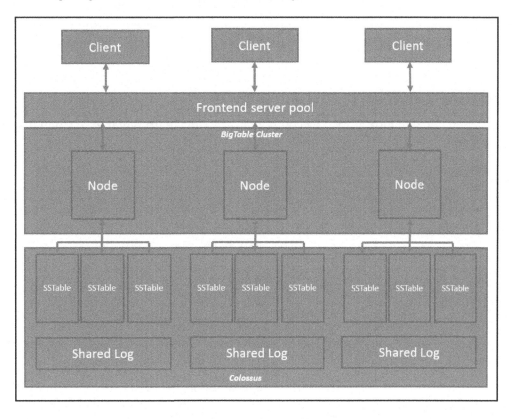

We can see that the client's requests go through a frontend server before they are sent to a Bigtable node. These nodes make up a Bigtable cluster belonging to a Bigtable instance, which acts as a container for the cluster.

Each node in the cluster handles a subset of the requests. We can increase the number of simultaneous requests a cluster can handle by adding more nodes. The preceding diagram shows only a single cluster, but replication can be enabled by adding a second cluster. With a second cluster, we can send different types of traffic to specific clusters and, of course, availability is increased.

To help balance out the workload of queries, Bigtable is sharded into blocks on contiguous rows. These are referred to as tablets and are stored on Google's filesystem – **Colossus** – in SSTable format. SSTable stands for **Sorted Strings Table** and stores immutable row fragments in a sorted order based on row keys. Each table will be associated with a specific Bigtable node, and writes are stored in the Colossus shared log as soon as they have been acknowledged. We should also note that data is never stored on Bigtable nodes. However, these nodes have pointers to a set of tablets that are stored in Colossus, meaning that if a Bigtable node fails, then no data loss is suffered.

Now that we understand the high-level architecture, let's look at the configuration of Bigtable.

Bigtable configuration

In this section, we will look at the key components that make up Bigtable. We will discuss the following:

- Instances
- Clusters
- Nodes
- Schema
- Replication

Instances

Cloud Bigtable is made up of instances that will contain up to four clusters that our applications can connect to. Each cluster contains nodes. We should imagine an instance as a container for our clusters and nodes. We have the option of two instance types:

- **Production**: This is a standard instance with one or two clusters, as well as three or more nodes in a cluster. We are unable to downgrade a production instance to a development instance once it's deployed.
- **Development**: This is a low-cost instance and is used for development and testing. Performance is equivalent to a one-node cluster, and Google offers no SLA guarantees. We can, however, upgrade to a production instance if needed.

Once we have decided on our instance type, we are also given the option of SSD or HDD storage. This is another permanent choice, and every cluster in our instance must use the same type of storage. Therefore, it is important to make sure that you're selecting the correct storage for your needs.

Exam tip: Remember that a development instance offers Bigtable at a lower cost but has no SLA. The HDD storage tier will also cost less but will not be as performant. Ensure that you are meeting requirements when you're selecting production or development instance types.

Clusters

A Bigtable cluster represents the service. Each cluster belongs to a single Bigtable instance, and, as we've already mentioned, each instance can have up to four clusters. When our applications send a request to an instance, it is handled by one of the clusters in the instance. Each cluster is located in a single zone, and an instance's clusters must be in unique zones. If our configuration means that we have more than one cluster, then Bigtable will automatically start to replicate our data by storing copies of the data in each of the cluster's zones and synchronizing updates between the copies. In order to isolate different types of traffic from each other, we can select which cluster we want our application to connect to.

Nodes

Each cluster in a production instance has a minimum of three nodes. Nodes are, as you may expect, compute resources that Bigtable will use to manage our data. Bigtable will try to distribute read and writes evenly across all nodes and also store an equal amount of data on each node. If a Bigtable cluster becomes overloaded, we can add more nodes to improve its performance. Equally, we can scale down and remove nodes.

Schema

It's worth noting that designing a Bigtable schema is very different from designing a schema for a relational database. There are no secondary indices as each table only has one index. Rows are sorted lexicographically by row key (the only index), from the lowest to the highest byte string. If you have two rows in a table, it's possible that one row will be updated successfully while the other row will fail. Therefore, we should avoid designing schemas that require atomicity across rows. Poor schema designs can be responsible for overall poor Bigtable performance.

Exam tip: Schemas can also be designed for **time series data**. If we want to measure something along with the time it occurred, then we are building a time series. Data in Bigtable is stored as unstructured columns in rows, with each row having a row key. This makes Bigtable an ideal fit for time series data. When we have to think about schema design patterns for time series, we should use tall and narrow tables, meaning that one event is stored per row. This makes it easier to run queries against our data.

Replication

The availability of data is a very big concern. Bigtable replication copies our data across multiple regions or zones within the same region, thus increasing the availability and durability of our data. Of course, to use replication, we must create an instance with more than one cluster or add clusters to an existing instance. Once this is set up, Bigtable will begin to replicate straight away and will store separate copies of our data in each zone where our instance has a cluster. Since this replication is done in almost real time, it makes for a good backup of our data. Bigtable will perform an automated failover should a cluster become unresponsive.

Application profiles

If we require an instance to use replication, then we need to use **application profiles**. By storing settings in these application profiles, we can manage incoming requests from our application and determine how Bigtable handles them. Every Bigtable instance will have its own default application profile, but we can also create our own custom profiles. Our code should be updated to specify which app profile we want our applications to use when we connect to an instance. If we do not specify anything, then Bigtable will use the default profile.

The configuration of **application profiles** will affect how an application communicates with an instance that uses replication. There are **routing policies** within an application profile. The **single-cluster routing** will route all the requests to a single cluster in your instance. The **multi-cluster routing** will automatically route traffic to the nearest cluster in an instance. If we create an instance with one cluster, then the default application profile will use single-cluster routing. If we create an instance with two or more clusters, then the default application profile will use multi-cluster routing.

We can create a custom application profile from the GCP console by browsing to the hamburger menu and going to **Bigtable** and then clicking on the instance where we wish to create the app profile. Finally, browse to the **Application profiles** option in the left-hand pane and click **CREATE APPLICATION PROFILE**.

In the following screenshot, we are creating an application profile for an instance called
tst001:

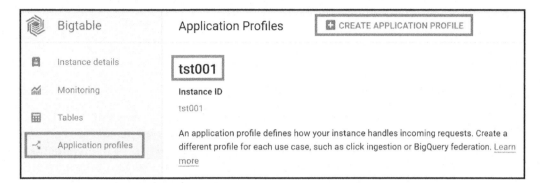

Then, we need to give the profile an ID and enter a description if we feel that's necessary.
Afterward, we select the routing policy we require:

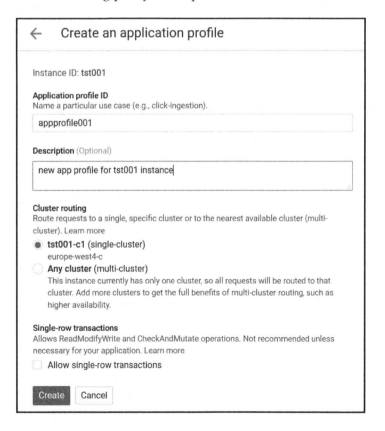

You will notice that we can check the box for single-row transactions. Bigtable does not support transactions that atomically update more than one row; however, it can use single-row transactions to complete read-modify-write and conditional writes operations. We should note that this option is only available when using a single-cluster routing policy to prevent conflicts.

Data consistency

One important aspect to understand is that Bigtable is eventually consistent by default, meaning that when we write a change to one of our clusters, we will be able to read that change from other clusters, but only after replication has taken place. To overcome this constraint, we can enable **Read-Your-Writes** consistency when we have replication enabled. This will ensure that an application won't read data that's older than the most recent writes. To achieve Read-Your-Writes consistency for a group of applications, we should use the single-cluster routing policy in our app profiles in order to route requests to the same cluster. The downside to this, however, means that if a cluster becomes unavailable, then we need to perform the failover manually.

Creating a Bigtable instance and table

Let's take a look at creating a Bigtable instance from our GCP console:

1. Browse to **STORAGE** | **Bigtable**, as shown in the following screenshot:

2. Click on **CREATE INSTANCE**:

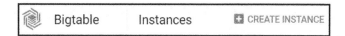

3. Provide a name and instance ID for our instance and select an instance type. Also, select the type of storage we require:

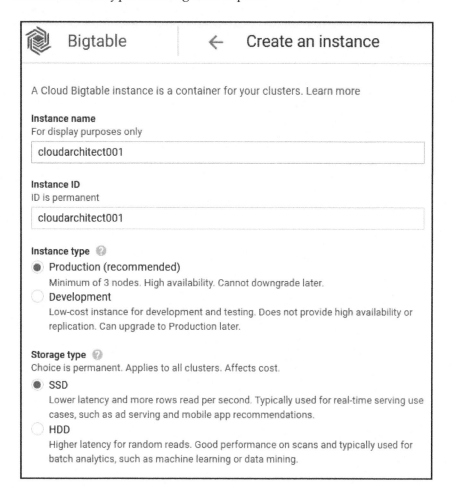

4. Provide the cluster details, that is, the location and the number of nodes needed. We can also set up replication if needed. Click **Done** to accept the cluster changes and click **Create** to complete the instance configuration:

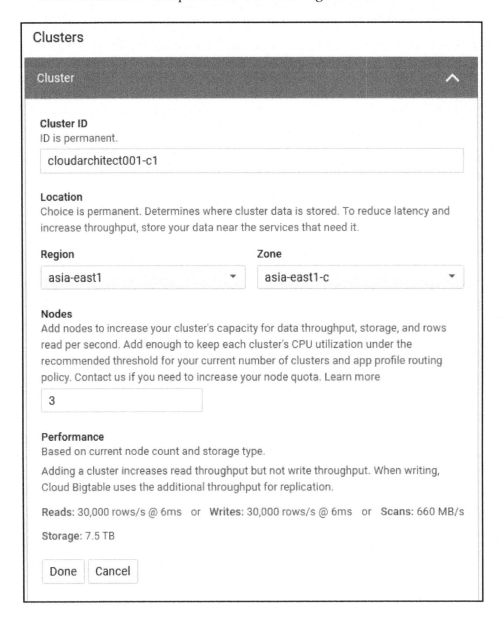

Once we have our instance and clusters, we can create a table. We touched on this earlier, but Bigtable has its own command-line tool, `cbt`, and creating a table is simplistic when we use it. Once again, we will make assumptions that you are familiar with this tool. Open up Cloud Shell so that we can configure the `cbt` tool. We looked at `cbt` and Cloud Shell in more detail in `Chapter 11`, *Google Cloud Management Options*:

1. Before we create a table, run the following syntax to mitigate the need to specify them in future command lines:

```
echo project = <project ID>\ninstance > ~/.cbtrc
echo instance = <instance ID> >> ~/.cbtrc
```

Here, we have the following:

- `<project ID>` is the ID of the project our Bigtable instance is associated with.
- `<instance ID>` is the ID of our instance.

2. Once this has been configured, we can create a table using some very simple syntax:

```
cbt createtable table001
```

Here, we have created a table called `table001`.

IAM

Access to Google Cloud Bigtable is secured with IAM. The following is a list of predefined roles, along with a short description of each:

- **Bigtable Admin**: This has rights to all Bigtable features, and is where you can create new instances. This role should be used by project administrators.
- **Bigtable User**: This has Read-Only access to the data stored within tables. This role should be used by application developers or service accounts.
- **Bigtable Reader**: This has Read-Only access to the data stored within tables. This role should be used by data scientists.
- **Bigtable Viewer**: This role should be used to grant the minimal set of permissions for Cloud Bigtable.

Quotas and limits

Google Cloud Bigtable comes with predefined quotas. These default quotas can be changed via the **Navigation** menu and via **IAM & Admin** | **Quotas**. From this menu, we can review the current quotas and request an increase for these limits. We recommend that you are aware of the limits for each service as this can have an impact on your scalability. For Cloud Bigtable, we should be aware of the following limits:

- There is a limit of 2.5 TB of SSD storage per node.
- There is a limit of 8 TB of HDD storage per node.
- There is a limit of 1,000 tables in each instance.

For Cloud Bigtable, we should also be aware of the following quotas:

- By default, you can provision up to 30 SSD or HDD nodes per zone in each project.
- There are numerous operational quotas that should be reviewed.

Pricing

Bigtable charges based on a number of factors:

- Instance types are charged per hour, per node.
- Production instances have a minimum of three nodes. Development instances are a single node.
- Storage is charged per month and costs vary depending on the use of SSD or HDD.
- Internet egress rates are charged depending on monthly usage. Ingress traffic is free.

For more specific details, please see the Bigtable pricing URL in the *Further reading* section.

Summary

In this chapter, we covered Cloud Spanner and Bigtable.

In terms of **Cloud Spanner**, we now understand that this is a scalable and globally distributed database. It is strongly consistent and was built to combine the benefits of relational databases with the scalability of a non-relational database. Cloud Spanner can scale across regions for workloads that might have high availability requirements.

We covered **Bigtable** at a high level in order to make sure you are aware of what is expected in the exam. It is a fully managed NoSQL database service that can scale massively and offer low latency, is ideal for IoT as it can handle high-speed transactions in real time, and it also integrates well with machine learning and analytics and can support over a petabyte of data.

We have now come to the end of a large chapter with a lot of information to take in. We have looked at the key storage services offered by GCP. We advise that you look over the exam tips in this chapter and make sure that you are aware of the main features of each service. Some of the key design decisions that we have spoken about are relational versus non-relational, structured data versus non-structured data, scalability, and SQL versus NoSQL.

In the next chapter, we will look at big data.

Further reading

Read the following articles to find more information about what was covered in this chapter:

- **Cloud Spanner**: https://cloud.google.com/spanner/docs/
- **Cloud Spanner Pricing**: https://cloud.google.com/spanner/pricing
- **Bigtable**: https://cloud.google.com/Bigtable/docs/
- **Bigtable Pricing**: https://cloud.google.com/Bigtable/pricing

11
Analyzing Big Data Options

If you have been looking into cloud computing, then the chances are you have come across the term **big data**. This is used to describe the large volumes of data that modern-day businesses are processing. We are not so worried about the mass of data, but more about how we can use this data. Almost everything carries a digital footprint these days, and there are challenges to ingest this data and to extract meaningful information. Google offers services that work together to allow us to first gather data, and then process it, before finally analyzing it. The faster we can analyze this means the faster business decisions can be made. Big data is becoming very important to many organizations.

In this chapter, we will look at Google big data services:

- Pub/Sub
- Dataflow
- BigQuery
- Dataproc
- Cloud IoT

In this chapter, we want to introduce the main Google big data services and concepts to a level expected by the exam. Of course, deeper dives are available.

End-to-end big data solution

Before we begin looking at the services, let's look at a very simple diagram. This represents the end-to-end big data solution. GCP provides us with all of the tools to architect an elastic and scalable service where we can import huge amounts of data, process events, and then execute business rules.

Exam tip: It is important to understand this flow and which services map to each stage. As we go through this chapter, we will map each big data service to a stage in our end-to-end solution.

We can ingest data from multiple sources, execute code to process this data, and then analyze the data to ensure that we maximize our business capabilities:

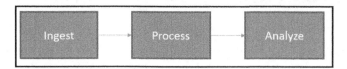

Of course, this is a very simplistic view of it and there are complexities when architecting our solutions, but we should expect, at least for the exam, to understand this at a high level. Let's look further into the services that map to each stage of the process.

Cloud Pub/Sub

Pub/Sub is a messaging and event ingestion service that acts as the glue between the loosely coupled systems. It allows us to send and receive messages between independent applications whilst **decoupling** the publishers of events and subscribers to those events. This means the publishers do not need to know anything about their subscribers. Pub/Sub is fully managed and therefore offers scale at ease, making it perfect for a modern stream analytics pipeline.

There are some core concepts that you should understand:

- A **publisher** is an application that will create and send messages to a topic.
- A **topic** is a resource to which messages are sent by publishers.
- A **subscription** represents the stream of messages from a single topic to be delivered to the subscribing application. Subscribers will either receive the message through pull or push, meaning the Pub/Sub pushes the messages to the endpoint using a webhook, or the message is pulled by the application using HTTPS requests to the Google API.
- A **message** is the data that a publisher will send to a topic. Put simply, it is data in transit through the system.

Publishers can be any application that can make HTTPS requests to `googleapis.com`. This can be existing GCP services, **Internet Of Things (IoT)** devices, or end user applications.

As we mentioned earlier, subscribers receive the messages either by a pull or push delivery method. Similar to publishers, pull subscribers can be any application that can make HTTPS requests to `googleapis.com`. In this case, the subscriber application will initiate requests to Pub/Sub to retrieve messages. On the other hand, push subscribers must be webhook endpoints that can accept POST requests over HTTPS.

In this case, Cloud Pub/Sub initiates requests to the subscriber application to deliver messages. Consideration should be given as to the best method for our requirements. As an example, if you are expecting a large volume of messages (for example, more than one message per second), then it is advisable to use the pull delivery method. Alternatively, if you have multiple topics that must be processed by the same webhook, then it is advisable to use the push delivery method:

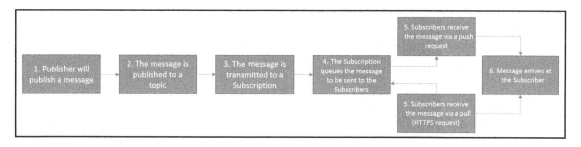

To summarize this, let's look at how this works in practice in the preceding diagram. When all of the deliveries are complete, the message will be removed from the queue.

As Cloud Pub/Sub integrates well with other GCP products, it opens up a lot of use cases.

Let's have a look at the most common use cases:

- **Distributed event notifications**: Let's take a service that needs to send a notification whenever there is a new registration. Pub/Sub makes it possible for a downstream service to subscribe and receive notifications of this new registration.
- **Balancing workloads**: Tasks can be distributed among multiple Compute Engine instances.
- **Logging**: Pub/Sub can write logs to multiple systems. For example, if we wish to work with real-time information, we could write to a monitoring system, and if we wish to analyze data at a later time, we could write to a database.

Creating a topic and subscription

Pub/Sub can ingest data from several data sources. The following diagram shows key services that can pass data to Pub/Sub. This is the first step into our solution:

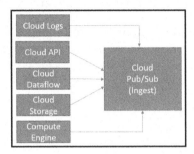

Let's now look at creating a Pub/Sub topic and subscription. We will then publish a message and pull it via Cloud Shell. Please refer to `Chapter 14`, *Google Cloud Management Options*, for more information on Cloud Shell. At this point, we are assuming you can open this up:

1. From the Navigation menu, browse to **BIG DATA** | **Pub/Sub**, as shown in the following screenshot:

2. Click on **Create a topic**:

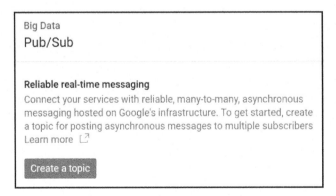

3. Append the auto generated name with a new topic name. In this example, we will name it `newTopic`. Click **CREATE**, as shown in the following screenshot:

4. Select **New subscription**, as shown in the following screenshot:

5. Append the auto generated subscription name. In this example, we will call it `newSub`. We will also leave the rest of the settings as their default settings, but we should note what each of these are:

   - **Subscription expiration**: If there are no active connections or pull/push successes, then the subscription expires.
   - **Acknowledgment Deadline**: The subscriber should acknowledge the message within a specific timeframe or Pub/Sub will attempt to deliver this message.
   - **Message retention duration**: Pub/Sub will try to deliver the message within a maximum of 7 days. After that, the message is deleted and is no longer accessible.

Notice that we keep the **Delivery Type** as **Pull**, as shown in the following screenshot:

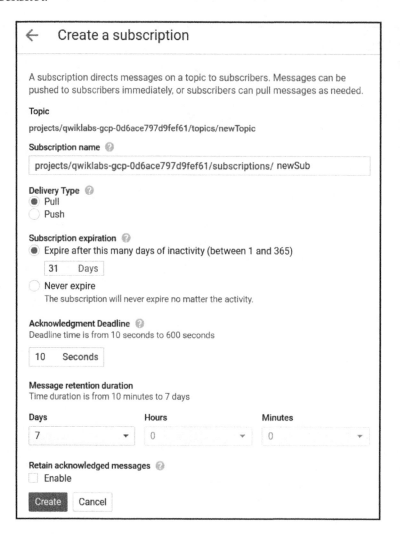

6. Select **Publish message**:

7. Enter the message content and select **Publish**, as shown in the following screenshot:

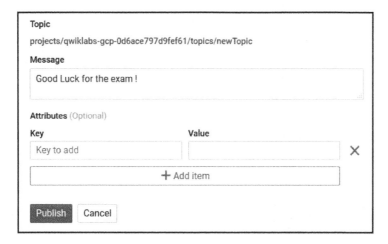

8. From Cloud Shell, we can now pull down the message:

This concludes how to publish and retrieve messages to and from Pub/Sub.

IAM

Access to Pub/Sub is secured with IAM. Let's have a look at the list of predefined roles together with a short description for each:

- **Pubsub Publish**: This has permission to publish a topic.
- **Pubsub Subscriber**: This has permission to consume a subscription or attach a subscription to a topic.
- **Pubsub Viewer**: This has the right to list topics and subscriptions.
- **Pubsub Editor**: This has the right to create, delete, and update topics, and create, delete, and update subscriptions.
- **Pubsub Admin**: This has the right to retrieve and set IAM policies for topics and subscriptions.

Quotas and limits

Pub/Sub comes with some limits. We recommend that you are aware of the limits for each service as this can have an impact on your scalability. For Pub/Sub, we should be aware of the following limits:

- There is a limit of 10,000 topics and 10,000 subscriptions per project.
- There is a limit of 10,000 attached subscriptions per topic.
- There is a limit of 1,000 messages and 10 MB total size per publish request.
- There is a limit of 10 MB per message.

Pricing

Pub/Sub is billed per message ingestion and delivery. There is also a storage charge for retained acknowledged messages.

Cloud Dataflow

Cloud Dataflow is a service based on Apache Beam, which is an open source software for creating data processing pipelines. A pipeline is essentially a piece of code that determines how we wish to process our data. Once these pipelines have been constructed and input into the service, they become a Dataflow job. This is where we can process our data ingested by Pub/Sub. It will perform steps to change our data from one format to another, and can transform both real-time stream or historical batch data. Dataflow is completely serverless and fully managed. It will spin up and destroy the necessary resources to execute our Dataflow job. As an example, a pipeline job might be made up of several steps. If a specific step requires execution on 15 machines in parallel, then Dataflow will automatically scale to these 15 machines and remove them when the job is complete. These resources are based on Compute Engine, referred to as workers, and Cloud Storage for a temporary staging area and I/O, and are based on our location settings.

 Exam tip: Dataflow will transform and enrich data in stream and batch modes. Its serverless architecture can be used to shard and process very large batch datasets or a high volume of live streams in parallel.

Cloud Dataflow is the next stage of our end-to-end solution and will process the data passed by **Cloud Pub/Sub**. Let's look at how this impacts our diagram:

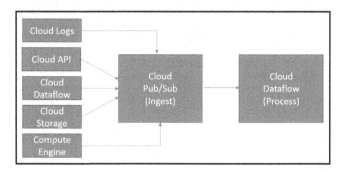

Let's now create a streaming pipeline using one of Google's open source Dataflow templates. Take the following scenario:

We have a Pub/Sub subscription and we wish to write the data to a data warehouse service for analysis. In this example, we will use BigQuery to analyze our data. We will discuss this service in the next section. We need Dataflow to convert JSON-formatted messages from Pub/Sub to BigQuery elements. For this example, we will use a Google public GCP project, which has the **Pub/Sub Topics** set up. We will also assume that we have a BigQuery table ready for the data to be written to:

1. From the Navigation menu, browse to **BIG DATA | Dataflow**:

2. Click on **CREATE JOB FROM TEMPLATE**:

3. We can now populate the required parameters for our Dataflow job:

    - We select a location to deploy our Dataflow workers and store our metadata. We will leave this as the default setting.
    - We insert the Pub/Sub input topic. This is a public project made available by Google as part of the template.

- We insert the BigQuery output table where our data will be written.
- We insert a Cloud Storage bucket to store temporary files:

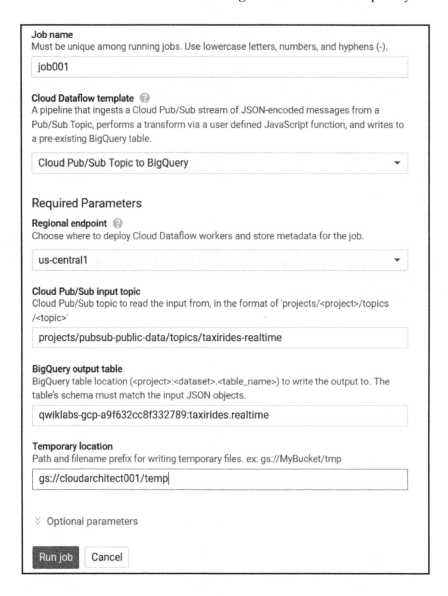

Job name
Must be unique among running jobs. Use lowercase letters, numbers, and hyphens (-).

job001

Cloud Dataflow template ⓘ
A pipeline that ingests a Cloud Pub/Sub stream of JSON-encoded messages from a Pub/Sub Topic, performs a transform via a user defined JavaScript function, and writes to a pre-existing BigQuery table.

Cloud Pub/Sub Topic to BigQuery ▼

Required Parameters

Regional endpoint ⓘ
Choose where to deploy Cloud Dataflow workers and store metadata for the job.

us-central1 ▼

Cloud Pub/Sub input topic
Cloud Pub/Sub topic to read the input from, in the format of 'projects/<project>/topics/<topic>'

projects/pubsub-public-data/topics/taxirides-realtime

BigQuery output table
BigQuery table location (<project>:<dataset>.<table_name>) to write the output to. The table's schema must match the input JSON objects.

qwiklabs-gcp-a9f632cc8f332789:taxirides.realtime

Temporary location
Path and filename prefix for writing temporary files. ex: gs://MyBucket/tmp

gs://cloudarchitect001/temp

⌄ Optional parameters

Run job | Cancel

4. Once we have run the job, we can see the flowchart as an output to see the status. This chart shows the stages of our pipeline. It reads JSON-formatted messages from a Cloud Pub/Sub topic, transforms them using a JavaScript user-defined function, and then writes them to our BigQuery table. This is a quick way to move Cloud Pub/Sub data to BigQuery:

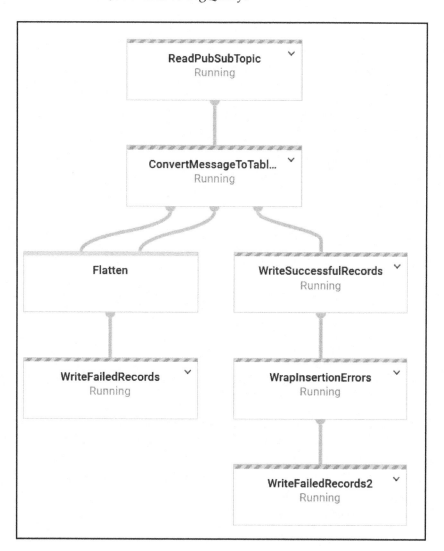

5. If we go to our BigQuery table and run a SQL query, we can see we are pulling in data from the Pub/Sub topic:

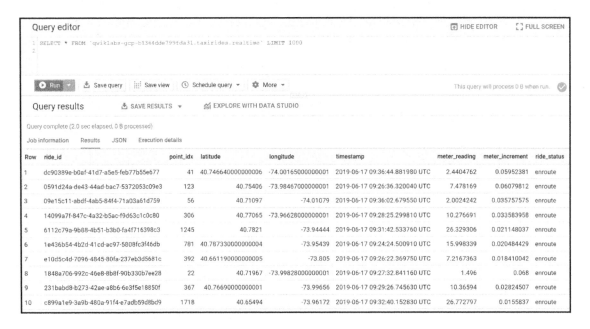

Of course, this query would be refined rather than selecting all.

IAM

Access to Cloud Dataflow is secured with IAM. Let's have a look at the list of predefined roles, together with a short description for each:

- **Dataflow Admin**: This has the right to create and manage Dataflow jobs.
- **Dataflow Developer**: This has the right to execute and manipulate Dataflow jobs.
- **Dataflow Viewer**: This has read-only rights to all Dataflow-related resources.
- **Dataflow Worker**: This has rights for a GCE service account to execute work units for a Dataflow pipeline.

Quotas and limits

Google Cloud Dataflow comes with predefined quotas. These default quotas can be changed via the navigation menu and **IAM & Admin** | **Quotas**. From this menu, we can review the current quotas and request an increase to these limits. We recommend you are aware of the limits for each service as this can have an impact on your scalability. For Cloud Dataflow, we should be aware of the following limits:

- Dataflow uses Compute Engine to execute pipeline code, and then we are subject to Compute Engine quotas.
- There is a limit of 1,000 workers per pipeline.
- There is a limit of 10 MB for a job creation request.
- There is a limit of 20,000 side input shards.

Pricing

Dataflow is billed in per-second increments on a per-job basis. Prices vary by region depending on the location.

BigQuery

BigQuery is a fully managed, serverless analytics service. It can scale to petabytes of data and is ideal for data warehouse workloads. It is, of course, the analysis stage of our solution, and once Dataflow processes our data, BigQuery will provide the value to our business by querying large volumes of data in a very short period of time. Queries are executed in the SQL language; therefore, it will be easy to use for many. We should emphasize that BigQuery is enterprise-scale and can perform large SQL queries extremely fast—all without the need for us to provision any underlying infrastructure.

 Exam tip: BigQuery is ideal for data warehouse workloads as it has the capacity for PB of storage.

BigQuery features

In this section, we will take a look at datasets and tables. These are two important concepts of BigQuery, and we need to understand them in order to be successful in the exam.

Datasets

Datasets are used to organize and control access to tables. We require at least one dataset before we can load data into BigQuery. Dataset names are unique to each project, and we are required to specify a location. Locations can be either regional or multi-regional, and we cannot change our location once the dataset has been created. Some consideration should be taken when selecting a location depending on export or ingestion requirements. For example, if we plan to query data from an external data source such as Cloud Storage, the data we are querying must be in the same location as our BigQuery dataset.

We can create a new dataset by browsing to the hamburger menu, | **BIG DATA** | **BigQuery**, and selecting **Create Dataset**:

An additional consideration when creating a dataset is whether or not to apply a default table expiration. BigQuery charges for both storage of data and per query. We should think about setting an expiration date if our tables will be for temporary use. The following example shows the same screenshot as the preceding one after the **Data location** has been selected:

We are setting an expiration value of 14 days for any table in our dataset.

Tables

Once we create a dataset, we can then create a table and load data into it. Tables will contain individual records that are organized into rows. Each table is defined by a schema that will describe the column names and data types, for example, a string or integer. The schema is decided when we create our table. We can also set an expiration date for our tables when we create them. If we set an expiration value when we create our dataset, then this value will be overwritten by the expiration value set when the table is created. If no value is set on either, then the table will never expire.

Partitioned tables make it easier to manage and query data. These are tables that are split into smaller partitions, meaning it will improve the query performance and reduce costs as the number of bytes read by a query is also reduced.

BigQuery offers two types of table partitioning:

- **Tables partitioned by ingestion time**: BigQuery will automatically load data into daily, data-based partitions.
- **Partitioned tables**: These allow us to bind data to a specific **TIMESTAMP** or **DATE** column.

 Exam Tip: It is possible to set expiration data on partitioned tables. Use this if you have, for example, a requirement to delete sensitive data after a period of time.

Using BigQuery

Let's look at the power of BigQuery. Google offers several example datasets available for public use to get a feel for BigQuery. In this example, we will use a dataset called **Chicago Taxi Trips** and we will execute a query to see which drop-off areas give the highest tip:

1. Browse to **BIG DATA** | **BigQuery** in the GCP console, as shown in the following screenshot:

Expand **ADD DATA** and select **Explore public datasets**, as shown in the following screenshot:

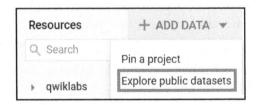

3. In the marketplace, search for `taxi` and select the **Chicago Taxi Trips** dataset:

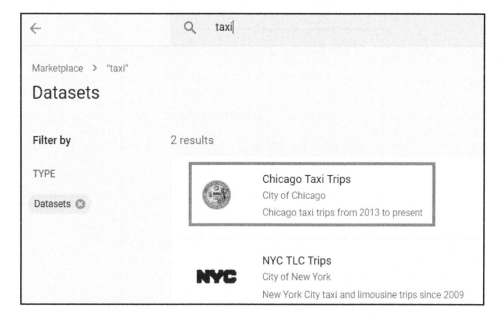

4. View the dataset:

5. You will now see the public datasets that are available for our use. Browse to the Chicago Taxi Dataset:

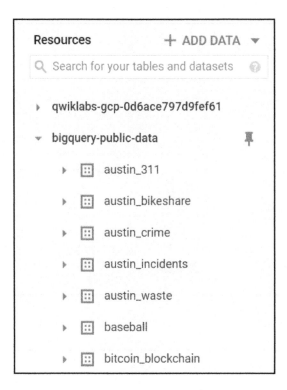

6. We can now execute a query on this dataset. This query will provide some valuable information. We will retrieve both the average and the highest tip given to drivers grouped by drop-off communities. We can see that this query uses standard SQL language:

Query editor

```
 1  SELECT
 2    dropoff_community_area,
 3    FORMAT('%3.2f', AVG(tips)) AS average_tip,
 4    FORMAT('%3.2f', MAX(tips)) AS max_tip
 5  FROM
 6    `bigquery-public-data.chicago_taxi_trips.taxi_trips`
 7  WHERE
 8    dropoff_community_area IS NOT NULL
 9  GROUP BY
10    dropoff_community_area
11  ORDER BY
12    average_tip DESC
13  LIMIT
14    10
```

No cached results

▶ Run ▾   ⬆ Save query   ⠿ Save view   🕐 Schedule query ▾   ⚙ More ▾

Query results   ⬇ SAVE RESULTS ▾   📈 EXPLORE IN DATA STUDIO

Query complete (2.6 sec elapsed, 1.5 GB processed)

Job information   Results   JSON   Execution details

Row	dropoff_community_area	average_tip	max_tip
1	31	98.10	9700.00
2	3	96.64	45000.00

Notice from the results that we have processed the query in only 2.6 seconds. It may not be a large amount of data queried, but it shows that we can quickly load a dataset and execute our query. There were no prerequisite steps to deploy infrastructure.

One thing regarding BigQuery that we should mention is that it has its own command-line tool, called bq. We will look more into bq in Chapter 14, *Google Cloud Management Options*.

Importing and exporting data

Of course, the preceding example was based on a public dataset. BigQuery allows us to upload from the console or Cloud Shell. Let's look at using the console to upload a CSV file we have locally. In this example, we'll assume we have a CSV already created called `airports.csv`:

1. From our BigQuery dataset, we can click on **CREATE TABLE**, as shown in the following screenshot:

2. We are then given several methods to create our table. Select **Upload** and then simply browse to the location of our CSV file:

3. We can then populate the dataset we want to add the table to and build our schema. In this example, we are adding entries to our schema with different types. We can see that `airport` and `city` are both **STRING**, but `arrival_data` is set to **DATE**:

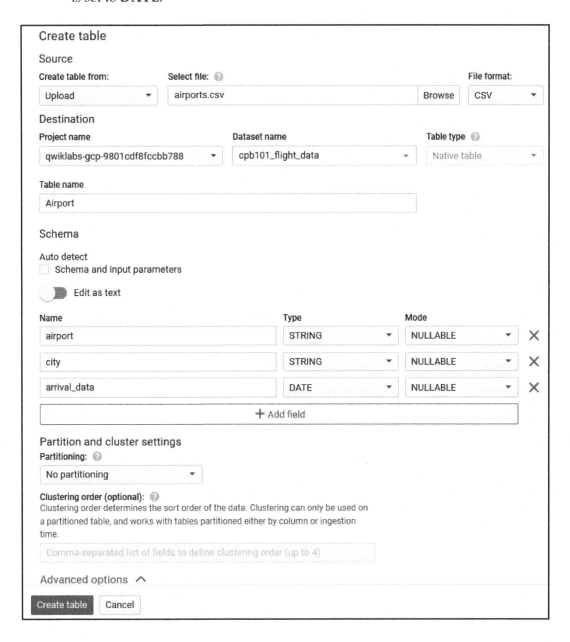

We will, at times, also need to export our tables to an external source as well. This is again a very simple process.

Let's export our table to a Cloud Storage bucket:

1. From our table view, we can click **EXPORT**:

2. Then, we populate our bucket name and export:

Let's move on now to take a brief look at BigQuery as a storage service.

Storage

Although we are discussing BigQuery as big data, let's remind ourselves that it is also a storage service. There is no need to export older data to another storage platform. With BigQuery, we can enjoy the same inexpensive long-term storage as we would expect from services such as Cloud Storage. As long as we are not editing tables for 90 consecutive days, then our cost will drop by 50%, which would match the cost of the Cloud Storage Nearline class.

We now have some valuable information from our data. Putting our full services together, at a high level, our solution would now look like this:

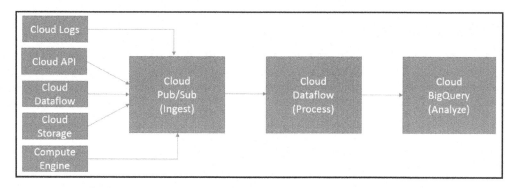

Take a moment to review the preceding diagram.

IAM

Access to BigQuery is secured with IAM. Let's have a look at the list of predefined roles together with a short description for each:

- **BigQuery User**: This has rights to run jobs within the project. It can also create new datasets. Most individuals in an organization should be a user.
- **BigQuery Job User**: This has rights to run jobs within the project.
- **BigQuery Read Sessions User**: This has rights to create and read sessions within the project via the BigQuery storage API.
- **BigQuery Data Viewer**: This has rights to read the dataset metadata and list tables in the dataset. It can also read data and metadata from the dataset tables.
- **BigQuery Metadata Viewer**: This has rights to list all datasets and read metadata for all datasets in the project. It can also list all tables and views and read metadata for all tables and views in the project.
- **BigQuery Data Editor**: This has rights to read the dataset metadata and to list tables in the dataset. It can create, update, get, and delete the dataset tables.
- **BigQuery Data Owner**: This has rights to read, update, and delete the dataset. It can also create, update, get, and delete the dataset tables.
- **BigQuery Admin**: This has rights to manage all resources within the project.

Quotas and limits

BigQuery comes with predefined quotas. These default quotas can be changed via the Navigation menu and **IAM & Admin | Quotas**. From this menu, we can review the current quotas and request an increase to these limits. We recommend you are aware of the limits for each service, as this can have an impact on your scalability. For BigQuery, we should be aware of the following limits:

- There is a limit of 100 concurrent queries.
- There is a query execution time limit of 6 hours.
- There is a maximum number of table operations per day of 1,000.
- There is a maximum of 100,000 streamed rows of data per second, per project.
- There is a maximum of 300 concurrent API requests per user.

Pricing

Storage costs for BigQuery are based on the amount of data we store. We can be charged for both active and long-term storage. Of course, long-term storage will be a lower monthly change. Additionally, we are charged for running queries. We are offered two pricing models for queries:

- **On-demand**: This charges based on the amount of data processed by easy query.
- **Flat-rate**: This allows us to purchase dedicated resources for processing and, therefore, we are not charged for individual queries.

Pricing is also determined by the location of our BigQuery dataset.

Dataproc

Dataproc is GCP's big data-managed service for running Hadoop and Spark clusters. Hadoop and Spark are open source frameworks that handle data processing for big data applications in a distributed manner. Essentially, they provide massive storage for data, whilst also providing enormous processing power to handle concurrent processing tasks.

If we refer back to the *End-to-end big data solution* section of this chapter, Dataproc is also part of the processing stage. It can be compared to Dataflow; however, Dataproc requires us to provision servers, whereas Dataflow is serverless.

Exam tip: Dataproc should be chosen over Dataflow if we have an existing Hadoop or Spark Cluster. Also, skill sets of existing resources are needed. If we need to create new pipeline jobs or to process streaming data, then we should select Dataflow.

As an alternative to hosting these services on-premises, Google offers Dataproc, which has many advantages—mainly cost saving, as you are only charged for what you really use, with no large initial outlay for the required processing power and storage. Traditional on-premises Hadoop clusters are generally expensive to run because you are paying for processing power that is not being utilized regularly, and we cannot remove the cluster because our data would also be removed. In comparison, Dataproc moves away from persistent clusters to ephemeral clusters. Dataproc integrates well with Cloud Storage. Therefore, if we have a requirement to run a job, we can spin up our cluster very quickly, process our data, and store it on Cloud Storage in the same region. We can then simply delete our cluster. Dataproc clusters are not made to run 24/7 but are, in fact, job-specific, and this is where we can really gain cost savings. This approach allows us to use different cluster configurations for individual jobs, scale clusters to suit individual jobs or groups of jobs, and, of course, reduce any maintenance of the clusters as we are simply spinning up a freshly configured cluster each time we need to run a job.

Exam tip: The whole point of an ephemeral cluster is to use them only for the job's lifetime.

Architecture

The following diagram shows the high-level architecture of Dataproc:

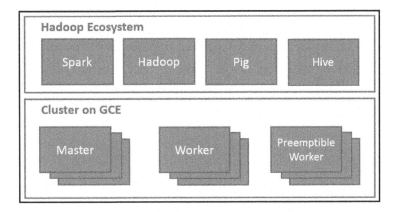

The underlying Dataproc infrastructure is built on Compute Engine, which means we can build on several machine types depending on our budget and take advantage of predefined and custom machine types.

 Exam tip: Cost savings are also increased by using preemptible instances.

When Dataproc clusters are created, we have the option to set a maximum combination of 96 CPU cores and 624 GB RAM. We can also select between SSD and HDD storage. Please refer to `Chapter 4`, *Working with Google Compute Engine*, for more details on machine types.

In a Dataproc cluster, there are different classes of machines:

- **Master nodes**: This machine will assign and synchronize tasks onto worker nodes and process results.
- **Worker nodes**: These machines will process data. These can be expensive due to high CPU and memory specifications.
- **Preemptible worker nodes**: These are secondary worker nodes and are optional. They do the same job, but lower the per-hour compute costs for non-critical data processing.

When we create a new cluster, we can select different cluster modes:

- **Standard**: This includes one master node and *N* worker nodes. In the event of a Compute Engine failure, in-flight jobs will fail and the filesystem will be inaccessible until the master nodes reboot.
- **High availability**: This includes three master nodes and *N* worker nodes. This is designed to allow uninterrupted operations despite a Compute Engine failure or reboots.
- **Single node**: This combines both master and worker nodes. This is not suitable for large data processing and should be used for PoC or small-scale non-critical data processing.

By default, when we create a cluster, standard Apache Hadoop ecosystem components will be automatically installed on the cluster:

- Apache Spark
- Apache Hadoop
- Apache Pig
- Apache Hive
- Python
- Java
- **Hadoop Distributed File System (HDFS)**

 The process of migrating from on-premises to Google Cloud Storage is explained further here at `https://cloud.google.com/solutions/migration/hadoop/hadoop-gcp-migration-data.`

We can also specify initialization actions in executables or scripts that Dataproc will run on all nodes in your cluster immediately after the cluster is set up. These are often used to set up job dependencies to ensure jobs don't require the installation of any dependencies.

IAM

Access to Dataproc is secured with IAM. Let's have a look at the list of predefined roles together with a short description for each:

- **Dataproc Editor**: This has full control over Dataproc.
- **Dataproc Viewer**: This has rights to get and list Dataproc machine types, regions, zones, and projects.
- **Dataproc Worker**: This is for service accounts only and provides the minimum permissions necessary to operate with Dataproc.

Quotas and limits

As Dataproc clusters utilize other GCP products, Compute Engine's limits and quotas apply to Dataproc. When we create a Dataproc cluster, then the compute resources will affect our regional quota limit.

We recommend that you review the *Further reading* section to review Compute quotas.

Cloud IoT Core

The **Internet of Things**, or **IoT**, is a collective term for physical objects that are connected to the internet. You will no doubt be using many IoT devices today, such as smartwatches, Google Home, or wirelessly controlled light bulbs.

Cloud IoT Core is a fully managed service that allows us to securely connect, manage, and ingest data from devices spread around the globe. It is also completely serverless, meaning no upfront software installation. Cloud IoT Core integrates with other GCP services to offer a complete solution for collecting, processing, and analyzing data in real time. Let's look at the following diagram. It shows us where Cloud IoT Core sits in the overall end-to-end solution we have discussed in this chapter and the protocols that IoT devices can use to communicate with it—MQTT and HTTP:

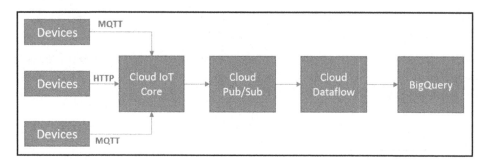

MQTT is a Publish/Subscribe protocol and is often used with embedded devices. MQTT is considered data-focused and better suited to IoT.

HTTP is a connection-less protocol, and devices will maintain a connection to Cloud IoT Core. HTTP is considered document-focused.

Both protocols communicate with Cloud IoT Core across a **protocol bridge**, which provides the following:

- MQTT and HTTS protocol endpoints
- Automatic load balancing
- Global data access with Pub/Sub

The other key component is the **device manager**. This is used to do the following:

- Register individual devices
- Configure individual devices
- Update and control devices
- Provide role-level access control
- Provide a console and APIs for device deployment and monitoring

IAM

Access to Cloud IoT Core is secured with IAM. Let's have a look at the list of predefined roles, together with a short description for each:

- **Cloudiot Viewer**: This has read-only access to all Cloud IoT resources.
- **Cloudiot Device Controller**: This has access to update the configuration of devices. It does not have rights to create or delete devices.
- **Cloudiot Provisioner**: This has rights to create and delete devices from registries but not to modify the registries.
- **Cloudiot Editor**: This has read-write access to all Cloud IoT resources.
- **Cloudiot Admin**: This has full control of all Cloud IoT resources and permissions.

Quotas and limits

There are many limits for Cloud IoT core, ranging from project limits to device limits, and are split into three categories:

- **Project, device, and telemetry limits**: These limits refer to the number of devices per project, device metadata, telemetry event payloads, and MQTT connections per device.
- **Rate**: These limits refer to device-to-cloud and cloud-to-device throughput limits, MQTT incoming messages per second and per connection, and device manager API limits.
- **Time**: These limits refer to MQTT connection time and timeout limits.

We recommend that you refer to the *Further reading* section for more information.

Pricing

Cloud IoT Core is charged according to the data volume used per calendar month. Google recommends the use of the pricing calculator to estimate the price according to the volume of data exchanged.

Additional considerations

There are other services offered by Google that we wish to highlight.

Exam tip

Dataprep: This is a web application that allows us to define preparation rules for our data by interfacing with a sample of the data. Like many of the other services we have discussed, Dataprep is serverless, meaning no upfront deployments are required. It can accept raw data and preprocess this before handing over to Cloud Dataflow to refine the data. Refer to https://cloud.google.com/dataprep/ for more information.

We recommend that you refer to the *Further reading* section if you are interested in learning more.

Exam tip

Datalab: This is built on **Jupyter** (formerly **IPython**), which is an open source web application. Datalab is an interactive data analysis and machine learning environment. We can use this product to visualize and explore data using Python and SQL interactively. This would be treated as part of the data usage stage of our end-to-end solution and would use data passed from BigQuery. Datalab is free of charge, but runs on Compute Engine instances, so charges will be applicable. For more information, refer to https://cloud.google.com/datalab/.

We recommend that you refer to the *Further reading* section if you are interested in learning more.

Exam tip

Data Studio: This is a **Business Intelligence (BI)** solution that turns your data into informative and easy-to-read dashboards and reports. It is a fully managed visual analytics service. Refer to `https://datastudio.google.com/overview/` for more information

This is a web application that allows us to define preparation rules for our data by interfacing with a sample of the data. Like many of the other services we have discussed, Dataprep is serverless, meaning no upfront deployments are required. It can accept raw data and preprocess this before handing over to Cloud Dataflow to refine the data. Refer to `https://cloud.google.com/dataprep/` for more information.

Summary

In this chapter, we have covered the main aspects of big data relating to the exam. We have covered each service and shown that these can be used at different stages of our end-to-end solution. We took the time to see how we can configure Pub/Sub, Dataflow, and BigQuery from the GCP console and discussed Dataproc and Cloud IoT Core.

Exam tip: The key takeaway from this chapter is to understand which services map to the ingest, process, and analysis stages of data.

We looked at the processing stage of our solution. Cloud Dataflow will deploy Google Compute Engine instances to deploy and execute our Apache Beam pipeline to process data from Pub/Sub and pass onto further stages for analysis or storage. We have shown how we can easily create a pipeline in the GCP console, which pulls information from Pub/Sub to analyze in BigQuery.

We covered BigQuery and understand now that it is a data warehouse. It is designed to make data analysts more productive, crunching petabytes of data in small amounts of time. It is completely serverless, so we do not have to worry about provisioning any infrastructure before we can use it, which saves a lot of upfront cost and time. We have looked at how easy and quick it is to set up a dataset and start to query it.

We also covered Dataproc. We have covered the architecture of the service and established that Dataproc is an alternative to hosting Hadoop clusters on-premises. We should now understand that Dataproc can be used to process data that has been injected from Cloud Pub/Sub.

We also covered Cloud IoT Core. This service is used to connect IoT devices. We have shown how we can ingest the real-time data generated by these devices. We also introduced Dataprep.

In the next chapter, we will take a look at machine learning.

Further reading

Read the following articles for more information:

- **For Cloud Pub/Sub**: Refer to the following:
    - **Pub/Sub**: https://cloud.google.com/pubsub/docs/
    - **Pricing**: https://cloud.google.com/pubsub/pricing
    - **Quotas**: https://cloud.google.com/pubsub/quotas
    - **Complex event processing**: https://cloud.google.com/solutions/architecture/complex-event-processing
    - **Use cases**: https://cloud.google.com/pubsub/docs/overview
- **For Cloud Dataflow**: Refer to the following:
    - **Dataflow**: https://cloud.google.com/dataflow/docs/
    - **Pricing**: https://cloud.google.com/dataflow/pricing
    - **Quotas**: https://cloud.google.com/dataflow/quotas
- **For BigQuery**: Refer to the following:
    - **BigQuery**: https://cloud.google.com/bigquery/docs/
    - **Pricing**: https://cloud.google.com/bigquery/pricing
    - **Quotas**: https://cloud.google.com/bigquery/quotas
- **For Dataproc**: Refer to the following:
    - **Dataproc**: https://cloud.google.com/dataproc/docs/
    - **Quotas**: https://cloud.google.com/compute/quotas
    - **Pricing**: https://cloud.google.com/dataproc/pricing
- **For Cloud IoT Core**: Refer to the following:
    - **Cloud IoT Core**: https://cloud.google.com/iot/docs/
    - **Quotas**: https://cloud.google.com/iot/quotas
    - **Pricing**: https://cloud.google.com/iot/pricing

Putting Machine Learning to Work

12

As we have already mentioned, **machine learning (ML)** is one of the differentiators of the **Google Cloud Platform (GCP)**. You should pay special attention to this chapter, as you will be learning that you don't actually need to be a data scientist to leverage ML in your applications. Google has options for both beginners and highly experienced consumers. ML can be quite an intimidating topic for many people but, hopefully, we will be able to explain the basic underlying concepts by means of easy examples. Having that understanding, we will then be able to look at the ML services that we can use in GCP. Hopefully, you are as excited about this chapter as we were when writing it.

In this chapter, we will cover the following topics:

- An introduction to AI and ML
- The seven steps of ML
- Learning models
- GCP ML options
- TensorFlow
- Cloud ML Engine
- Pretrained ML models
- Dialog flow
- AutoML

 Exam tip: For the exam, make sure that you can differentiate between different GCP ML services and that you are able to identify the proper one for your use case. It may be the case that two services satisfy requirements, but *which of them will entail less effort when it comes to their use?* Remember what types of ML models there are and understand the differences. And don't be scared – no one will ask you to develop your own model!

An introduction to AI and ML

Artificial intelligence (**AI**) is described as the ability of a digital computer to perform tasks that intelligent human beings can perform. ML is a subset of AI. It is used by machines to make decisions based on data without getting specific instructions. It can be used, for example, to indicate whether an email that's been received is spam, to recognize objects, or to make smart predictions. The ML concept is illustrated in the following diagram:

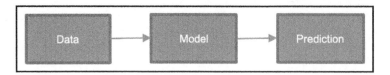

As we can see, ML relies on mathematical models that have been created from an analysis of samples called **training data**. The process of developing the model is called **model training**. The purpose of the model is to answer our question with the highest possible degree of accuracy. The better the accuracy, the better the model. You may be confused as to how this model is created. We will look at this in the following section.

The seven steps of ML

Google indicates that there are seven steps for ML:

1. Gathering the data
2. Preparing the data
3. Choosing a model
4. Training
5. Evaluation
6. Hyperparameter tuning
7. Prediction

Let's go through each of the steps with an example. Let's say we are training the model to check whether a piece of fruit is an apple or a lemon. We need to choose the features that we will use to train our model. There are lots of possible alternatives, including shape, color, taste, and skin smoothness:

For this particular training, we will use color and sugar content. The second measurement is probably not the simplest one to obtain, but for this test, let's assume that we have the proper equipment to do so.

Gathering and preparing the data

Let's start gathering data by buying multiple apples and lemons. We will start with the creation of tables with two features – **color** and **sugar content**.

 Color is described in terms of wavelength interval in **nanometers (nm)**.

This is an example involving a couple of fruits, but we need far more samples in order to obtain accurate predictions:

Color [nm]	Sugar content [g]	Fruit
590	10	Apple
570	2	Lemon
610	15	Apple
500	3	Lemon

At this stage, we should try to visualize the data to make sure we haven't collected too many fruits of one kind; otherwise, the model will be biased toward that fruit.

Now, we need to split the data into **training** and **evaluation data**. The data that's used for training should not be used for evaluation if our model is correct as we will always get good results. A good rule of thumb is that we should use 80% of the data for training and the remaining 20% as evaluation data. Once we have this division, additional steps may be required to prepare the data, such as normalization and deduplication. In our case, these are not required.

Choosing a model

Now, we need to establish which model we want to use. There are thousands of models that have been developed that we can choose from. They can be suitable for images, text, or numerical-based data. The model should be chosen according to the use case. Since we have only two features in our case, the model can be a simple linear model.

Training

Now, we'll get to the heart of ML: the actual training. Let's look at the model we have chosen for training. Here, we have $X = W * Y + b$, where W is **weight** and b is **bias**. During training, we will manipulate the W and b values and use the training data to verify whether we are getting correct predictions. Each of these manipulations is referred to as a training step:

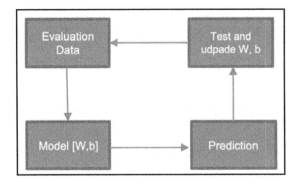

While, at the outset, we may obtain poor results, gradually, we will get accurate predictions for the W and b values. If we are not getting the results we anticipated, we may need to change the model:

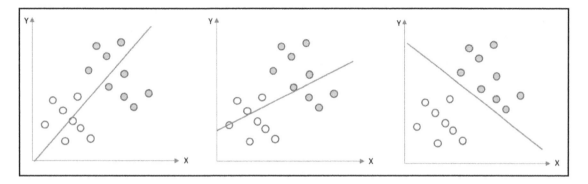

In the preceding plots, we can see how the line changes when we manipulate W and b. In the beginning, we may get results that do not appear to be fit for purpose, but eventually, we achieve values for which we get satisfying results.

Evaluation

Once the training is complete, it is time to evaluate the model. This is where our validation data will be used. You will test this data against your trained model and see how correct it is:

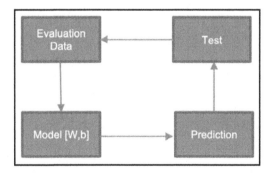

This is supposed to simulate how the model would work with real-world data.

Hyperparameter tuning

When we were training our models, we made some assumptions regarding parameters. Those parameters are so-called hyperparameters. By tuning them, we can get higher accuracy rates. For example, we can use **learning rate parameters**, which indicate the extent of the changes made to W and b. If these parameters are too small, it can take a long time for our model to converge. If these parameters are too big, our model may never converge, thereby missing the ideal state. The other parameter we might want to tune is how many times we run through the training process. By changing it, we could potentially obtain higher accuracy.

Keep in mind that this process is rather experimental and requires some experience to get it set right. Have a look at the *Further reading* section for more information on hyperparameter tuning.

Prediction

Finally, it is time to use our model to evaluate whether a given fruit is an apple or a lemon based on sugar content and color. There are a couple of ways in which we can do this. As you will see in the *Cloud ML Engine* section of this chapter, we can host our model on GCP and access it via API whenever we need to make a prediction.

Of course, this is a very simple example, but it should be good enough for you to grasp the idea of how ML works.

Learning models

Now that we have a basic understanding of ML and how to train a model, let's have a look at three types of ML learning. These are as follows:

- Supervised learning
- Unsupervised learning
- Semi-supervised ML

The preceding three types of ML are defined as follows:

- **Supervised learning**: Supervised learning is the most common model. It is used when the training data and validation data is labeled. What the model does is learn how to set a label for input data. It does this based on what it has learned from some labeled training data. We can further classify supervised learning into the following categories:
    - **Classification**: This occurs when the output data is a category, for example, *apple*, *pear*, or *orange*.
    - **Regression**: This occurs when the output data is a value, such as *cost* and *temperature*.

- **Unsupervised learning**: Unsupervised learning is used when the training data is not labeled. The model attempts to learn the structure of the data and export information or features that might be useful for classification. Since the data isn't labeled, the accuracy cannot be measured. As an example, the model can be used on data that consists of attributes such as weight and height for people of different genders. The height and weight information can be extracted from the data to perform classification into groups. If you draw a plot from the data, you may observe that the data can be used to create patterns and groups.

Again, as the labels are not known, we cannot explicitly say which group represents which gender, but we can presume that one of the groups can be represented by males and the other by females. We can further classify unsupervised learning into the following categories:

- **Clustering**: This occurs when you want to group the data, for example, consumers, according to their preference for coffee or tea.
- **Association**: This occurs when you want to link two different actions or behaviors, for example, a customer buying product *A* also bought product *B*.

- **Semi-supervised ML**: Semi-supervised training occurs when part of the training data is labeled and part of it isn't. You can use a mix of both of the preceding methods. Unsupervised learning can be used to structure the data. Supervised learning can be used to label unlabeled data.

GCP ML options

With GCP, you have multiple options when it comes to leveraging ML. Which one you choose largely depends on your use case and how knowledgeable you are on the topic. The following options are available:

- **TensorFlow (for data scientist)**: This is an option for those who want to work with ML from scratch. It is a software library that's developed and open-sourced by Google. There are more libraries on the market, but this one is the most popular and is used by other cloud providers for their managed ML services.
- **ML Engine (for data scientist)**: This is an option for those who want to train their own models, but who use Google for training and predictions. It is a managed TensorFlow service that offloads all infrastructure and software bits from users.
- **Pretrained ML models (for developer)**: This is an option for those who want to leverage ML without having any knowledge of it. It allows Google-developed models to be used to perform predictions.
- **AutoML (for developer)**: This is an option for those who want to leverage ML without having any knowledge of it, and where the pretrained models are not fit for purpose. It allows models to be trained by supporting labeled data.

TensorFlow

TensorFlow is the most popular open source ML library in the world for developing and training ML models. As a library, it is now part of the GCP offering and can be used on different platforms. For the development phase, you can use your laptop. For the run phase, you can still use your laptop, or go to the public cloud or even a mobile device.

As you know, Google has the biggest datasets in the world. For this reason, it developed TensorFlow to be highly scalable. Google uses it for services such as Gmail, Google Search, and Photos. You can have a look at how TensorFlow works using TensorFlow Playground, which is available at the following link: `https://playground.tensorflow.org`:

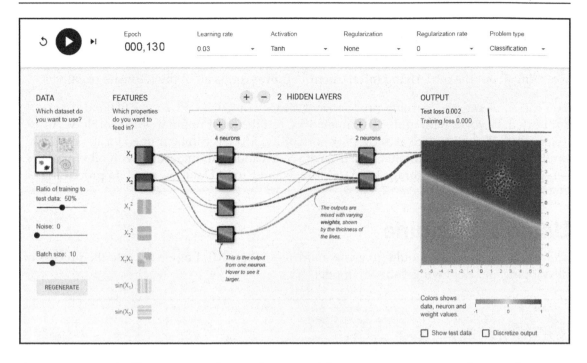

As you can see, it allows you to choose the type of dataset you want to analyze, and you can experiment with all of the parameters we discussed in the *Seven steps of ML* section. Visualization of the process allows you to understand how changes in parameters affect the final output.

Exam tip: For the exam, you don't really need to have in-depth knowledge of TensorFlow. Just be aware of what it is and what it is used for. However, it may be an idea to test TensorFlow Playground.

Even if it is not tested as part of the exam, you may want to have a look at an example of TensorFlow usage. The following video demonstrates how to classify clothing images: `https://www.youtube.com/watch?v=FiNglI1wRNk`.

Cloud ML Engine

Cloud ML is a managed service that allows you to train and host ML models without worrying about the underlying infrastructure. It provisions all of the requisite resources.

You can accelerate the learning process since a range of CPU, GPU, and TPU nodes are supported. It works with multiple frameworks, but the most popular is TensorFlow. As TensorFlow is open source, it allows for portability. Models can be trained locally on limited data and then sent to GCP to train at scale. Cloud ML integrates with other GCP services, such as Cloud Storage for data storage and Cloud Dataflow for data processing.

Using ML Engine

The following diagram should give you an idea of where ML Engine fits into the process of developing and deploying your ML model:

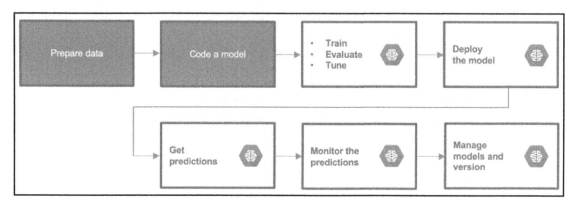

Now, think about the seven steps we discussed previously. You can see that ML Engine will allow you to progress from training your model to deploying it in production. From there, the model can be consumed. You will also be able to version your models to see how well each version works.

Interacting with ML Engine

ML Engine can be managed with a couple of tools. To manage ML Engine's model versions and jobs, Google recommends using the following:

- Google Cloud Console
- The `gcloud ml-engine` command

To make predictions, use the following:

- A RESTful API
- The Python API client

ML Engine scale tiers

Running a training job on Cloud ML requires you to specify machines that you require for the job.

You can choose from predefined clusters (scale tiers) or use a custom configuration. With a custom configuration, you need to specify what machines your cluster will consist of. Note that there are different types of servers that build the cluster:

- **Masters**: These manage other nodes
- **Workers**: These work on a chunk of a training job
- **Parameter servers**: These manage the shared model state

There are a couple of cluster options you can choose from:

- **BASIC**: One worker instance.
- **STANDARD_1**: One master instance, plus four workers and three parameter servers.
- **PREMIUM_1**: One master instance, plus 19 workers and 11 parameter servers.
- **BASIC_GPU**: One worker instance with a single GPU.
- **BASIC_TPU**: One master VM and a Cloud TPU.
- **CUSTOM**: This allows you to use your own cluster specification.

Cloud Tensor Processing Units (TPUs)

In this section, we will explain what TPUs are. They are Google's custom-developed, **application-specific integrated circuits (ASICs)**, which are used to speed up ML workloads.

They enhance the performance of linear algebra computation, which is used heavily in ML applications. TPUs facilitate a reduction in model training time from weeks to hours. In the following photograph, we can see a rack of servers using TPUs, which was presented at the Google Next conference:

As indicated by Google, the following factors make your model suitable for being trained with TPUs:

- Models using matrix computations
- Models without custom TensorFlow operations inside the main training loop
- Models that take a long time to train; for example, weeks
- Models with very large batch sizes

In other cases, you may still consider using CPUs or GPUs.

Submitting a training job

Before you run a training job in the ML Engine, you can actually run the job locally on your machine, or in Cloud Shell using the `gcloud ml-engine` local command.

This allows you to adjust the job quickly and not have to pay for ML Engine resources.

 Exam tip: Remember that you can use ML Engine locally when you develop your model to save time and costs.

Once you are ready to execute training with large datasets, use Cloud ML Engine.

To submit a training model job to ML Engine, you can use either Google Cloud Console or the `gcloud ml-engine jobs submit` command. Let's have a look at the syntax for a job submission:

```
gcloud ml-engine jobs submit training $JOB_NAME \
        --scale-tier basic \
        --package-path $PACKAGE_PATH \
        --module-name $MODULE_NAME \
        --job-dir $JOB_DIR \
        --region $REGION
```

The preceding parameters are explained as follows:

- `$JOB_NAME`: A name to use for the job
- `$PACKAGE_PATH`: A packaged training application that is staged in a Cloud Storage location
- `$MODULE_NAME`: The name of the main module in your package
- `$REGION`: The region where you want your job to run
- `$JOB_DIR`: The path to a Cloud Storage location to use for the job's output

Once you've submitted the job, you can go to Stackdriver Logs to monitor the training model's progress.

Deploying the model

Once the model has been trained and stored, we can use `gcloud ml-engine versions create` to deploy the model. The command is as follows:

```
gcloud ml-engine versions create $VERSION \
--model=$MODEL \
--origin=$ORIGIN \
--runtime-version=$RUNTIME_VERSION
```

The preceding parameters are explained as follows:

- `$VERSION`: The name of the model version
- `$MODEL`: The name of the model
- `$ORIGIN`: The location of the model's directory can be a Google Cloud Storage (`gs://`) path or a local file path
- `$RUNTIME_VERSION`: The Google Cloud ML Engine runtime version for this job

Predictions

Before we learn how to request predictions, let's have a look at the options that are available to us.

Cloud ML provides two types of predictions – **online** (HTTP) and **batch**. In both cases, a trained model is used. The input data is delivered to the model and a response is received. However, there are certain differences:

- **Online**: This minimizes the response time while processing one or more instances per request. The requests are synchronous, and data is passed as a JSON file. The prediction is received in the response message.
- **Batch**: This handles large volumes of instances in a job and runs more complex models. The requests are asynchronous and the data is passed from Cloud Storage input files. The prediction is written to Cloud Storage output files.

If we look at the use cases, online prediction should be leveraged when your application requires a quick response, for example, to recognize an object. Batch prediction should be used when you want to process accumulated data and a delay in the response is acceptable.

Submitting predictions

Let's have a look at the `gcloud` command to submit a batch job:

```
gcloud ml-engine jobs submit prediction $JOB \
--data-format=$DATA_FORMAT \
--input-paths=$INPUT_PATH \
--output-path=$OUTPUT_PATH \
--region=$REGION \
--model=$MODEL \
--version=$VERSION
```

The preceding parameters are explained as follows:

- `$JOB`: The name of the batch prediction job
- `$DATA_FORMAT`: The data format of the input files
- `$INPUT_PATH`: The Google Cloud Storage paths to the instances to run the prediction on
- `$OUTPUT_PATH`: The Google Cloud Storage path to which to save the output, for example, `gs://my-bucket/output`
- `$REGION`: The Google Compute Engine region in which to run the job
- `$MODEL`: The name of the model to use for prediction
- `$VERSION`: The model version to be used

Pretrained ML models

Google's pretrained models can be used to perform predictions without us needing any knowledge of how ML works. All of the models are accessible using APIs and can be directly consumed from your application. The data for prediction is delivered using a JSON file or is stored on Cloud Storage. There are currently a number of models available, as follows:

- The Cloud Speech-to-Text API
- The Cloud Text-To-Speech API
- Google Cloud Translation
- Cloud Natural Language
- Cloud Vision
- Cloud Video Intelligence

Let's have a quick look at each of them.

The Cloud Speech-to-Text API

The Cloud Speech-to-Text API empowers developers with the ability to turn speech into text. This API accepts received audio and returns a text transcription. This API can be used synchronously, asynchronously, or in a streaming model. Many languages and dialects are supported. For a full list, check the *Further reading* section.

The Cloud Text-To-Speech API

 The Cloud Text-to-Speech API empowers developers with the ability to transform text into a form of **Synthesis Markup Language** (**SSML**) input into audio data of natural human speech. Many languages are supported, with multiple voices available per language. There are two types of voice to choose from, that is, **Standard** and **WaveNet**, the latter constituting an advanced module that narrows the gap to human speech.

The Cloud Translation API

The Cloud Translation API enables the translation of thousands of languages. If the language is unknown, the service can auto-detect it. Cloud Translation comes with libraries for the most popular languages, so you can use it directly in your code without using the REST API.

The Cloud Natural Language API

The Cloud Natural Language API allows you to leverage the deep learning models that Google uses for its search engine to analyze text. It is also leveraged by Google Assistant.

It is able to perform the following operations:

- Extract information regarding entities, including places, people, and events
- Categorize the entities
- Perform sentiment analysis
- Perform syntax analysis

Exam tip: Expect to see questions on the Natural Language API in the exam. Remember that it is an easy way to analyze natural human language. It is quicker to use this than to develop your own model. Keep the preceding capabilities in mind so that you can adapt them to the use case you are given in the exam.

In view of the preceding capabilities, this API can be used for the following use cases.

It can be leveraged to analyze documents, news, social media, or blog posts. In combination with the Speech API, it can analyze customer satisfaction from a call center call. Be aware that a limited number of languages are supported. If your language is not supported, you can use the Translation API to convert the text into a supported language.

Let's put this into practice! The API can be accessed both through the REST API and the `gcloud ml language` command, and the text can be provided as a parameter or uploaded from Cloud Storage. For better visualization, we will use a GUI tool provided by Google to analyze some sample text:

```
Packt has released a new book to help IT geeks learn GCP. The readers
really love it!
```

Looking at **Entities**, we can see that five entities have been found. Each entity comes with a **Salience** attribute (ranging from 0-1), which stipulates how important that entity is in the sentence. The higher the value, the more salient it is. For some entities, you also get a Wikipedia link so that you can obtain further information:

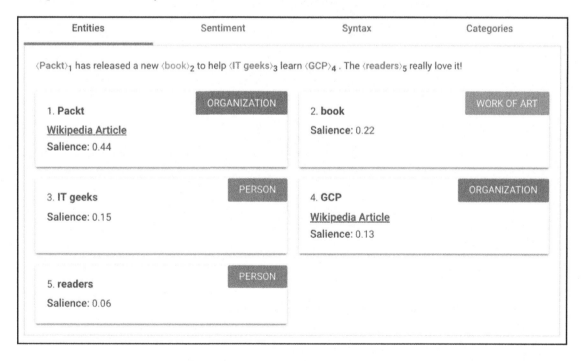

For sentiment analysis, we see two **Sentiment** attributes:

- **Score**: Ranging from -1 (very negative) to 1 (very positive)
- **Magnitude**: Ranging from 0 to infinity, showing the strength of the statement:

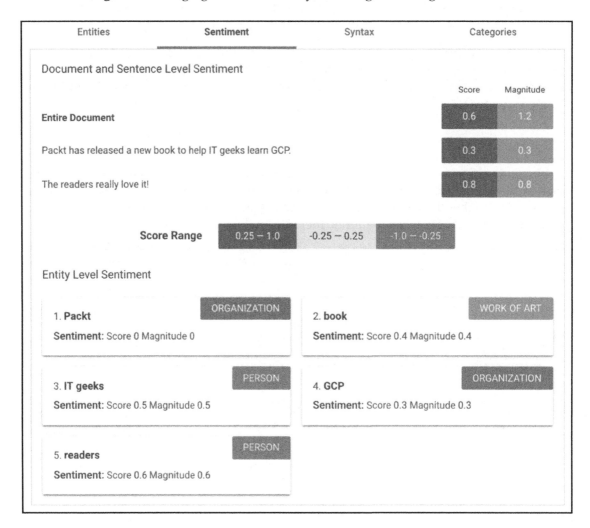

Now, we change the preceding sentence to the following:

```
Packt has released a new book to help IT geeks learn GCP. The readers think
it is ok.
```

We can see that both **Score** and **Magnitude** have dropped to zero for the second sentence:

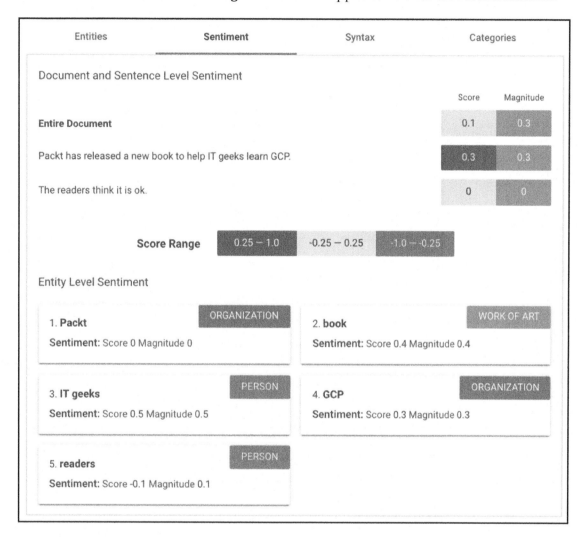

The **Syntax** tab shows detailed syntax information:

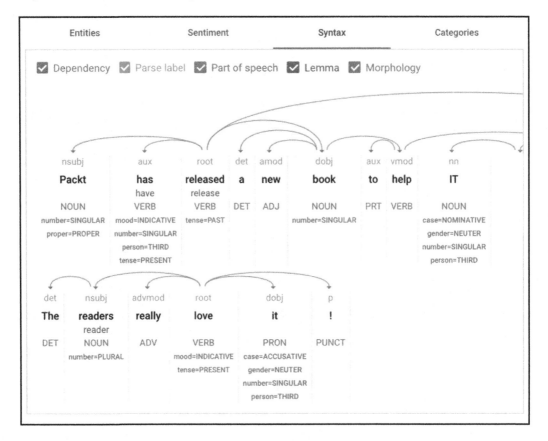

Finally, the text was categorized as **Computer & Electronics** with a **Confidence** of 0.67:

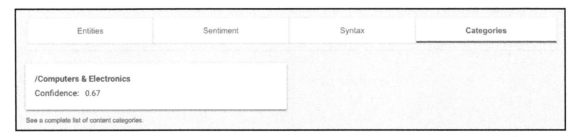

As you can see, this is a very powerful API that can help you perform a deep analysis on text.

Remember that this is still under development and that new features will be added over time.

The Cloud Vision API

The **Cloud Vision API** provides vision detection features, including the following:

- Image labeling
- Face and landmark detection
- **Optical Character Recognition (OCR)**
- Tagging explicit content

You can test this API using `https://cloud.google.com/vision/`. You simply upload the image and see what analysis is possible.

If we look at the **Faces** tab, we can see that a face and a hat were detected correctly. The service was also able to detect the feeling of joy, which I can confirm, as it is me in the photograph having a lot of fun:

Picture1.png

In the **Objects** tab, we can see that most of the objects have been identified correctly, although I don't remember wearing a skirt that day:

The **Labels** tab reveals the analysis of how the image is to be labeled. Again, most of the labels make sense, with the exception of the tennis racket:

Arm	89%
Recreation	76%
Shoulder	75%
Elbow	75%
Tennis Racket	72%
Sports	65%

Picture1.png

When we look at the OCR capabilities, there is some good analysis, especially when we look at **+Block 3**, where the API has detected an **S** from the logo with an odd font:

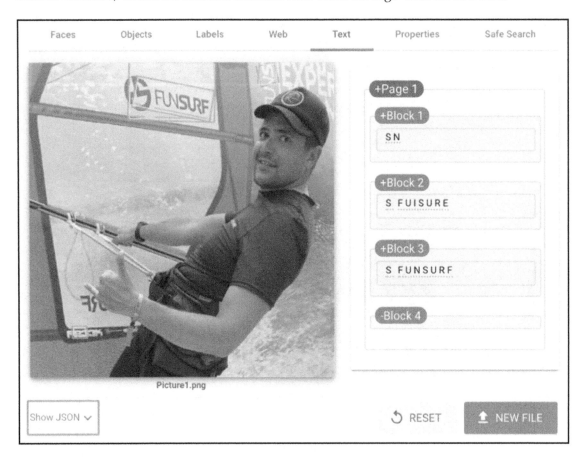

Finally, if we expand the **Show JSON** link under the image, we can also see how the REST API's call and response would appear:

Request URL

```
https://vision.googleapis.com/v1/images:annotate
```

Request

```
{
  "requests": [
    {
      "features": [
        {
          "maxResults": 50,
          "type": "LANDMARK_DETECTION"
        },
        {
          "maxResults": 50,
          "type": "FACE_DETECTION"
        },
        {
          "maxResults": 50,
          "type": "OBJECT_LOCALIZATION"
        },
        {
          "maxResults": 50,
          "type": "LOGO_DETECTION"
        },
        {
          "maxResults": 50,
          "type": "LABEL_DETECTION"
```

Response

```
{
  "cropHintsAnnotation": {
    "cropHints": [
      {
        "boundingPoly": {
          "vertices": [
            {
              "x": 84
            },
            {
              "x": 492
            },
            {
              "x": 492,
              "y": 503
            },
            {
              "x": 84,
              "y": 503
            }
          ]
        },
      "confidence": 1,
```

As we can see in the preceding screenshot, we get the response in JSON format. This allows us to easily parse it and use the results of the query in the code of the application.

The Google Cloud Video Intelligence API

Google Cloud Video Intelligence allows you to analyze video that's been uploaded to Cloud Storage.

Currently, the following features are available:

- **Labels**: These detect and label entities, such as animals, plants, and people.
- **Shots**: These detect scene changes within the video and label them.
- **Explicit content**: These are explicit content annotations for pornography.

This can have a number of use cases. Video metadata can be created with labels that describe its connect to allow improved searching in media libraries. In addition, videos with inappropriate content can be identified and removed from general access.

Dialogflow

This is actually a tool outside of GCP and has its origins in a product called **Api.ai**. It was developed to perform human-to-computer interaction using natural language processing.

It allows you to create so-called **Agents** and **Intents** that have definite possible conversation scenarios. Dialogflow able to train itself on possible variations of phrases that the user uses to demonstrate particular intent. The more phrases that are provided, the better it can learn to trigger the intent:

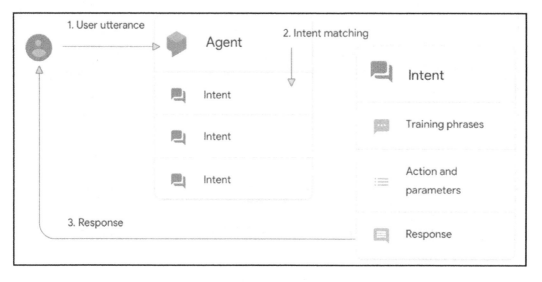

When a user calls an intent, the **Agent** can answer with a simple response or more advanced actions can take place. For example, **Intent** can be analyzed in relation to defined parameters.

The parameters can get extracted and passed to so-called **Fulfillment**, which are basically Firebase functions. The developer can produce Node.js code to integrate with third-party systems outside Dataflow. This can be used to retrieve information or asked to perform specific actions. As an example, a call can be made to a weather service to get a forecast for a particular location, or a smart home system can be called to turn off the light in the living room. Dialogflow can integrate with your application or website using the REST API, or you can use one of the one-click integrations for applications such as the following:

- Google Assistant
- Slack
- Facebook Messenger
- Twitter
- Skype
- Amazon Alexa
- Microsoft Cortana

AutoML

AutoML comes into play when pretrained models are not fit for purpose. As an example, the Vision API can recognize a table, but *what if we want to recognize a particular table that our company produces?* The Vision API cannot do that for us.

In such a case, we need to use AutoML or train our own model. As you have probably already guessed, the former is a much easier method. What AutoML does is it takes datasets from you, trains and deploys the model, and then serves it through the REST API. This sounds a little bit like magic, right? Take a look at the following diagram:

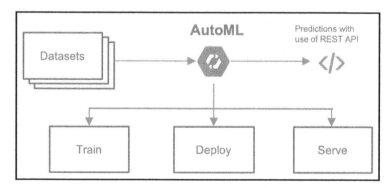

Note that there are five services available that allow you to train your custom model:

- **AutoML Vision**: This classifies your images according to your own defined labels.
- **AutoML Translation**: This performs translation queries, returning results specific to your domain.
- **AutoML Natural Language**: This classifies English language content into a custom set of categories.
- **AutoML Tables**: This turns structured data into predictive insights.
- **AutoML Video Intelligence**: This allows you to classify segments of video.

Let's have a look at an example. See how you would actually use AutoML, using the example of the Vision API, to recognize a table that your company produces. In short, what you would do is the following:

1. Make multiple photos of your table.
2. Upload it to Cloud Storage.
3. Create a CSV file with a label for your photos.
4. Provide the CSV file to AutoML to train the model.

Once the model has been trained, you can access the model through the REST API, like you would with any other pretrained model. Quite amazing, right? Check the *AI adventures* video from the *Further reading* section if you want to see AutoML Vision in action.

 At Google NEXT '19, new AutoML services were announced: AutoML Tables and AutoML Video Intelligence. Check the Cloud AutoML link in the *Further reading* section for more details. As these are very new services, they are unlikely to crop up in the exam.

Summary

In this chapter, we learned about the ML services offered by GCP. We started with the theory of ML to introduce basic concepts and nomenclature so as to better understand the actual services. We learned that, depending on your role and use case, you need to make the correct choice as to which service will be the most effective for you to use. One goal can sometimes be achieved using two or more different services. We also learned that you don't need to be a data scientist to leverage ML. Those of you who have very limited knowledge can use pretrained models. If those models are not good enough for your use case, you can try AutoML, which allows new models to be created without us having to develop the model ourselves. We just need to deliver proper datasets to GCP.

Finally, for those of you who have the knowledge, and are capable of developing your own models, ML Engine is the service you can use to develop and host your models.

In the next chapter, we will have a closer look at how to secure our environment in GCP.

Further reading

Read the following articles for more information regarding what was covered in this chapter:

- **ML building blocks**: https://cloud.google.com/products/ai/
- **Dialogflow**: https://Dialogflow.com/docs
- **ML Engine**: https://cloud.google.com/ml-engine/docs/
- **Cloud AutoML**: https://cloud.google.com/automl/docs/
- **TensorFlow**: https://www.tensorflow.org/
- **AI adventures video**: https://www.youtube.com/watch?v=nKW8Ndu7Mjw
- **Speech-to-Text**: https://cloud.google.com/speech-to-text/docs/basics

Section 3: Designing for Security and Compliance

In this section, we will focus on GCP security and compliance, including industry-standard certifications.

This section contains the following chapter:

- Chapter 13, *Security and Compliance*

13
Security and Compliance

Security in GCP was built in from the start and certainly not an afterthought! In each service that GCP provides, you will see that security is paramount. In the public cloud era, it's true that a single breach of security cannot only cause direct financial implications but can also have a detrimental effect on future business for a company. For this reason, GCP takes the view that the best way is in-depth defense rather than a single piece of technology, and it offers a lot more security that a customer can usually afford by replicating on premises. In this chapter, we will look at the key topics that we need to understand in order to be successful in the exam and try to give an overview of security and the importance GCP places on it.

In this chapter, we will cover the following topics:

- Introduction to security
- Cloud Identity
- Resource Manager
- IAM
- Service accounts
- Fire rules and load balancers
- Cloud Security Scanner
- Monitoring and logging
- Encryption
- Penetration testing in GCP
- Industry regulations
- Additional security services

Code in Action

Check out the following video to see the Code in Action:
`http://bit.ly/31i6wpz`

Introduction to security

Let's start this chapter with a brief introduction to GCP's approach to security. As we mentioned previously, security is not an afterthought and is built into its services. But before we even think about securing our services, we need to acknowledge the fact that GCP has a holistic view of security. This can be seen by restricting physical data center access and using custom hardware and hardened versions of operating systems in the software stack.

Google uses custom hardware with security in mind and uses a hardened version of Linux for the software stack, which is monitored for binary modifications and enforces trusted server boots.

Storage is a key service for any cloud provider, and GCP offers encryption at rest by default on all storage services. This can support customer encryption keys or manage keys on behalf of the customer. On physical storage disks, retired disks will have sectors zeroed and if data cannot be deleted, disks are destroyed in a multi-stage crusher. It should, however, be noted that if a customer deletes data, it can take 180 days to be physically deleted.

Additionally, one of the main security concerns is attacks from outside organizations. To protect us from internet attacks, Google offers the ability to register against the frontend, which will check incoming network connections for correct certificates, and offers protection against DDoS attacks. In addition, using GCP load balancers will offer extra protection, while cloud VPNs and direct connections offer more encryption options. This chapter will touch on services that will be covered in more detail in later chapters of this book.

Exam tip: We will talk about security in more depth than what is expected in order for you to be successful in the exam; however, it is vital to understand the information in the role of a cloud architect. For the exam, there are several areas that we recommend you focus on:

- Understanding Cloud IAM roles
- Understanding what Cloud Identity is
- Understanding what **Key Management System** (KMS) does
- Understanding the difference between **Customer-Supplied Encryption Keys** (CSEKs) and **Customer-Managed Encryption Keys** (CMEKs)
- Being aware of encryption at rest and in transit
- Being aware of PCI compliance

Cloud Identity

Cloud Identity is a key GCP service that's offered by Google as an **Identity as a Service (IDaaS)** solution. This is an optional service, and a more basic approach can be taken to apply individual permissions to services or projects. However, for enterprise organizations, using an identity service makes far more sense. It enables businesses to manage who has access to their resources and services within a GCP organization, all from a single pane of glass. Cloud Identity can be used as a standalone product for domain-based user accounts and groups. We should note early on in this chapter that Google also offers a similar management pane for G Suite users. The console works in the same way, and user and domain management have a lot of similarities. You may wish to investigate this further in detail, but for the purpose of this book and, more importantly, the exam, we will focus solely on GCP Cloud Identity.

Like many on-premises directories that can reduce the overhead of user administration, GCP gives us the opportunity to centrally manage our users in the cloud through Cloud Identity. It offers a central, single pane of glass to administer users, groups, and settings and is referred to as the Google Admin console. To utilize Cloud Identity, your domain name should be enabled to receive emails, hence allowing your existing web and email addresses to be used as normal. Your GCP organization will have a single Cloud Identity, and the organization is the root node in the resource hierarchy. It is deemed the super node of your projects.

It should be noted that there are two editions of Cloud Identity. One is free and one is a premium subscription. The premium subscription offers additional features, such as device management and security and application management. Finally, you must understand that Cloud Identity is not controlled through the GCP console, but in fact through the Google Admin console. Once logged in to the admin console, you will be able to add users, create groups, and assign members and disable users.

The following is a screenshot of what the **Google Admin** console page looks like:

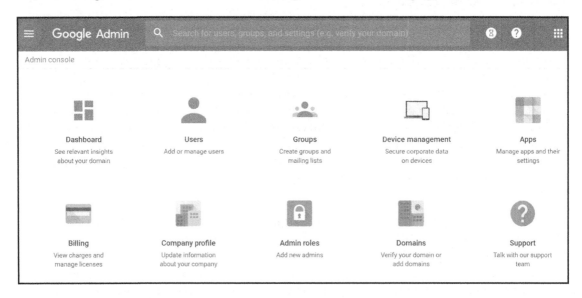

Adding users manually is classed as overhead in terms of effort and is not scalable if you have a large environment to manage. The whole point of Cloud Identity is to simplify the management of users and groups as it's unlikely that an organization can afford one person to add, remove, and manage things. This is where **Google Cloud Directory Sync (GCDS)** comes in. Many organizations will have an LDAP DB such as Microsoft **Active Directory (AD)**. GCDS can synchronize an organization's AD or LDAP database onto Cloud Identity and it is highly scalable. Synchronization is only one-way, that is, from on premises to GCP, and so your on-site DB is never compromised. GCDS allows the administrator to perform delta syncs and scheduled synchronizations and perform tasks manually. If we require permissions to be revoked from a user, or indeed disabled, then the results are immediate.

Google authentication means Google stores and manages all authentications and passwords by default, but there is an option to disable this. A two-step verification can be added to this by using multi-factor tools. There is also an alternative to using **Single Sign-On (SSO)**, which is an SAML 2.0-based authentication that also includes **Multi-Factor Authentication (MFA)**. Finally, password complexity can be set within Cloud Identity's password management to align with existing policies your business may have:

Password management
Locally applied

Configure password policies for your organization. Some of these policies can't be enforced for users who are authenticated by a third party identity provider via SAML, or if you upload a cryptographic hash of the password using our API.
Learn more

Password strength
Require strong passwords in line with security best practices. ❓

☑ Enforce strong password

Password length
Passwords must be between 8 and 100 characters.

Minimum length

8

Maximum length

100

In the preceding screenshot, we can see an example of the **Password management** screen.

Resource Manager

GCP Resource Manager allows you to create and manage a hierarchical grouping of objects such as organizations, folders, and projects together. Let's look at an example where we have an organization, `brgerrard.co.uk`, and several folders underneath that add to the structure. Folders are optional but can be used to group projects. Access to these folders will work on a hierarchical model, meaning that if you have full access to the `Departments` folder, then this will be inherited down to, for example, the `Google Cloud Architect Project` folder, as shown in the following screenshot:

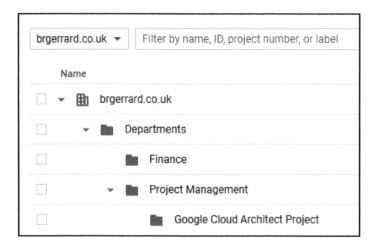

A good example to think of would be the separation of development, testing, and production environments in GCP. Separate projects for each environment allow you to grant access to only those who need access to the resources. The following screenshot shows how the hierarchy of GCP is set up:

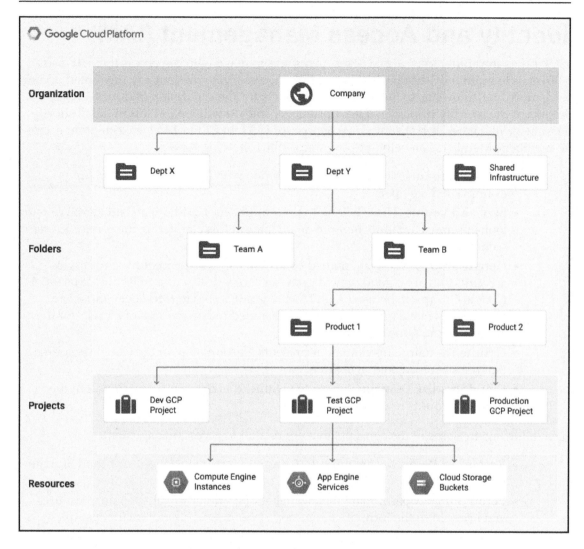

It's important to understand that setting permissions at a higher level results in permission inheritance. For example, granting a user permission to the **Dept Y** folder means that the user will also have the same permissions applied to all subfolders and projects. It is therefore important to design your organization and permissions in such a way that they grant access only to the resources that are required to fulfill the requested role.

Identity and Access Management (IAM)

GCP offers the ability to create GCP resources and manage who can access them. It also allows us to grant only the specific access that's necessary, to prevent any unwanted access, and, moreover, allows us to meet any requirements for the separation of duties. This is known as the security principle of least privilege, and we will look at this in detail shortly. First, we will have a look at some key concepts of IAM. In Cloud IAM, we can grant access to members. Members can belong to any one of the following types:

- **Google accounts**: These represent someone who interacts with GCP, for example, a developer.
- **Service accounts**: These belong to your application and not an end user. We will look at service accounts in more detail later in this chapter, in the *Service accounts* section.
- **Google groups**: These are named collections of Google accounts and service accounts and are a good way to grant an access policy to a collection of users. A Google Group can be used with IAM to grant access to roles. One important exception is that a group can only be assigned the owner role of a project if they are part of the same organization.
- **G Suite Domain**: This domain represents a group of all of the Google accounts that have been created in G Suite.
- **Cloud Identity Domain**: Similar to G Suite, this domain represents all of the Google accounts in an organization.

The following are some of the concepts that are related to access management:

- **Resources:** Resources are projects, Compute Engine instances, or Cloud Storage buckets.
- **Permissions**: A permission dictates what operations are allowed on a resource and are seen in the form of `<service>.<resource>.<verb>`, for example, `compute.instance.list`. Permissions cannot be assigned directly to a user.
- **Role**: Roles are a collection of permissions. To provide a user with access to a resource, we grant them a role rather than assigning permissions directly to the user. There are three kinds of roles, that is, **Primitive**, **Predefined**, and **Custom**, and we will discuss them later in this chapter.
- **IAM Policy**: An IAM Policy is a collection of statements that will define who has what type of access. You attach a policy to a resource and use it to enforce access control whenever it is accessed.

The following IAM entities can be assigned to a role: Google Group, Google Account, service account, and Cloud Identity or G Suite Domain.

Now that we have some background knowledge of IAM, let's continue with some examples. We previously mentioned the principle of least privilege, and we now know that we should only grant access to exactly what is necessary.

Let's look at the `Google Cloud Architect Project` folder permissions in the following example. We may have a user who should be able to create projects in all folders, but we may also have another user who should only create projects in a specific folder. In the following screenshot, we are granting the user, `konrad@brgerrard.co.uk`, the **Project Creator** role:

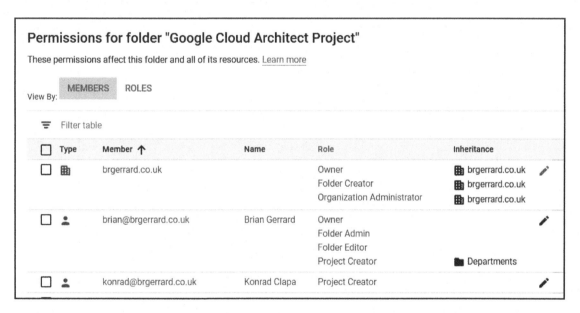

Primitive roles existed prior to Cloud IAM. These were legacy **owner**, **editor**, and **viewer** roles. Since these roles are limited, applying any of these roles means granting a wide spectrum of permissions. This doesn't exactly follow our least-permission principle! However, we should understand that there may be some cases where we wish to use primitive roles. For example, we may work in a small cross-functional team where the granularity of IAM is not required. Similarly, if we are working in a testing or development environment, then we may not wish full granular permissions to be applied.

If we want to be more granular, we should use predefined roles and base our roles on job functions. If we want to create roles with specific permissions and not the Google-provided collection, then we can utilize custom roles. These provide more granularity, but it should be noted that they are user-managed and therefore come with overhead.

Applying individual members to each role can be tedious, however, and ideally, we should use groups to control access and apply roles to those groups and not to individual users. As an example, let's create a new group from our Cloud Identity admin console called `Project Creator`. Looking back at our previous screenshot from the *Identity and Access Management (IAM)* section, we can do this by browsing to the **Groups** field and clicking **Add new group**:

1. Give the group a name, as shown in the following screenshot:

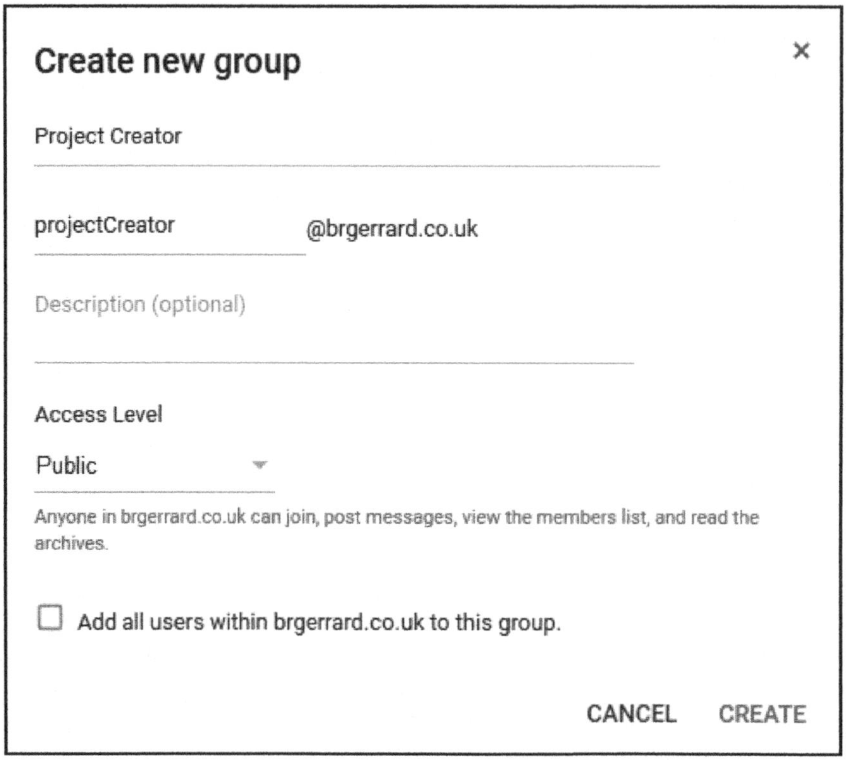

Create new group   ✕

Project Creator
_____

projectCreator   @brgerrard.co.uk
_____

Description (optional)

_____

Access Level

Public   ▾
_____

Anyone in brgerrard.co.uk can join, post messages, view the members list, and read the archives.

☐   Add all users within brgerrard.co.uk to this group.

                                                  CANCEL   CREATE

2. Apply this to a resource in our GCP console. In this example, we are assigning the group to a folder:

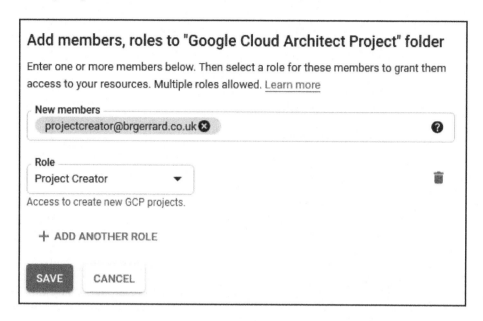

Now, we can centrally control permission to our resources rather than drilling down into folder structures in our GCP console. This also offers a separation of duties to increase security. Now that we have created our project, we want to allow a user to only create a VM instance.

Let's say that, as a project owner, we want to allow an engineer to create a VM instance, but we want a separate engineer to have read-only access to this compute resource. Again, we can create two new groups in Cloud Identity for this purpose; let's call them `vmviewer` and `vmadmin`. We can assign these groups the relevant roles. Using predefined roles means that they are managed by Google, and any additional permissions that are added to a role would mean that your member automatically gets these.

Our `vmviewer` group is now assigned the **Compute Viewer** role on a project level, as shown in the following screenshot:

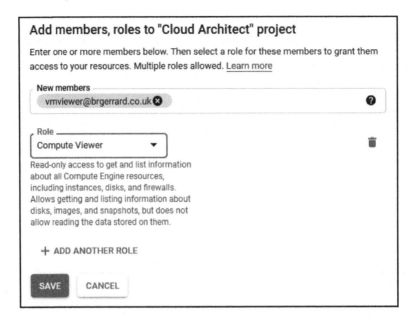

Our `vmadmin` group is now assigned the **Compute Instance Admin** role on the project level:

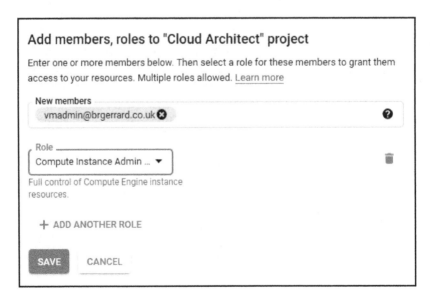

We can also use the gcloud CLI to add permissions. This command line allows us to manage interactions with GCP APIs. As an example, if I want to assign the editor role to brian@brgerrard.co.uk within the redwing project, then I can run the following command:

```
gcloud projects add-iam-policy-binding redwing
-member='user:brian@brgerrard.co.uk' -role='roles/editor'
```

The output of this command will confirm that brian@brgerrard.co.uk has been granted the role of editor.

This gcloud projects command line can also be used for many more functions. Please note that we will take a deeper dive into the gcloud command line in Chapter 14, *Google Cloud Management Options*.

 Please refer to the official documentation if you are keen on using this in more depth: https://cloud.google.com/sdk/gcloud/reference/projects/.

Finally, regarding IAM, we have spoken about who has permission to perform actions on resources. We should also be mindful of what organizational policies focus on. These policies allow us to set restrictions on resources. An organizational policy would allow us to disable certain options that are available to a user. These restrictions are done using constraints and can be applied to a GCP service or a list of GCP services. For example, let's say that we didn't want a default network to be available. We could set a constraint to skip default network creation, therefore preventing any new VM instances on this network.

Previously, we mentioned the importance of service accounts. We will look at these in more depth now.

Service accounts

Service accounts are Google accounts that are used to call the API of a service, hence removing users from any direct involvement. They belong to an application or VM instance. By default, every GCP project we create will have a default service account created when we enable our projects to use Compute Engine:

1. We can create a new service account through **IAM** | **Service accounts** on our GCP console. We can also create a new service account using the gcloud CLI. As an example, let's say we need to have a VM that has access to Cloud Storage. The following screenshot shows us creating a new service account named `AccessCloudStorage`:

2. Once we decide that we will be using service accounts for our resources, we can then decide whether we want to grant specific roles to the service account. The following screenshot shows that we have optional choices when assigning a role:

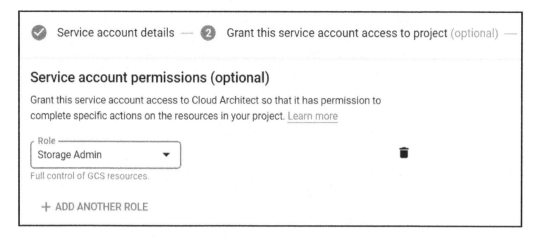

3. During the process of creating our VM instance, assign this service account under the **Identity and API access** option:

This will allow the service account to assume the service account identity for authenticating API requests. As we mentioned previously, we can see that we have the option to assign accounts we have created as a service account.

If you select the default service account, you will notice that there is an option to select an access scope. An access scope determines the level of access the API call is allowed to a service. It is good practice to select each API access individually per service to improve security. The following is the full list of APIs that are currently available:

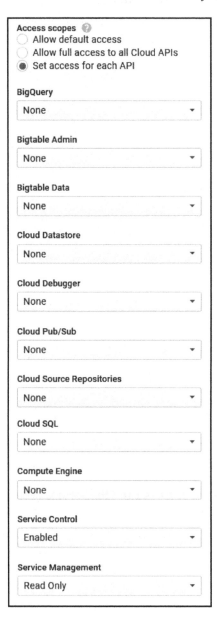

Service accounts are secured with a key pair:

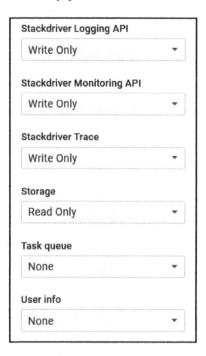

There are two types of service account keys—GCP-managed and user-managed. GCP-managed keys are used by services such as Compute Engine and App Engine and cannot be downloaded. User-managed keys are created and can be downloaded and managed by users of GCP. You are fully responsible for user-managed keys. We will speak about key management in the *Encryption* section of this chapter.

Before we finish talking about service accounts, one final thing to note is that service accounts should still follow the same principles we learned about for IAM. Service accounts should only get the minimum set of permissions required for that service.

Exam tip: For the exam, this topic is key so that you understand identities, roles, and resources. We have briefly touched on IAM in previous chapters, but now we want to look at it in a bit more detail. Some principles to note before you read any further, which will be explained in more detail in this chapter, are as follows:

- IAM roles are groups of permissions that can be assigned to users, groups, or service accounts.
- There are different types of roles.
- We should follow the principle of least privilege.
- Use groups to control access rather than granting access to individual users, if possible.

In this section, we covered service accounts. We explained that they are a special type of account that removes a user from direct involvement and that they are an important part of Google IAM. In the next section, we will look at ACLs, which are an alternative to IAM.

Cloud Storage access management

On top of using IAM permissions to restrict access to Cloud Storage, it can also be secured using **Access Control Lists** (**ACLs**). ACLs should be used when you want to set permissions on objects rather than the whole bucket, for example, to gain access to an individual object in a specific bucket. This is because Cloud IAM would apply permissions to all of the objects in a bucket. It's vital to understand this because, from a manageability perspective, it is not ideal to manage these individually and if there is commonality of permissions across all objects in the bucket, then you should use IAM to control access.

An ACL is made up of the permission that defines what can be performed, as well as the scope that defines who can perform the action. When a request is made to a bucket, the ACL will grant the user permissions, if applicable; otherwise, the request will result in a **403 Forbidden** error. An object inside a bucket can only be granted **Owner** or **Reader** permission, as shown in the following screenshot. On top of the ACLs, GCP also offers legacy roles of bucket **Owner**, bucket **Reader**, and bucket **Writer**:

gcp-bucket-file.txt permissions

If you don't rely on individual object-level permissions, you can start managing all permissions uniformly at the bucket-level. Go to the bucket's Permissions tab to get started. Learn more

ENTITY	NAME	ACCESS
Project ▾	owners-951071968842	Owner ▾ ✕
Project ▾	editors-951071968842	Owner ▾ ✕
Project ▾	viewers-951071968842	Reader ▾ ✕
User ▾	brian@brgerrard.co.uk	Owner ▾ ✕

＋ Add item

CANCEL   SAVE

As with IAM, we should follow the principle of least privilege. If you need to use ACL, then do not apply the owner role if it is not needed. You should be careful to ensure that buckets are not unnecessarily made public (by assigning the `allUser` role).

One final piece of information you should be aware of before the exam is the use of signed URLs. This option allows you to grant access to a visitor so that they can upload or download from storage without the need for a Google Account. Access can be time-limited and access can be granted for read or write to anyone who has the URL. We can create a signed URL with `gsutil` by running the following command:

```
gsutil signurl -d 10m Desktop/private-key.json gs://example-bucket/cat.jpeg
```

In this example, we are using `private-key.json` as our service account private key in order to expose the `cat.jpeg` bucket object from `example-bucket`.

Firewall rules and load balancers

We already covered networking in `Chapter 8`, *Networking Options in GCP*, but we would like to recap what is important from a security standpoint.

If Compute Engine instances don't need to communicate with each other, then we should host them on different **Virtual Private Cloud** (**VPC**) networks. Additionally, if we have an application made up of servers on different network tiers, then each server should be on a different subnet. Let's take a traditional web app and DB application as an example. We want to segment each tier on a different subnet.

Firewall rules are the obvious choice for securing a network. As you now know, a VPC lets you isolate your network to allow for segmentation between computing resources. Firewall rules let you control the flow of inbound and outbound traffic by allowing or denying the traffic based on direction, source or destination, protocol, and priority. The following screenshot shows the creation of a new firewall rule:

It's important to note that firewall rules in GCP are stateful, meaning that if a rule is initiated by an **Allow** rule in one direction, the traffic will automatically be allowed to return. Likewise, you should also understand that all VPCs have two default rules. The first one permits all outgoing connections to any IP address, and the second blocks all incoming traffic. These are assigned the lowest priority, which means they can easily be overwritten by your custom rules. Additional rules that are applied to a new VPC allow ingress connections for all protocols and ports between instances. Others allow for ICMP traffic (`ping`/`trace route`), SSH, and RDP from any source to any destination in the VPC.

As with IAM, for firewall rules, we should also use the principle of least privilege. By this, we mean that we should only allow communications that are needed by our applications and tie down anything that's not required. It is seen as good practice to create a rule with a low priority that will block all traffic and then layer the relevant rules on top with higher priority.

Load balancers in GCP also offer additional security. Load balancers support SSL and HTTPS proxies for encryption in transit. There is a requirement for at least one signed SSL certificate to be installed on the target HTTPS proxy for the load balancer, and you have a choice of using self-managed SSL certificates or Google-managed SSL certificates. It seems obvious but if you need to use HTTPS traffic, then you should select the HTTPS load balancer, but for non-HTTPS traffic, you should use the SSL load balancer.

Cloud Security Scanner

It's important to take application security as seriously as we take infrastructure security. Applications are one of the main sources of attacks, and GCP aids in this through the Cloud Security Scanner service. Of course, we know security is an extremely important topic and Cloud Security Scanner supports us in the early detection of vulnerabilities in our services.

When you create a scan, you can set this to scan URLs that your Compute Engine instance, App Engine instance, or GKE instance hosts and likewise exclude URLs. It will detect common vulnerabilities such as flash injection, mixed content, clear-text password, and cross-site scripting. We can also set a schedule for scans or perform them manually. It should be noted that Cloud Scanner can generate a real load against your application, so performance should be taken into consideration as some scans can take hours to complete. Likewise, caution should be exercised when using this service as it can post comments into the comments section of a web page or generate multiple emails if prompted for signup on a page. It is, therefore, good practice to scan your applications in a test environment and have a backup of your application state before a scan is initiated.

The following screenshot shows us creating a new scan:

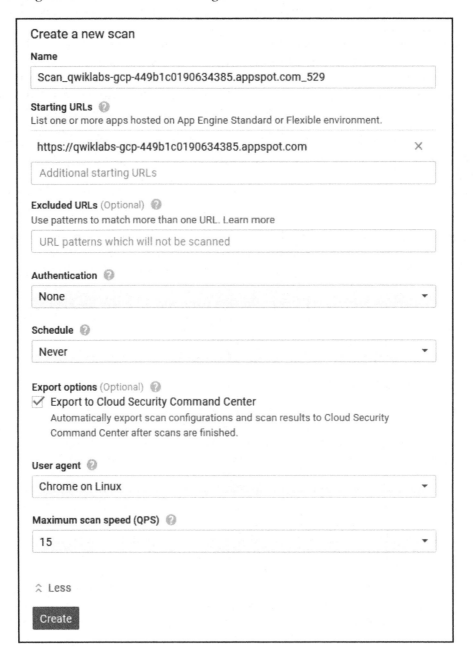

When we have run the scan, we will receive our results, which will flag any vulnerabilities, as shown in the following screenshot:

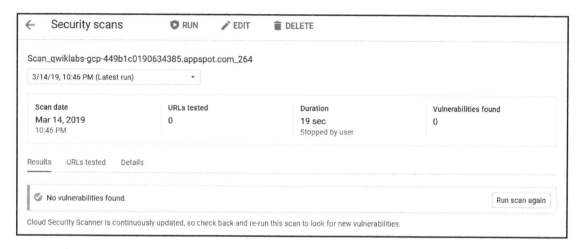

In this section, we have looked at Cloud Security Scanner and shown you how to set up a new scan. In the next section, we will touch on monitoring and logging.

Monitoring and logging

We will look at monitoring in a lot more detail in `Chapter 15`, *Monitoring Your Infrastructure*, but it is wise to mention this again in terms of security. Stackdriver is Google's service for the monitoring and management of services, containers, applications, and infrastructure. Stackdriver's features offer error reporting, debugging, alerts, tracing, and logging.

Logging assists in securing GCP and minimizing the downtime of your applications. Monitoring allows you to monitor application metrics that can flag an anomaly. Moreover, Stackdriver Debugger inspects the state of your production data and compares your source code without any performance overhead. Logging allows for real-time metrics logging and retains a set period, depending on the log type. If you have security requirements to keep logs for a longer period, then they can be exported to Cloud Storage, which offers inexpensive storage for extended periods.

Encryption

Encryption is a basic form of security for sensitive data. In its simplest form, encryption is the process of turning plaintext data into a scrambled string of characters. We cannot read those strings and, more importantly, a system cannot read if it doesn't hold the relevant key to migrate it back to plaintext format.

Encryption is a key element of GCP security. By default, GCP offers encryption at rest, which means that data stored on GCP's Storage services is encrypted without any further action from users. This means that there is no additional configuration needed and even if this data did somehow get into the wrong hands, then the data would be unreadable as they wouldn't have the proper encryption key to make sense of the data.

The ability to encrypt sensitive data over GCP assures customers that confidential data will stay just there. At the core of this protection is GCP KMS, which Google uses to manage cryptographic keys for your cloud services. Cloud KMS allows you to generate, use, rotate, and destroy cryptographic keys, which can either be Google-generated or, indeed, imported from your own KMS system. Cloud KMS is integrated with Cloud IAM, and so you can manage permissions on individual keys. When we create a new disk, for example, the default option is to use a Google-managed key.

Now, let's take a look at data encryption keys and key encryption keys.

Data encryption keys versus key encryption keys

The key that's used to encrypt a piece of data is known as a **Data Encryption Key (DEK)**. These keys are then wrapped by a **Key Encryption Key (KEK)**. KEKs are stored and managed within Google Cloud's KMS, allowing Google to track and control access from a central point. It isn't possible to export your KEK from KMS, and all of the encryption and decryption of keys must be within KMS. In addition to this, KMS-held keys are backed up for disaster recovery purposes. KEKs are also rotated over a period of time, meaning that a new key is created. This allows GCP to comply with certain regulations, such as **Payment Card Industry Data Security Standard (PCI DSS)**, and is considered a security best practice. GCP will rotate the keys every 90 days by default.

CMEKs versus CSEKs

GCP offers additional methods for managing encryption keys that might fit better with customer security policies.

GCP offers the ability for the customer to manage KEKs, allowing us to control the generation of keys, the rotation of keys, and the expiration of a key. Keys will still be stored in KMS, but we will have control of their life cycle. This is known as CMEK. In order to organize keys effectively, Google Cloud KMS uses the concept of key rings to group keys together and push inherited permissions to keys.

We can create our key through a number of steps. Let's get started:

1. By browsing to **Security** | **Cryptographic keys** from our GCP console, we can create a new key ring within Cloud KMS. Key rings group keys together:

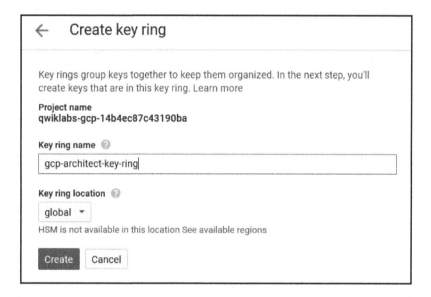

Once we have created the key ring, we will be prompted to create a key. We can create a number of keys under the key ring, and those keys will be responsible for encrypting and decrypting data. When creating a new key, you can see that we have options when setting the key's purpose, for example, whether the key is only for encryption, decryption, or both.

Note that key rings belong to a project and reside in a location. In our previous example, we selected the global location, which means it will be available from multiple data centers. We can also select from the following:

- **Regional**: This consists of zones in a specific geographical location.
- **Dual-Regional**: This consists of zones in two specific geographical locations.
- **Multi-Regional**: This consists of zones spread across a general geographical area.

Tip: When deciding on which location to chose, network performance should be considered.

2. Furthermore, we can select rotation periods and when the validity of the key begins. Once the key has been created, we can manage the rotation period, disable and re-enable the key, or delete the key completely through the GCP console. The following screenshot shows us creating a new key:

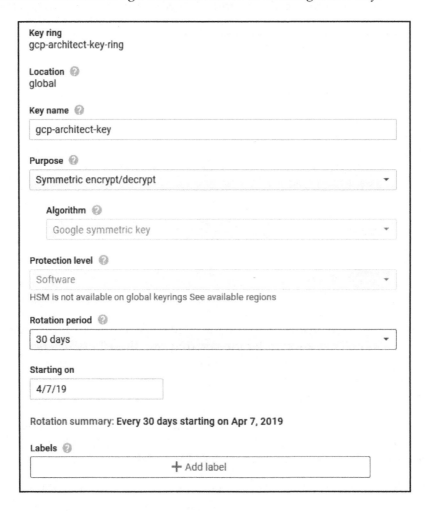

An important aspect of the KMS key structure is the key version. Each key can have many versions, which are numbered sequentially, starting with 1. We may have files encrypted with the same key but with different key versions. Cloud KMS will automatically identify which version was used for encryption and will use this to decrypt the file if the version is still in an *enabled* state. We will not be able to decrypt the file is the version has been moved to a state of *Disabled*, *Destroyed*, or *Scheduled for destruction*.

3. Now that we have created our key, let's use it. If, for example, we want to create a new disk in GCP, we have a number of options under the encryption settings. To use our newly created key, we should select **Customer-managed key** and select our key from the drop-down menu when prompted, as shown in the following screenshot:

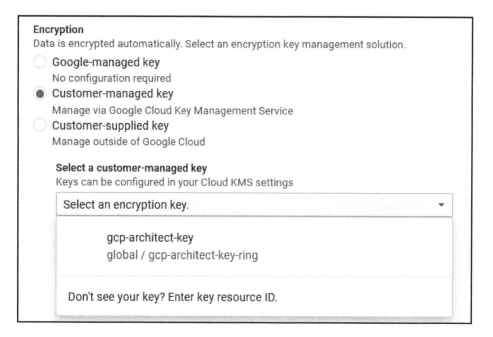

A second option that is available is CSEK, where the key is not stored in KMS and Google doesn't manage the key. CSEK allows us to provide our own AES-256 key. If we supply this key, Cloud Storage doesn't permanently store it on Google's own servers or in any way manage our key. Once we have provided the key for a Cloud Storage operation, then the key is purged from Google's memory. This means that the key would have to be provided each time storage resources were created or used. The customer would have sole responsibility, which means that, if the key was lost, then you would be unable to decrypt your data. Here, we would select the **Customer-supplied key** option and input the relevant key.

Industry regulations

It's also important to understand that security is more than just firewall rules or encryption. Google needs to adhere to global regulations and third-party certifications. Examples of the regulations that GCP adheres to can be found on their web page at `https://cloud.google.com/security/compliance/#/`. It is recommended that you review this page to familiarize yourself with the various standards that should be met. Some of these will be well known, for example, regulations from the financial industry such as PCI DSS or ISO 27017 address who is responsible for interactions between cloud vendors and customers.

In this section, we will look at PCI compliance and the shared responsibility model.

PCI compliance

Many organizations handle financial transactions, and Google has to go to great lengths to secure information residing on their servers. An example of PCI can tie what we learned previously into a real-life example. If there is a need to set up a specific payment processing environment, then Google can assist in helping customers to achieve this. At the core of this architecture would be what we have learned in this chapter. To secure the environment, we should use Resource Manager to create separate projects to segregate our gaming and PCI projects. We can utilize Cloud IAM and apply permissions to those separate projects. Remember the rule of least privilege! We can also secure the environment with firewall rules to restrict the inbound traffic. We want the public to be able to use our payment page, so we need HTTPS traffic to be secured by an HTTP(S) load balancer, and any additional payment processing applications may need bi-directional access to third parties. Take a look at the article here, `https://cloud.google.com/solutions/pci-dss-compliance-in-gcp`, for more in-depth knowledge of how GCP would handle PCI DSS requirements.

Shared responsibility model

Like the other main public cloud vendors, GCP has what is known as a shared responsibility agreement.

Google is not responsible for what resides in the operating system. It's important to understand the principle of shared responsibility for the exam. Google won't be responsible for everything in your architecture, so we must be prepared to take our share of the responsibility. For the exam, we should understand that the different GCP services that are offered mean that Google and the customer will have different levels of responsibility. As an example, let's look at Cloud Storage. Google will manage the encryption of storage and the hardware providing the service and will allow audit logging. However, it will not be responsible for the content that resides on Cloud Storage or the network security that's used to access it. Likewise, access to and authentication of the content will be the owner's responsibility. Compare this to, let's say, BigQuery, which is a PaaS offering. In this case, Google would take responsibility for network security and authentication.

The following diagram shows what the customer is expected to manage in each service model. From left to right, we can see the difference between fully self-managed on-premises data centers and SaaS offerings:

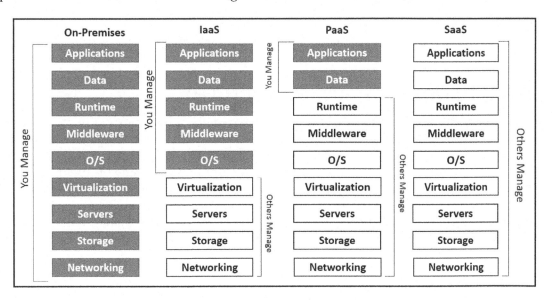

Data Loss Prevention (DLP)

Removing **Personal Identifiable Information** (PII) is also a concern within the industry. Cloud DLP provides us with a powerful data and de-identification platform. An example of how Cloud DLP can assist us is that we can perform the automatic redaction of sensitive data by removing email addresses, driver's license numbers, or passport numbers, which may be stored in GCP storage repositories.

Penetration testing in GCP

It's worth noting that, if you have a requirement to perform penetration testing on your GCP infrastructure, you don't need permission from Google, but you must abide by the Acceptable Use Policy to ensure that tests only target your projects. Interestingly, Google offers an incentive program should bugs or vulnerabilities be found, and rewards range from $100 to $31,337!

Additional security services

GCP offers a number of advanced services to help to secure your infrastructure and resources. In this section, we will take a short look at other key services.

Cloud Identity-Aware Proxy (IAP)

Google offers additional access control to your Cloud Engine instances or applications running on GCP via Cloud IAP. This allows the user identity to be verified over HTTPS and grants access only if permitted. This service is especially useful for remote workers as it negates the need for a company VPN to authenticate user requests using on-premises networks. Instead, access is via an internet-accessible URL. When remote users need to access an application, a request is forwarded to Cloud IAP and access will be granted (if permitted). Additionally, without the overhead of a traditional VPN, manageability is simplified for the administrator.

Enabling Cloud IAP is a simple process, but there are some prerequisites that must be met. You will need to configure firewall rules to block access to the VMs that are hosting your application and only allow access through IAP. Next, you need to navigate to **Security** | **Identity-Aware Proxy** in the GCP console, where you will find a list of your application or Compute Engine resources. Simply click on the blue radio button to enable IAP. Finally, you can populate the IAP access list with the relevant membership from the information panel that will become available. The following screenshot shows IAP enabled for an HTTPS resource:

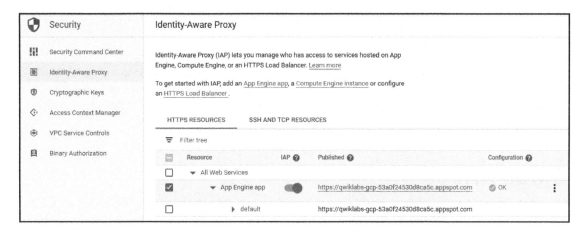

In the next section, we will look at Security Command Center.

Security Command Center (SCC)

SCC gives enterprises an overarching view of their cloud data across a number of GCP services. The real benefit of SCC comes from it assisting in gathering data and identifying threats, and it can actually act on these before any business impact occurs. It also provides a dashboard that reflects the overall health of our resources. It can also integrate with other GCP tools such as Cloud Security Scanner and third parties, such as Palo Alto Networks. GCP refers to possible security threats in SCC as *findings*. To access these *findings*, you must first have the relevant IAM role, which includes the permissions for the Security Center Findings Viewer and then browse to the **Findings** tab of the SCC. Of course, like all GCP services, there is API integration, which allows us to list any findings. SCC also offers the ability to use *security* marks, which allow us to annotate assets or findings and search or filter using these marks.

To use SCC, you must view it from your GCP organization. Additionally, you must be an organization administrator and have the Security Center Admin roles for the current organization. This allows you to select all of the current and future projects to be included (if you wish). Alternatively, we can include or exclude individual projects, should any security risk be found.

Forseti

Forseti is an open source security tool that assists in securing your GCP environment. It is useful if you wish to monitor resources to ensure that access control is the same as you intended it to be and can be used to create an alert when anything changes, via email or a post on a Slack channel. Additionally, it offers the ability to take snapshots of resources so that you always know what your cloud looks like. It can also enforce rules on sensitive GCP resources by comparing a policy to the current state and correcting any violations using GCP APIs.

Cloud Armor

Cloud Armor uses Google's global infrastructure to provide defense at scale against DDoS attacks. It is used to blacklist or whitelist access to your HTTPS load balancer. This can be used to prevent malicious users or traffic from contacting your resources, or—worse—taking control of your VPC based on rule sets. The following screenshot shows a policy that is set to deny a specific IP and give a 404 error:

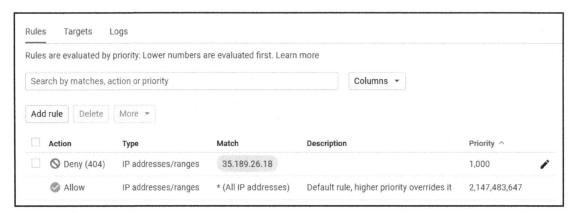

By clicking on the **Targets** tab, we can see that the policy is targeting a backend load balancer, as shown in the following screenshot:

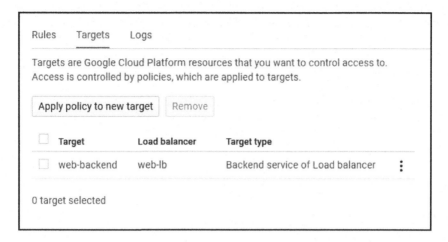

Cloud Armor logs allow us to see any access attempts and tells us which source requested access. We should be aware that these logs are provided through Stackdriver, which was described in the *Monitoring and logging* section of this chapter. This will be covered in more detail in `Chapter 15`, *Monitoring Your Infrastructure*.

The following screenshot shows some example output from Cloud Armor logs:

Summary

There are much bigger, deeper dives into security, but for the purpose of the exam, it's critical that you understand that security is key to all of Google's services and was not an afterthought. In this chapter, we covered a number of services that are offered to make sure that your GCP infrastructure is secure. We introduced Cloud Identity, covered the IAM model, and looked at encryption.

 Exam tip: Remember that we should never grant a user or service more permissions than what's required. Always use the principle of least privilege.

In the next chapter, we will look at management options in GCP.

Further reading

Read the following articles for more information on what was covered in this chapter:

- **Cloud Identity**: https://cloud.google.com/identity/docs/
- **IAM**: https://cloud.google.com/iam/docs/
- **Encryption**: https://cloud.google.com/storage/docs/encryption/
- **Cloud IAP**: https://cloud.google.com/iap/docs/
- **Security Command Center**: https://cloud.google.com/security-command-center/docs/
- **Cloud Armor**: https://cloud.google.com/armor/docs/

4
Section 4: Managing Implementation

In this section, we will focus on how to use various tools to manage GCP.

This section contains the following chapter:

- Chapter 14, *Google Cloud Management Options*

14

Google Cloud Management Options

This chapter describes how to utilize the various management options available so that you can administer your **Google Cloud Platform (GCP)** services in an easier way. In the previous chapters, we touched on the command-line tools that are available so that we can manage Google services. We can now go into more detail about these tools, which includes gcloud, cbt, bq, and gsutil.

Exam tips: It's vital that you know about the most efficient command-line tool for managing a particular service. Review and understand each command-line tool in them chapter and ensure that you can quickly map this to a GCP service. For example, if we are asked to create a new storage bucket using a command-line tool, we should know instantly that we need to use gsutil.

We also recommend that you take a deeper look at the gsutil command lines and understand them so that you can set life cycle policies.

As we cover each management option in this chapter, you can expect to understand how to access it and gain hands-on knowledge from examples. You can also expect to see code-based commands that can be used in the real world but are important to understand for exam success. We will begin by looking at using **Application Programming Interfaces (APIs)** and will then look at the remaining tools.

In this chapter, we will introduce the various management options that you can use. Specifically, we will cover the following topics:

- Using APIs
- Google Cloud Shell
- GCP **Software Development Kit (SDK)**
- Cloud Deployment Manager
- Pricing Calculator
- Additional things to consider

Code in Action

Check out the following video to see the Code in Action:
`http://bit.ly/31i6wpz`

Using APIs

API usage is extremely common now. APIs are access points to an application that offer developers flexibility in the way they communicate with them, dramatically increasing their efficiency.

GCP offers full documentation on the APIs for their services. We recommend that you check out `https://cloud.google.com/apis/` and click on the specific service you wish to read more about.

APIs use different authentication services, depending on where the API calls come from and the resource(s) they are requesting:

- **API keys**: These are encrypted strings that can be used when API calls don't need to access user data. These are great for getting developers up and running quickly. Keys are created from the GCP console under **API | Services | Credentials**. The key is then used in the API request.
- **OAuth client IDs**: These are based on the scope, meaning that different privileges will be granted to different IDs. This method is used if a developer needs to request user data.
- **Service Accounts**: These belong to an application of a VM instance. Please refer to `Chapter 13`, *Security and Compliance*, for more in-depth information on service accounts.

Let's look at an example of using an API. As we mentioned previously, we can browse to **API | Services** from the GCP console to view and enable APIs. If we search for Compute Engine, as shown in the following screenshot, we can select **TRY THIS API**:

This will take us to the APIs Explorer page. This is a nice feature that GCP offers to assist us in using our API calls for all of its services. The following screenshot shows the search results for the **Compute Engine API**:

If we click on this, we will see a list of all the API calls that are related to GCE. Let's look for the method that we can use to create a new instance, that is, `compute.instances.insert`:

If we click on this method, it will bring us to a page that allows us to request a VM instance via the API. The first thing that we should notice is the menu on the right-hand side, where we select OAuth 2.0 as our authentication method. This allows us to authorize the API call using the same user we used to log in to the GCP console. There is some mandatory information to populate, and this is specified in red:

- **project**: This is the ID of your GCP project.
- **zone**: This is the zone where you would like the VM to reside.

The following screenshot shows an example of these fields populated:

We also need to populate the request body with information about our request. Let's look at what is required in the following example. We are required to provide information regarding the machine's type, the machine's name, and the disk and image type:

```
{
  "machineType":"zones/us-central1-f/machineTypes/n1-standard-1        "
  "name":"instance001             "
  "disks":
  [
    {
      "type":"PERSISTENT               "
      "initializeParams":
      {
        "sourceImage":"projects/debian-cloud/global/images/family/debian-9       "
      }
      "boot": ☑
    }
  ]
}
```

After the initial validation, we can execute our request by clicking **Authorize and execute**. Response code **200 OK** means that our request was successfully executed. By taking a closer look, we can see information on the user, URI, and zone:

```
200 OK

- Show headers -

- {
    "kind": "compute#operation",
    "id": "1506986924064556374",
    "name": "operation-1554742199982-58607a08c18ac-71978ce0-e8119a6d",
    "zone": "https://www.googleapis.com/compute/v1/projects/qwiklabs-gcp-7463f770b17e1dc7/zones/us-central1-f ",
    "operationType": "insert",
    "targetLink": "https://www.googleapis.com/compute/v1/projects/qwiklabs-gcp-7463f770b17e1dc7/zones/us-central1-f/instances/instance-1 ",
    "targetId": "4032531473407329623",
    "status": "RUNNING",
    "user": "google3004538_student@qwiklabs.net",
    "progress": 0,
    "insertTime": "2019-04-08T09:50:01.662-07:00",
    "startTime": "2019-04-08T09:50:01.665-07:00",
```

Now, let's look at another example by creating a new disk. We can simply search for the `compute.disks.insert` method. Again, we have the project and zone to populate. The request body is also required:

```
{
    "name":"newdisk001          "          "
    "sizeGb":"10               "          "
}
```

After clicking **Authorize and execute**, we can, once again, see the response:

```
200 OK

- Show headers -

- {
    "kind": "compute#operation",
    "id": "971166634079601434",
    "name": "operation-1554742773093-58607c2b5151c-1b31c368-c00bd32b",
    "zone": "https://www.googleapis.com/compute/v1/projects/qwiklabs-gcp-7463f770b17e1dc7/zones/us-central1-f ",
    "operationType": "insert",
    "targetLink": "https://www.googleapis.com/compute/v1/projects/qwiklabs-gcp-7463f770b17e1dc7/zones/us-central1-f/disks/newdisk001 ",
    "targetId": "4908396006527648538",
    "status": "RUNNING",
    "user": "google3004538_student@qwiklabs.net",
    "progress": 0,
    "insertTime": "2019-04-08T09:59:33.945-07:00",
    "startTime": "2019-04-08T09:59:33.953-07:00",
```

We recommend that you explore the GCP APIs Explorer page to review what APIs are available in the core GCP services. In the upcoming sections, we will be looking at more command-line tools that are available to us.

Google Cloud Shell

The main management tool in the GCP suite is Google Cloud Shell. This is a free `g1-small` **Google Compute Engine** (**GCE**) instance that provides command-line access so that you can manage your GCP infrastructure through a Linux shell. The interesting thing here is that it can be accessed directly from your GCP console simply by clicking on the shell access in the top-right-hand side:

Once activated, the console screen will split in two and Google Cloud Shell will become visible inside the browser:

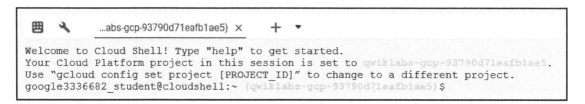

No additional steps are required for authorization, so we can manage projects and resources securely without the need to install any other management toolset. Moreover, the SDK command lines that we will look at in this chapter are packaged as standard. Additionally, Google Cloud Shell has preinstalled admin tools such as MySQL client, Docker, and kubectl. Finally, your developers can also access different languages, including Go, Python, Node.js, and Ruby. For a full and up-to-date list of features that have been installed, we recommend that you visit `https://cloud.google.com/shell/docs/features#tools`.

Google Cloud Shell comes with 5 GB of persistent disk storage, which is mounted to your `$HOME` directory. This means that you can store scripts or user configurations safely between sessions and install any required packages. Note that anything saved outside the `$HOME` directory will be lost when the session terminates, that is, after it has been idle for an hour.

We can upload and download from our local machine using the console shell settings, as shown in the following screenshot:

Google Cloud Shell's code editor can also be used to browse the folder path from persistent storage. We can easily access this by clicking the pencil icon in the Cloud Shell menu bar:

From here, we can update our scripts or files directly in Cloud Shell. The Cloud Shell virtual instance also comes with standard Linux-based editors such as `nano` and `vim`. Note that, at the time of writing, the code editor is in the beta stage:

```
Cloud Shell

File  Edit  Selection  View  Go  Help

  brian                example.json ×
    ~key.json       1  {
    example.json    2      "glossary": {
                    3          "title": "example glossary",
                    4          "GlossDiv": {
                    5              "title": "S",
                    6              "GlossList": {
                    7                  "GlossEntry": {
                    8                      "ID": "SGML",
                    9                      "SortAs": "SGML",
                   10                      "GlossTerm": "Standard Generalized Markup Language",
                   11                      "Acronym": "SGML",
                   12                      "Abbrev": "ISO 8879:1986",
                   13                      "GlossDef": {
                   14                          "para": "A meta-markup language, used to create markup languages such as DocBook.",
                   15                          "GlossSeeAlso": ["GML", "XML"]
                   16                      },
                   17                      "GlossSee": "markup"
                   18                  }
                   19              }
                   20          }
                   21      }
                   22  }
```

Now that we have covered Google Cloud Shell, let's move on and look at the GCP SDK that's available to us.

The GCP SDK

This section will describe how to use the Google Cloud SDK. The SDK is a set of tools that allows you to manage your GCP resources and applications and includes the `gcloud`, `gsutil`, and `bq` command-line tools. There are, as expected, some prerequisites to installing this kit. The SDK can run on Linux, macOS, and Windows OSes and requires you to have Python 2.7.x installed. Some tools that come bundled may have additional requirements. Please refer to `https://cloud.google.com/sdk/install` for specific system and operating system requirements.

gcloud

`gcloud` is the primary command-line tool for GCP and allows you to perform common tasks in your GCP environment. There are many use cases for `gcloud`; for example, creating and managing GCE instances, cloud SQL instances, Kubernetes Engine clusters, Dataproc clusters, DNS zones, and Cloud Deployment Manager deployments.

When you are using `gcloud` for the first time, it is advisable to check out the usage guidelines. Adding `-h` to a command will offer the following guidelines:

```
google3167498_student@cloudshell:/home (qwiklabs-gcp-cf3e4b1a188f0368)$ gcloud -h
Usage: gcloud [optional flags] <group | command>
  group may be             access-context-manager | alpha | app | asset | auth |
                           beta | bigtable | builds | components | composer |
                           compute | config | container | dataflow | dataproc |
                           datastore | debug | deployment-manager | dns |
                           domains | endpoints | filestore | firebase |
                           functions | iam | iot | kms | logging | ml |
                           ml-engine | organizations | projects | pubsub | redis |
                           resource-manager | services | source | spanner | sql |
                           topic
  command may be           docker | feedback | help | info | init | version

For detailed information on this command and its flags, run:
  gcloud --help
```

For detailed information about this command and its flags, we can run the following command:

```
gcloud --help
```

This will list far more details—try it out and take a look at the output you receive! Press the spacebar to continue looking through the detailed output or press *Q* to exit.

 `gcloud` has a command reference for features and resources hosted on GCP, which we recommend you review. This can be found at `https://cloud.google.com/sdk/gcloud/reference/`.

Let's have a look at how we can use `gcloud` to create a new VM instance.

We will also show you how we can use `gcloud` to connect to our VM via SSH, create a new disk, and attach it to our VM instance. Follow these steps:

1. In order to create a VM, we should use the following syntax:

    ```
    gcloud compute instances create <instance name> --zone <zone
    name>
    ```

    Here, `<instance name>` is the name of your VM instance and `<zone>` is the zone where your instance will be deployed.

2. The following example will create a new VM instance named `myinstance` in `zone us-central1-f`:

    ```
    gcloud compute instances create myinstance --zone us-central1-f
    ```

3. Once we have created our instance, `gcloud` also allows us to connect to the instance and manage it. This is a thin wrapper around the SSH command that will deal with the authentication and instance name to IP address resolution. The connection will, by default, initiate the SSH session using the user credentials that are running the command:

    ```
    gcloud compute ssh <instance name> --zone <zone name>
    ```

    Here, `<instance name>` is the name of your GCE VM instance and `<zone>` is the zone where your instance will be deployed.

4. The following example will connect to a new VM instance named `myinstance` in `zone us-central1-f` using the following SSH command:

    ```
    gcloud compute ssh myinstance --zone us-central1-f
    ```

5. `gcloud` also allows us to perform day-two operations. As an example, let's add a disk to the VM instance we've already created. First, we need to create the disk using the following syntax:

```
gcloud compute disks create <disk name> --zone <zone name>
```

Here, `<disk name>` is the name of the disk we are creating and `<zone name>` is the zone where the disk will be created.

6. The following example will create a new disk named `newdisk001` in `zone us-central1-f`:

```
gcloud compute disks create newdisk001 --zone us-central1-f
```

We should note that, in the preceding example, I don't use the optional size flag. We should note that the default disk size for a standard HDD is 500 GB. Also, you can see that we have created the disk in the same zone as the instance.

7. Finally, we need to attach the disk to our instance. This can be accomplished using the following syntax:

```
gcloud compute instances attach-disk <instance name> attach-disk <disk name> --zone <zone>
```

Here, `<instance name>` is the name of your GCE VM instance, `<disk name>` is the name of the disk you want to attach to your VM instance, and `<zone name>` is the zone your instance resides in.

8. The following example will attach a disk called `newdisk` to a VM instance called `myinstance` in the `us-central1-f` zone:

```
gcloud compute instances attach-disk myinstance --disk newdisk001 --zone us-central1-f
```

Finally, it is wise to mention the alpha and beta commands that you may find in `gcloud`. Alpha commands are typically not production-ready and may still be in the development phase. They may change without any notice and some are only fully accessible via invitation. Beta commands are typically almost fully developed and being tested in production. However, these may also be changed without notice.

gsutil

In this section, we will describe the usage of `gsutil`. The main purpose of this is to ensure that you understand the primary use case of `gsutil` and show examples of real-life scenarios. `gsutil` is a Python application that can be used to manage Cloud Storage resources and can be triggered from Cloud Shell. By using `gsutil`, we can do the following:

- Create and delete buckets
- Manage access to these buckets and their objects
- Copy and move storage data
- List the contents of a bucket
- Transfer data in and out of our Cloud Shell instance (note that this is not limited to Cloud Shell)

 You need to understand that the `gsutil` syntax works in `gsutil <action> gs://<bucket name>/<resource name>` format. An example of `<action>` could be `mb`, which is used to create a bucket. Here, `gs://` is the prefix to indicate a resource in Cloud Storage. `<bucket name>/<object name>` could be `cloudarchitect/notes.txt`, for example. For a full range of `gsutil` commands, please refer to `https://cloud.google.com/storage/docs/gsutil`.

Creating a bucket is a good place to start with `gsutil`. Buckets are basic containers where you can store your data. We covered storage in detail in `Chapter 5`, *Networking Options in GCP*.

Let's look at some examples of common tasks that we can use `gsutil` for. Let's create a bucket, upload some content to it, list some files, and then remove the bucket:

1. The following syntax can be used to create a bucket:

   ```
   gsutil mb -l <zone name> gs://<bucket name>
   ```

   Here, `<zone name>` is the zone in which you will create your storage bucket, and `<bucket name>` is a globally unique bucket name. In the following example, we will create a bucket called `cloudarchitect001` in the `us-east1` zone:

   ```
   gsutil mb -l us-east1 gs://cloudarchitect001
   ```

2. Now that we have created a new bucket, let's add a file to it. In this example, I will create a new file on my local persistent Google Cloud Shell storage. Let's assume that we have a file called examnotes.txt in our Cloud Shell environment. This can be uploaded as we described in the *Google Cloud Shell* section. In order to copy this to our bucket, we can use the following syntax:

```
gsutil cp <file to copy> gs://<bucket name>
```

Here, <file to copy> is the file you wish to copy to your bucket and <bucket name> is a globally unique bucket name where you want the file to reside. In the following example, we will copy a file called examnotes.txt to a bucket called cloudarchitect001:

```
gsutil cp examnotes.txt gs://cloudarchitect001
```

The output from the previous command will confirm the success of this copy.

3. We can list the contents of our bucket to ensure that the file is there by using the following syntax:

```
gsutil ls gs://<bucket name>
```

Here, <bucket name> is the name of the bucket you wish to list resources in. Let's list the resources of our cloudarchitect001 bucket:

```
gsutil ls gs://cloudarchitect001
```

4. If we wish to remove files from our bucket, we can use the following syntax:

```
gsutil rm gs://<bucket name>/<object name>
```

Here, <bucket name> is the name of the bucket where your resource resides and <object name> is the object you wish to remove. Let's remove examnotes.txt from our cloudarchitect001 bucket:

```
gsutil rm gs://cloudarchitect001/examnotes.txt
```

5. Finally, if we wish to remove the bucket completely (remember, resources come at a cost!), we can use the following syntax:

```
gsutil rb gs://<bucket name>
```

Here, <bucket name> is the name of the bucket we wish to delete. Let's delete our cloudarchitect001 bucket:

```
gsutil rb gs://cloudarchitect001
```

Note that we could also run this command with the `-r` flag, which would remove the bucket and all its contents.

bq

Now, let's look at the command-line tools for BigQuery. BigQuery was described in more detail in `Chapter 11`, *Analyzing Big Data Options*, so in this section, we won't do a deep dive into the service. However, in general, the main ways to interact with BigQuery is to load, export, query, view, and manage data. One of the ways we can do this is from Cloud Shell using the `bq` command-line tool.

 BigQuery can be complex to use from the `bq` command line, and it is recommended to review the `bq` command-line tool reference page for full details at `https://cloud.google.com/bigquery/docs/bq-command-line-tool`.

Let's look at some common use cases. In the following examples, we will create a new dataset, create a table, and then query it. The following syntax is used to create a new dataset in its simplest form:

```
bq --location=<location> mk --dataset <dataset name>
```

Here, `<location>` is the dataset location and `<dataset name>` is the name of your new dataset. The location can be multi-regional, such as the US or EU, or it can be a regional location, such as `us-west2` or `europe-north1`. Let's create a new dataset called `newdataset` as a multi-regional location of the US:

```
bq --location=US mk --dataset newdataset
```

 There are some optional flags that can be set. It is good practice to configure the default table's expiration for the default tables of your datasets, the expiration time for your tables, and the partition expiration for your partitioned tables.

Now, let's create a new empty table in its simplest form. To do so, we can use the following syntax:

```
bq mk -t <dataset name>.<table name> <schema>
```

Here, `<dataset name>` is the name of the dataset you wish to create a new table in, `<table name>` is the name of the table to be created, and `<schema>` is the inline schema definition in `[FIELD:DATA_TYPE]` format. A path to a JSON file on your local machine can also be used. The `<schema>` parameter may be a bit confusing but, to clarify, this is like a column in an Excel file.

Let's create a new table called `newtable` inside our dataset with the name `newdataset`. We will create two new columns named `examname` and `result`, which we will want to populate with character (Unicode) data, that is, `STRING` data:

```
bq mk -t  newdataset.newdataset examname:STRING,result:STRING
```

Finally, let's look at how we can use `bq` to run queries. To do so, we need to use the following syntax:

```
bq query '<SQL query>'
```

Here, `<SQL query>` is the SQL query that you wish BigQuery to execute on the data. `<SQL query>` will contain information on the data to query from a specific dataset and table. If we want to connect to a project that isn't set as our default, we can also specify this in our SQL request. If we were to query the full path of the table, it would look as follows:

```
<projects>.<dataset>.<table>
```

To clarify this, let's look at an example. GCP provides some sample datasets and tables that we can make use of. Let's execute a `bq` query on a table called `shakespeare` from a dataset called `samples`. The dataset and the table reside under a `public` project that Google allows us to connect to called `bigquery-public-data`.

In this example, we want to see how many times the word `beloved` appears in Shakespeare's works. We will search by the columns in the table, which are `word` and `corpus`. Also, note that we are specifying `#standardSql` as the query type:

```
bq query "#standardSql SELECT word, corpus, COUNT(word) FROM \'bigquery-
public-data.samples.shakespeare\'
WHERE word LIKE '%beloved%' GROUP BY word, corpus"
```

This will return the following results:

```
| word    |        corpus          | f0  |
+---------+------------------------+-----+
| beloved | cymbeline              |  1  |
| beloved | romeoandjuliet         |  1  |
| beloved | winterstale            |  1  |
| beloved | tamingoftheshrew       |  1  |
| beloved | hamlet                 |  1  |
| beloved | twogentlemenofverona   |  1  |
| beloved | tempest                |  1  |
| beloved | timonofathens          |  1  |
| beloved | kinglear               |  1  |
| beloved | sonnets                |  1  |
| beloved | coriolanus             |  1  |
| beloved | 1kinghenryiv           |  1  |
| beloved | juliuscaesar           |  1  |
| beloved | 3kinghenryvi           |  1  |
| beloved | antonyandcleopatra     |  1  |
| beloved | comedyoferrors         |  1  |
| beloved | periclesprinceoftyre   |  1  |
| beloved | titusandronicus        |  1  |
| beloved | rapeoflucrece          |  1  |
| beloved | measureforemeasure     |  1  |
| beloved | midsummersnightsdream  |  1  |
| beloved | merchantofvenice       |  1  |
| beloved | asyoulikeit            |  1  |
| beloved | othello                |  1  |
| beloved | troilusandcressida     |  1  |
| beloved | 2kinghenryvi           |  1  |
| beloved | twelfthnight           |  1  |
| beloved | kinghenryviii          |  1  |
+---------+------------------------+-----+
```

For exam success, we should understand the power of the `bq` command line, but mostly ensure that we understand which command-line tool to use in order to query BigQuery tables.

cbt

In this section, we will discover the command-line tool for Cloud Bigtable—cbt. Written in Go, the CLI allows us to perform basic interactions with Bigtable. Unlike the previous command-line tools we've looked at, we must install the component using Cloud Shell and the gcloud command.

Again, we took a deeper look at this service in Chapter 10, *Exploring Storage Options in GCP – Part 2*, but before we look at the command-line tool, we should remind ourselves that Bigtable is a high-performance NoSQL database service that uses instances, clusters, and nodes. Bigtable is a container for your clusters and nodes. Tables belong to these Bigtable instances:

```
gcloud components install cbt
```

You may have noticed that the different tools we have looked at have slightly different syntax and that cbt is no different. The usage of cbt is as follows:

```
cbt <command>
```

Let's look at an example of creating a new instance in Bigtable called myfirstinstance. There are additional flags we must add. Let's look at the syntax:

```
cbt createinstance <instance id> <display name> <cluster id> <zone> <number of nodes> <storage type>
```

Here, <instance id> is an identifier you wish to give your Bigtable instance, <display name> is the display name of your Bigtable instance, <cluster id> is an identifier for the cluster of nodes, <zone> is the zone in which your instances will be deployed, <number of nodes> is the number of VM instances in the cluster, and <storage type> is the storage type we wish to use for our VM instances. This can be set as either SSD or HDD.

Let's look at the syntax that we'd have if we wanted to create a new instance with an ID of instance001, a display name of myfirstinstance, a cluster ID of cluster001, and three nodes deployed in the europe-west2-a zone using SSD storage:

```
cbt createinstance instance001 myfirstinstance cluster001 europe-west2-a 3 SSD
```

If we look inside our console, we are able to verify that this has been created correctly:

Instance details	✏ EDIT INSTANCE	🗑 DELETE INSTANCE	

myfirstinstance
Instance ID: **instance001**   Type: **Production**   Storage: **SSD**

cluster001

CPU utilization	Rows	Throughput	System error rate
Average: 0.2%	Read: 0/s	Read: 0 B/s	0%
Hottest node: 0.2%	Write: 0/s	Write: 0 B/s	

Cluster ID	Zone	Nodes	Storage utilization	
✅ cluster001	europe-west2-a	3	▦▦▦ ▦▦▦ ▦▦▦▦	0 B / 7.5 TB

You can also use `gcloud` commands to create Bigtable instances. `gcloud` offers us the ability to create production or development environments, where developments have limited performance and no SLA. If you need to create a development Bigtable instance, then use `gcloud`.

Cloud Deployment Manager

In this section, we will look at one of the most useful management tools—Google Cloud Deployment Manager. It's important to understand the concepts of Cloud Deployment Manager for exam success.

Deployment Manager allows us to automate the creation and configuration of a variety of GCP resources. We can write all the resources our application needs in a declarative format using YAML files, which ensure repeatable deployments with consistent results. YAML is a data sequencing language that humans can easily read. Overall, Deployment Manager can be referred to as **Infrastructure as Code (IaC)**. You may have some experience with tools such as Ansible or Terraform, and will recognize that the nesting of elements occurs through indentation, rather than any braces or brackets, which are used in some other languages.

Exam tip: Deployment Manager is a very large topic, and deep dive courses are available so that you can gain further knowledge. For the purpose of the exam, we will explain the fundamental knowledge that's needed to be successful.

There are some components that are fundamental to Deployment Manager. Configuration files contain all the resources we want to deploy, as well as their properties.

A configuration file starts with the resource string and is followed by a list of entries, each of which have the following fields:

- **Name**: The name of the resource we are deploying; for example, `vm001`.
- **Type**: This specifies the base type of this resource. There are many available resource types and they relate to the type of resource we wish to deploy. For example, the resource type for a new VM instance would be `compute.v1.instance`. Note that `v1` stands for production-ready.
- **Properties**: This specifies the properties that are required to create the resource. For example, if we wish to deploy a new VM instance from the GUI, we need to populate mandatory fields such as OS type, disk type, and image and network interfaces. These would be populated in the `properties` section of a configuration file.

> A full list of resource types can be found here: `https://cloud.google.com/deployment-manager/docs/configuration/supported-resource-types`.

Let's look at how we can construct our first example configuration file. In the *Google Cloud Shell* section of this chapter, we referred to the Cloud Shell editor. Let's open this up and create a new file. To do this, simply right-click on your user ID and select **New File**:

Give the file a name—for example, vm001.yaml—and click **OK** to create it. We are now ready to edit. In this example, the code will do the following:

- Create a VM in the europe-west4-a zone
- Size it as the g1-small machine type
- Use centos-6 as our image
- Create a persistent boot disk
- Add the VM to the default network
- Add access configurations as external NAT

A complete configuration file will look as follows:

```
resources:
 - name: vm001
   type: compute.v1.instance
   properties:
   zone: europe-west4-a
   machineType:
https://www.googleapis.com/compute/v1/projects/architectproject/zones/europ
e-west4-a/machineTypes/g1-small
   disks:
 - deviceName: boot
   type: PERSISTENT
   boot: true
   autoDelete: true
   initializeParams:
   sourceImage:
https://www.googleapis.com/compute/v1/projects/centos-cloud/global/images/c
entos-6-v20190423
   networkInterfaces:
 - network:
https://www.googleapis.com/compute/v1/projects/architectproject/global/netw
orks/default
   accessConfigs:
 - name: External NAT
   type: ONE_TO_ONE_NAT
```

Now, let's save it and use this configuration file to deploy a VM. Again, we will use the Cloud Shell tool to execute this using the Deployment Manager command-line syntax:

```
gcloud deployment-manager deployments create <deployment name> --config
<config file>
```

Here, `<deployment name>` is the name of your overall deployment name. Remember that the VM instance name is specified in our configuration file and that `<config file>` is the name of the configuration file we created previously. Let's look at an example of creating a new deployment called `deployment01` using our `vm001.yaml` configuration file:

```
gcloud deployment-manager deployments create deployment01 --config
vm001.yaml
```

If we browse to **Deployment Manager** in our GCP console, we can confirm that this was deployed:

We can also browse to Compute Engine in our GCP console and confirm that the VM instance exists:

So, although we have taken time to create a configuration file, we have only deployed a single VM instance. Deployment Manager gives us the opportunity to deploy full environments. To do this, we should use templates. A template allows us to abstract part of a configuration file into individual building blocks that can be reused across deployments.

A template is a separate file from your configuration file. It is also written in a different language—either Jinja or Python—and is imported and used as a type in a configuration file.

Templates allow us to pass variables from our configuration files, which means they can stay pretty static and we can just pass in the edited variables from our configuration file. We need to modify our configuration file to reflect the fact that we want to call a template file. This is done by adding a path from the template to the top of our configuration file. We could also edit the configuration file to reflect the variables we want to pass.

Let's look at an example. We want to keep a static template for creating debian-9 VMs, but we want to pass variables such as the hostname, zone, and machine type. Our configuration file will now look as follows. Note that we have added the vm-template.jinja file as a type and that our variables are set as properties:

```
imports:
  - path: vm-template.jinja

resources:
- name: newinstance
  type: vm-template.jinja
  properties:
    name: createdbytemplate
    zone: europe-west4-a
    type: g1-small
```

Now, we need to configure our template file. This will look like our old configuration file, but now we have set the values of our variables to be passed through. Note that our hostname, machine type, and zone are set inside our brackets in the following format:

```
{{ properties["variable name"] }}
```

Here, variable name is the string that's passed from the configuration file:

```
resources:
- name: {{ properties["name"] }}
  type: compute.v1.instance
  properties:
    zone: {{ properties["zone"] }}
    machineType: zones/{{ properties["zone"] }}/machineTypes/{{
properties["type"] }}
    disks:
    - deviceName: boot
      type: PERSISTENT
      boot: true
      autoDelete: true
```

```
        initializeParams:
          sourceImage: projects/debian-cloud/global/images/family/debian-9
    networkInterfaces:
    - network: global/networks/default
```

We can save this and call it `vm-template.jinja`. We can now use our `gcloud` commands to call our `vm001.yaml` file:

```
gcloud deployment-manager deployments create templatedeployment --config
vm001.yml
```

We can now check our console to verify that we have a new VM called `createdbytemplate`:

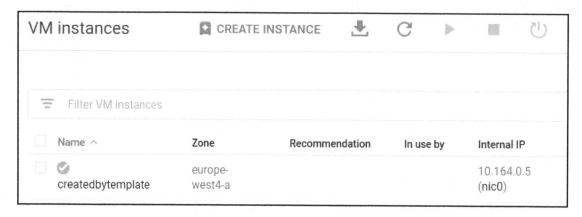

We can also specify the variable properties in our `gcloud` command. In the following example, we have our template file, which is expecting variables for a hostname and a zone:

```
resources:
- name: {{ properties["name"] }}
  type: compute.v1.instance
  properties:
    zone: {{ properties["zone"] }}
    machineType: zones/{{ properties ["zone"] }}/machineTypes/g1-small
    disks:
    - deviceName: boot
      type: PERSISTENT
      boot: true
      autoDelete: true
      initializeParams:
        sourceImage: projects/centos-cloud/global/images/centos-6-v20190423
    networkInterfaces:
    - network: global/networks/default
    accessConfigs:
```

```
- name: External NAT
  type: ONE_TO_ONE_NAT
```

Once again, let's use our `gcloud` commands to create this. However, we need to specify the name as `vm002` and the zone as `europe-west4-a`:

```
gcloud deployment-manager deployments create deployment002 --template vm-
template.jinja --properties name:vm002,zone:europe-west4-a
```

Let's check our GCP console and confirm that we now have a VM instance called `vm002` in the `europe-west4-a` zone:

So far, we have only looked at single VM deployments, but we can also deploy multiple VMs via Deployment Manager. Let's look at an example where we want to deploy a three-tier application made up of a web application and a DB server in different zones. We can expand on our previous template to add the information that's required. Note that we are now specifying three separate resources:

```
resources:
- name: {{ properties["webname"] }}
  type: compute.v1.instance
  properties:
    zone: {{ properties["webzone"] }}
    machineType: zones/{{ properties ["webzone"] }}/machineTypes/{{
properties["type"] }}
    disks:
    - deviceName: boot
      type: PERSISTENT
      boot: true
      autoDelete: true
      initializeParams:
        sourceImage: projects/centos-cloud/global/images/centos-6-v20190423
    networkInterfaces:
    - network: global/networks/default
      accessConfigs:
```

```
        - name: External NAT
          type: ONE_TO_ONE_NAT

  - name: {{ properties["appname"] }}
    type: compute.v1.instance
    properties:
      zone: {{ properties["appzone"] }}
      machineType: zones/{{ properties ["appzone"] }}/machineTypes/{{
properties["type"] }}
        disks:
        - deviceName: boot
          type: PERSISTENT
          boot: true
          autoDelete: true
          initializeParams:
            sourceImage: projects/centos-cloud/global/images/centos-6-v20190423
        networkInterfaces:
        - network: global/networks/default
        accessConfigs:
        - name: External NAT
          type: ONE_TO_ONE_NAT

  - name: {{ properties["dbname"] }}
    type: compute.v1.instance
    properties:
      zone: {{ properties["dbzone"] }}
      machineType: zones/{{ properties ["dbzone"] }}/machineTypes/{{
properties["type"] }}
        disks:
        - deviceName: boot
          type: PERSISTENT
          boot: true
          autoDelete: true
          initializeParams:
            sourceImage: projects/centos-cloud/global/images/centos-6-v20190423
        networkInterfaces:
        - network: global/networks/default
        accessConfigs:
        - name: External NAT
          type: ONE_TO_ONE_NAT
```

Now, we need to update our configuration file. Let's save this and call it `multi.yaml`:

```
imports:
  - path: vm-template.jinja

resources:
- name: newinstance
```

```
type: vm-template.jinja
properties:
  webname: web001
  webzone: europe-west2-a
  appname: app001
  appzone: europe-west4-b
  dbname: db001
  dbzone: europe-west6-c
  type: g1-small
```

We can now run the following command to trigger a deployment called
`multideployment`:

> **gcloud deployment-manager deployments create multideployment --config
> multi.yaml**

Now, let's check our results from Cloud Shell:

```
The fingerprint of the deployment is NdvSfAvJTKQnTfuTYocnBQ==
Waiting for create [operation-1556477906253-5879bc0b3f6a3-e71eb3bb-b27e918e]...done.
Create operation operation-1556477906253-5879bc0b3f6a3-e71eb3bb-b27e918e completed successfully.
NAME     TYPE                  STATE       ERRORS  INTENT
app001   compute.v1.instance   COMPLETED   []
db001    compute.v1.instance   COMPLETED   []
web001   compute.v1.instance   COMPLETED   []
```

We can confirm our deployment via the GCP console. Let's check out the **Deployment Manager** menu, where we can see that our deployments have been successful:

We can also see that each VM instance has been deployed to the correct zone:

Name ^	Zone	Recommendation	In use by	Internal IP	External IP	Connect	
✅ app001	europe-west4-b			10.164.0.3 (nic0)	None	SSH ▾	⋮
✅ db001	europe-west6-c			10.172.0.4 (nic0)	None	SSH ▾	⋮
✅ web001	europe-west2-a			10.154.0.3 (nic0)	None	SSH ▾	⋮

This is how we configure a template for VM instance types only. We can also extend our template to other types of services, such as networking. As a final example, let's look at how to create a template and configuration file in order to create a networking and firewall ruleset. In this example, we need to have three separate templates: one for our network, one for our subnetwork, and one for our firewall rule.

Let's look at our network first. This is pretty simple. Note that we are now using a type of `compute.v1.network` and that we have single properties. We set this to `false` to avoid the autocreation of a corresponding subnetwork. The name is a variable that's passed from our configuration file. Let's save this file as `network.jinja`:

```
resources:
- name: {{ env["name"] }}
  type: compute.v1.network
  properties:
    autoCreateSubnetworks: false
```

Next, we can create a subnetwork template. Again, we have the name as a variable that will be passed from our configuration file. We will also be passing information about the IP range and the network to attach it to, which we will create using the `network.jinja` template, as well as the region to create the subnet in. Let's save this as `subnet.jinja`:

```
resources:
- name: {{ env["name"] }}
  type: compute.v1.subnetwork
  properties:
    ipCidrRange: {{ properties["iprange"] }}
    network: {{ properties["network"] }}
    region: {{ properties["region"] }}
```

Finally, let's create a template to create a firewall rule. Once again, we will pass the name from our configuration file, but this time we will append the name with a hardcoded value. We will also set the network to attach this to and pass in the protocol for our firewall rule. Let's save this template as `firewall.jinja`:

```
resources:
- name: {{ env["name"] }}-firewall-rule
  type:  compute.v1.firewall
  properties:
    network: {{ properties["network"] }}
    sourceRanges: ["0.0.0.0/0"]
    allowed:
    - IPProtocol: {{ properties["Protocol"] }}
      ports: ["80"]
```

Now, we need our configuration file. We import all three of our templates rather than a single file, like we did in the previous examples. There is no real complexity to this—we just add an extra line for each template to import. One of the key things to note here is to make sure we connect the subnet and firewall rule to the correct network. We pass the variable as follows:

```
$(ref.custom-net.selfLink)
```

Here, `custom-net` is the name of the network we are creating. The name is passed as a variable. Let's save this configuration file as `config.yaml`:

```
imports:
- path: network.jinja
- path: subnet.jinja
- path: firewall.jinja

resources:
- name: custom-net
  type: network.jinja
- name: custom-subnet
  type: subnet.jinja
  properties:
    iprange: 10.10.0.0/16
    network: $(ref.custom-net.selfLink)
    region: us-central1
- name: custom
  type: firewall.jinja
  properties:
    network: $(ref.custom-net.selfLink)
    Protocol: TCP
```

Finally, let's upload these files to our Cloud Shell environment and trigger the `gcloud` commands that we have become familiar with:

```
gcloud deployment-manager deployments create networking --config
config.yaml
```

Let's see what the output of this command looks like in Cloud Shell:

```
The fingerprint of the deployment is 2A6YxCYsxQ_e04Se7N6Rpw==
Waiting for create [operation-1556741126674-587d909dcd9bd-c1d90539-9a25356a]...done.
Create operation operation-1556741126674-587d909dcd9bd-c1d90539-9a25356a completed successfully.
NAME                      TYPE                   STATE       ERRORS  INTENT
custom-firewall-rule  compute.v1.firewall    COMPLETED   []
custom-net            compute.v1.network     COMPLETED   []
custom-subnet         compute.v1.subnetwork  COMPLETED   []
```

There is one final file that we should also discuss. A schema file is used as a guide to show users how to interact with and use your template. For example, let's look at a configuration file that will require a zone to be passed as a variable to the template. We can provide our users with information on how it is used and which variables need to be set:

```
info:
  title: VM Instance Template
  author: Cloud Architect
  description: Creates a new instance
  version: 0.1

imports:
- path: vm-template.jinja

required:
- zone

properties:
  zone:
    type: string
    description: zone where VM will reside
```

There are some great Deployment Manager examples that are provided by Google, which we can download and use in our free-tier environment. We recommend that you download and look at a further, more complex, Cloud Deployment Manager template at `https://github.com/` `GoogleCloudPlatform/deploymentmanager-samples`.

Pricing Calculator

Google offers help when it comes to calculating the cost of running your apps in GCP. Instead of checking the prices in the documentation of each service, you can use the Google Cloud Platform Pricing Calculator. This calculator is available online via `https://cloud.google.com/products/calculator`. It allows you to choose the services and configuration you want to use for your application. You can also add estimated storage and network requirements. The total price will be calculated for you:

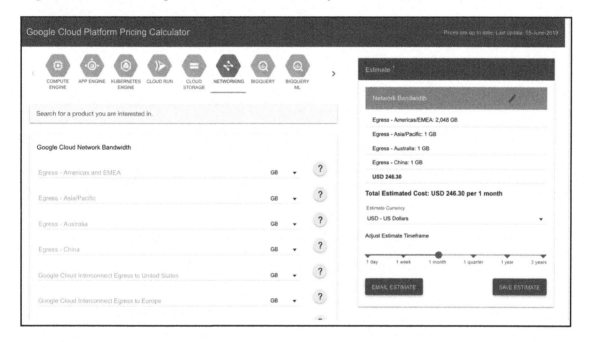

Here, you can see an example of the cost for five nodes on the GKE cluster with 500 GB disk space. To add estimated egress networking traffic, you just choose the **NETWORKING** icon and define where your traffic will go:

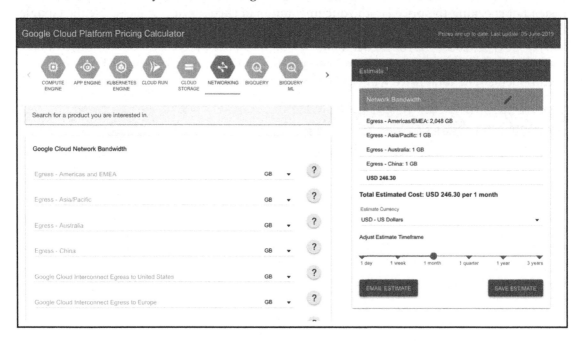

Let's look at another example, this time for **CLOUD STORAGE.** In this example, we are showing you how much it will cost to use 1 TB of cloud storage in Singapore. We have estimated that we will have 500,000 class A and 500,000 class B operations per month. Please note that when you are adding operations into the calculator, it expects the figure in millions. In our example, we have put 0.5 million:

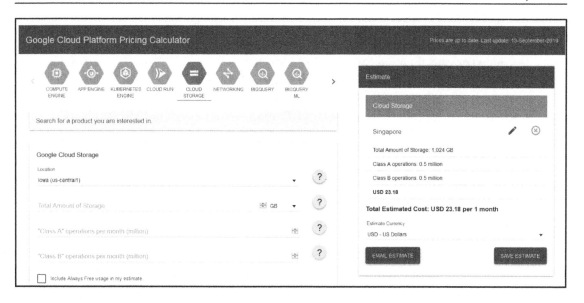

We encourage you to navigate to this website and familiarize yourself with different examples.

Additional things to consider

There are additional management tools that we need to consider. For the exam, it is also important to be aware of the following:

- **Cloud Source Repositories**: These are fully featured Git repositories that are hosted on GCP and support the collaborative development of an application. You can use `gcloud` commands to create code, commit code, and manage new repositories. More information can be found here: `https://cloud.google.com/source-repositories/docs/`.
- **Cloud Build**: This is a GCP CI/CD service that will execute your builds on the GCP infrastructure. It can import source code from Google Cloud Storage, Cloud Source Repositories, GitHub, or Bitbucket. More information can be found in `Chapter 5`, *Exploring Google Kubernetes Engine as a CaaS Offering*, and here: `https://cloud.google.com/cloud-build/docs/`.
- **Cloud Scheduler**: This is a fully managed cron job scheduler service. It can be used to trigger jobs on App Engine, send Pub/Sub messages, or even hit HTTP(S) endpoints.

- **Container Registry**: This provides us with private Docker repository storage on our GCP platform. We can use `gcloud` commands to push images to our registry, and then we can pull these images using an HTTP endpoint from any GCE instance or even our own hardware. More information can be found in `Chapter 5`, *Exploring Google Kubernetes Engine as a CaaS Offering*.
- **Cloud Endpoints**: This acts as an API management system that allows us to manage our APIs on any Google Cloud backend. Once you have deployed your API into Cloud Endpoints, you can create a developer portal that users can interact with and access and view documentation.

Summary

In this chapter, we looked over the main management tools that can be used to manage GCP services. It's important to reiterate that you should understand which services can be managed by which command-line tool and the basic command-line structure. Let's review what we would use each tool for:

- `gcloud` can be used to manage many GCP services, but it is most commonly used to manage Compute Engine VM instances, Cloud SQL instances, Kubernetes Engine clusters, and Cloud Deployment Manager deployments.
- Use `cbt` to manage Bigtable.
- Use `bq` to manage BigQuery.
- Use `gsutil` to manage Cloud Storage. We need to understand the different syntax for creating buckets, copying data, and removing buckets.
- Deployment Manager can be used to automate a variety of GCP services within templates and configuration files.
- Pricing Calculator.

Remember that Google offers a free tier where you can use these command-line tools and familiarize yourself with creating and managing different services.

In the next chapter, we will look at how to monitor our GCP services.

Further reading

Read the following articles for more information about what was covered in this chapter:

- **APIs Explorer**: https://cloud.google.com/storage/docs/gsutilhttps://developers.google.com/apis-explorer/#p/
- **gsutil**: https://cloud.google.com/storage/docs/gsutil
- **cbt**: https://cloud.google.com/bigtable/docs/quickstart-cbt
- **gcloud**: https://cloud.google.com/sdk/gcloud/
- **bq**: https://cloud.google.com/bigquery/docs/bq-command-line-tool
- **Cloud Deployment Manager**: https://cloud.google.com/deployment-manager/docs/

Section 5: Ensuring Solution and Operations Reliability

In this section, we will focus on monitoring service operations.

This section contains the following chapter:

- Chapter 15, *Monitoring Your Infrastructure*

15
Monitoring Your Infrastructure

In this chapter, we will look at GCP monitoring. We will discuss what Stackdriver is and why you need it. We will explain all of the services that it offers. We will also go through some basic configurations that will give you a good understanding of how you can leverage it, in order to monitor both **virtual machines** (**VMs**) and applications.

The following topics will be covered in this chapter:

- Introduction to Stackdriver
- Configuring Stackdriver
- Monitoring Stackdriver
- Stackdriver Logging
- **Application Performance Management** (**APM**)

Exam tips: Monitoring is a massive topic and can feel somewhat overwhelming. Once you understand the three main functionalities of Stackdriver, which are monitoring, logging, and APM, we want you to focus on what you will be tested on in the exam:

- Make sure that you know which GCP service you can monitor with Stackdriver.
- Pay special attention to **Google Compute Engine (GCE)**, both in terms of performance and availability monitoring.
- Understand audit logs well, and make sure that you know how to track who made the changes to your project and the associated resources.
- Log in to the GCP console, and browse the activity and audit logs.
- Anticipate that you may be asked where to find particular types of logs! Finally, Qwiklabs will allow you to understand the service better, and we strongly recommend that you have a look at the available labs.

Technical requirements

In order to gain hands-on experience with Stackdriver, we recommend that you use Qwiklabs. The Stackdriver quest can be found here: `https://www.qwiklabs.com/quests/35?locale=en`.

You need to purchase credits in order to enroll for the quest.

Introduction to Stackdriver

We have already learned about a number of services, and now it is time to take a closer look at the monitoring options. Google comes with a GCP-integrated tool called Stackdriver. Stackdriver was founded in 2012 as an **Software as a Service (SaaS)** platform that would allow consistent monitoring across different cloud layers. In 2014, it was acquired by Google and made publicly available in 2016 as a GCP service.

Currently, Stackdriver can monitor both GCP and AWS. However, integration with the former is much more robust. Stackdriver is a suite of tools that provides the following services:

- Monitoring
- Logging
- Debugging
- Tracing
- Error reporting
- Profiling

Monitoring and logging are agentless, but, in order to obtain more informative metrics and logs, an agent should be installed. There are actually two types of agents that can be installed on your instances: a monitoring agent, based on the `collectd` software, and a logging agent, based on the `fluentd` software.

In the following diagram, you can see a schema, which highlights a GCE VM instance and the agents that are installed on top of it. The VM instance, by default, talks to logging and monitoring. The agents report to their respective services:

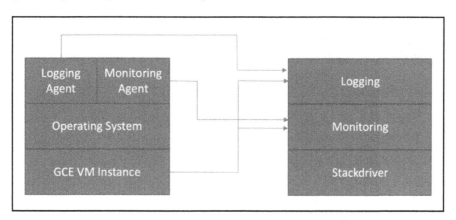

GCP is a developer-oriented platform, and it provides a lot of monitoring-related services that can be directly integrated with your application. Stackdriver allows you to monitor both the infrastructure and the applications. It is very important to understand that developers need to consider monitoring and logging from the very outset when designing applications. For each of the programming languages that are supported, there are libraries that facilitate log integration with Stackdriver. Make sure that you check the languages that are supported, so that you can take full advantage of them!

In this chapter, we will have a look at how Stackdriver is used to monitor GCP. Remember to read this chapter carefully and perform the recommended Qwiklabs, as this is a key exam topic.

As we now have a basic understanding of what Stackdriver is, let's have a look at the cost of each service.

Cost

With Stackdriver, you only pay for what you use. The cost can be controlled using Cloud Billing reports and alerts.

The following Stackdriver services can be used for free:

- Stackdriver Debugger
- Stackdriver Error Reporting
- Stackdriver Profiler

The following services may incur costs once monthly limits have been exceeded:

- Stackdriver Logging
- Stackdriver Monitoring
- Stackdriver Trace

We don't include the actual prices on purpose, given that they may change.

 Check the following link to learn about the most recent and detailed pricing list: https://cloud.google.com/stackdriver/pricing.

Configuring Stackdriver

Google Stackdriver is enabled on a project-by-project basis. Best practice says that, if you are going to use just one project, you should enable it for that project. If you have more than one project, you should have a separate project just for monitoring. From that project, you will be able to indicate which other projects you would like to monitor. Remember, you are not charged for additional projects, so this will not entail any additional costs.

Now, let's have a look at how to start working with Stackdriver:

1. To enable it, simply go to **Monitoring Service** in the left service pane. You will see the **Create your free Workspace** window, with the project you are currently logged into.
2. Click on **Create workspace** to continue, as shown in the following screenshot:

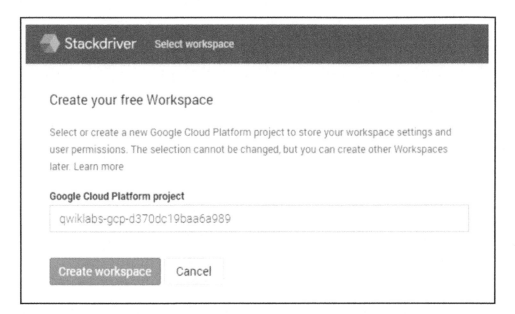

3. In the scenario of multiple projects, enable the monitoring for each project by ticking the checkboxes in front of them, as shown in the following screenshot:

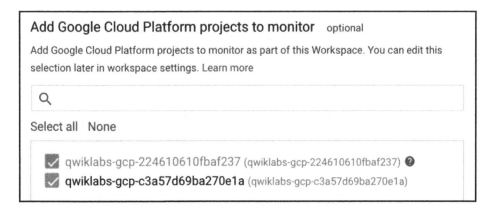

4. You can choose whether you want to monitor AWS resources. That will require the creation of an IAM role in AWS, with listed permissions. If you only work with GCP, then you can launch monitoring by clicking on **Skip AWS Setup**:

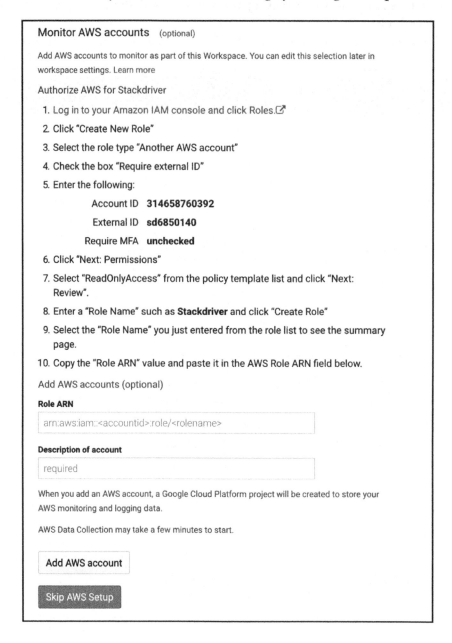

5. In the next window, click **Continue**. This will bring you to the main Stackdriver console. This is your starting point for any further configurations:

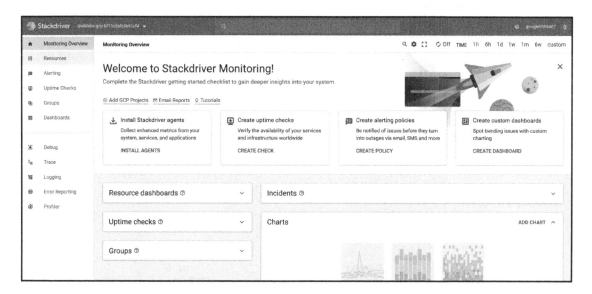

Now that we have configured Stackdriver, let's look at the monitoring service.

Stackdriver Monitoring

With the monitoring service, you can discover, and monitor, all GCP resources and services. The monitoring console allows you to view all of your resources, create alerting policies, and view uptime checks, groups, and custom dashboards. It also allows you to navigate to the debug, trace, logging, and error reporting consoles.

Let's have a look at what can be configured from here. We will look into the following topics:

- Groups
- Dashboards
- Alerting policies
- Change screen
- Uptime checks
- Monitoring agents

Groups

Resources such as VM instances, applications, and databases can be grouped into logical groups. This allows us to manage them together and display them in the dashboards. Constraints are used to define the criteria to filter the resources. They can be based on names, regions, applications, and more. The groups can be nested in one another, and the nesting can be six levels deep:

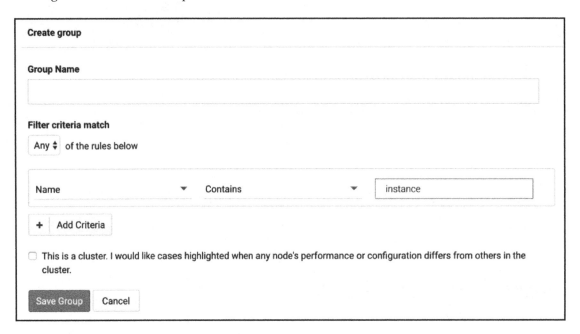

The preceding screenshot shows the screen for creating a new group. We can use multiple criteria in order to filter the resources that we want to be added to the group.

Dashboards

Dashboards allow us to give visibility to different metrics in a single pane of glass. We can create multiple dashboards that contain charts that are based on predefined or user-defined metrics. This allows us to create customized boards with the most important metrics. The charts visualize the metrics, allowing a good understanding of how your environment performs.

Note that, for instance, we can also see agent-based metrics on top of standard Stackdriver metrics, as shown in the following screenshot:

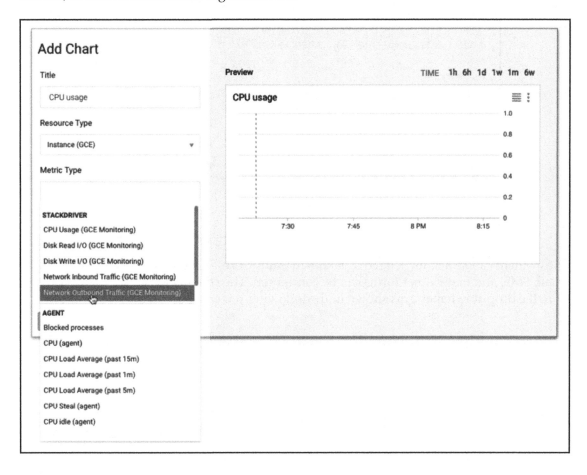

Alerting policies

Alerting policies can be configured in order to create notifications when event and metric thresholds are reached. The policies can have one or more conditions to trigger the alert, and will create an incident that is visible in the Stackdriver console.

The opened incident can be **Acknowledge**, **Resolve**, or **Comment**. The menu for these actions opens once you click on the three dots icon on the right-hand corner:

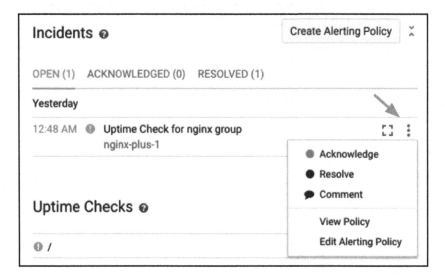

The incident can be acknowledged as a known issue, or resolved. In terms of notifications, email, SMS, and many other forms can be configured. The channel to be used can be chosen from the drop-down menu, as shown in the following screenshot:

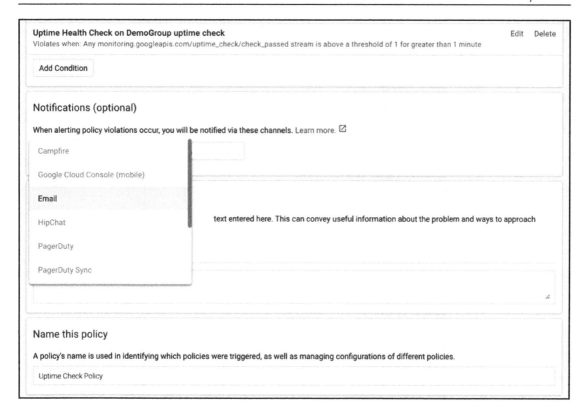

To further guide the operations to a possible solution, documentation links can also be attached to the alert.

Uptime checks

Uptime checks are used for checking the availability of your services from different locations around the globe. They can be combined with alerting policies and are displayed in the dashboards. Checks can be done using HTTP, HTTPS, or TCP, and are possible for URL, App Engine, **Elastic Load Balancer (ELB)**, AWS EC2, and GCE instances. The probing interval can be set to **1**, **5**, **10**, or **15 minutes**, as shown in the following screenshot:

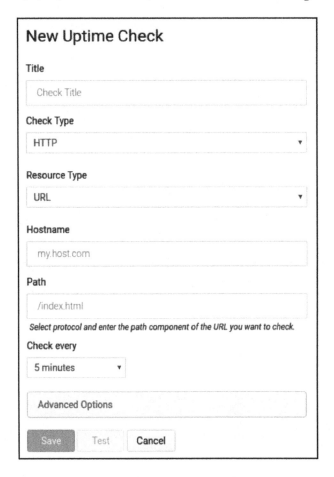

 Exam tip: Remember that, for the uptime check to work, the firewall rules need to be created. To check the IPs of the uptime servers, go to the uptime check console, and download the list of rules. For details on how to do it, check the documentation: `https://cloud.google.com/monitoring/uptime-checks/`.

Monitoring agents

To get more out of Stackdriver, a monitoring agent can be installed on the instance in order to collect additional metrics. By default, the monitoring agent collects disk, CPU, network, and process metrics; however, additional metrics can also be collected.

The Stackdriver monitoring agent is a collectd-based agent that can be installed both on GCP and AWS instances. The agent can be also configured to monitor many applications, including the Apache web server, Tomcat, Kafka, Memcached, and Redis.

The installation of the agent on Linux is very straightforward, and requires the following two commands to be executed:

```
curl -sSO https://dl.google.com/cloudagents/install-monitoring-agent.sh
sudo bash install-monitoring-agent.sh
```

To install the agent on a Windows machine, run the following command in PowerShell and then follow the instructions: https://cloud.google.com/monitoring/agent/install-agent#agent-install-windows.

Exam tip: To monitor the instance memory, you need to use the Stackdriver Monitoring agent!

Stackdriver Logging

Stackdriver Logging is the second most important service. It allows you to store and analyze logs, as well as events coming from GCP and AWS. Based on the logs, alerts can be created. It also provides a robust API, allowing logs to be both managed and injected. This means that any third-party application can leverage Stackdriver for logging purposes. The gathered logs are visible in the Logs Viewer, where they can be filtered and exported for further analysis or archival purposes, or integrated with third-party solutions. There are a number of types of logs, and some of them are not enabled by default. Log-based metrics use log entries, and can be leveraged to create dashboard charts and custom alerts. Now, let's take a closer look at how to use logging. We will be looking at the following topics:

- Logs Viewer
- Basic log filtering
- Advanced filtering
- Exporting logs

- Logging agent
- Log-based metrics
- Cloud audit logs
- Activity
- Retention

Logs Viewer

Logs Viewer is a console that allows you to view, filter, and export logs. Keep in mind that logs are associated with a single GCP project. To be able to view logs from other projects, you need to switch the view. An API can be used to get logs from multiple projects. The logs can be filtered, using either basic or advanced filtering, to pinpoint the exact event.

Basic log filtering

When you use basic filtering, there are a number of predefined filters available. The filters are placed above the log list, and each of them has a drop-down menu. The first filter allows you to choose the service for which the logs will be displayed, for example, the GCE VM instance. Note that the number of options depends on the resources that are provisioned in GCP:

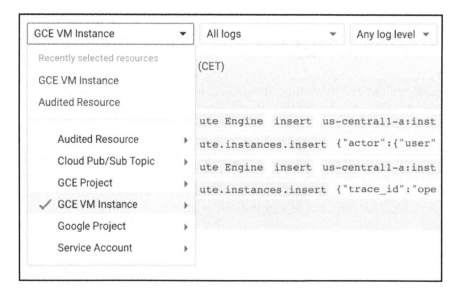

The second filter allows you to choose the type of logs to be displayed, as shown in the following screenshot:

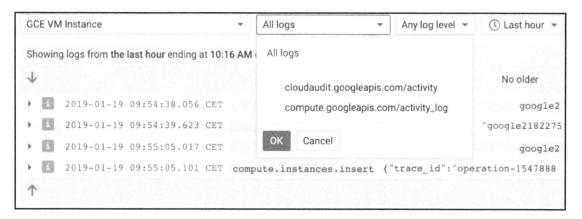

As shown previously, in the case of GCE, the following options are displayed:

- `compute.googleapis.com/activity_log`: This shows the activities that are related to the GCE API, for example, creating disk and updating metadata.
- `cloudaudit.googleapis.com/activity`: These are the cloud audit activity logs.

The third filter allows the level of severity to be chosen:

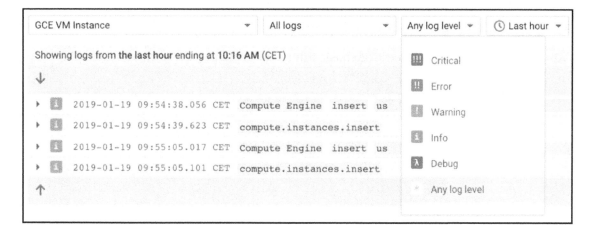

The fourth filter allows you to choose the time range:

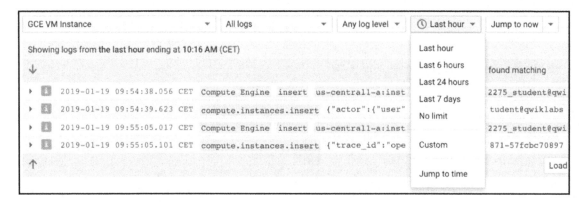

You can also choose from predefined time spans or a custom one.

Advanced filtering

An advanced logs filter is an expression that allows you to display logs based on the following constraints:

- Specific logs or log service entries
- Specific time period entries
- Conditions relating to metadata or user-defined field entries
- A specific percentage of all log entries

Advanced filters can be created from basic filters, or written by the user from scratch:

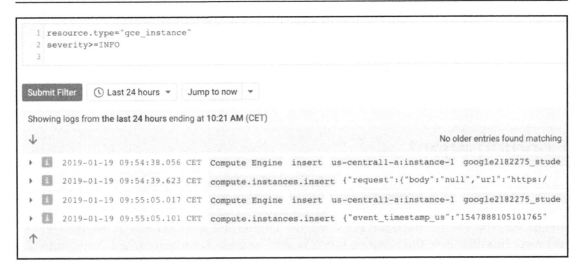

The preceding example shows logs with a resource type of the GCE instance and a severity of INFO and higher.

Exporting logs

Log entries that are received by logging can be exported (copied) to Cloud Storage buckets, BigQuery datasets, and Cloud Pub/Sub topics. You export logs by configuring log sinks, which then continue to export log entries as they arrive in logging. A sink includes a destination and a filter that selects the log entries to be exported. Remember, only the logs that were created after the sink configuration will be exported:

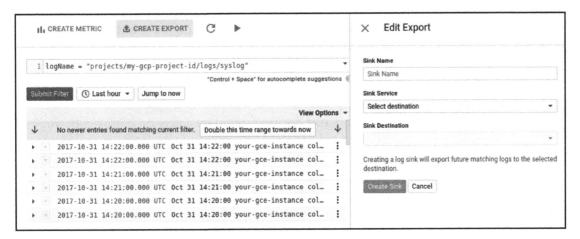

There are a couple of use cases for exporting the logs:

- BigQuery can be used for analytics and queries using the SQL language.
- Pubs/Subs export allows integration with third-party solutions.
- Cloud Storage export is the most cost-effective option for archiving the logs.

Logging agent

The logging agent is an application that is based on `fluentd`, and both Linux and Windows machines are supported. It allows the streaming of logs from common third-party applications and system software to Stackdriver Logging. The agent is included in the images for App Engine and GKE. For Compute Engine and Amazon EC2, it needs to be installed. Installation of the agent on Linux is very simple, and requires the following two commands to be executed:

```
curl -sSO https://dl.google.com/cloudagents/install-logging-agent.sh
sudo bash install-logging-agent.sh
```

By default, the agent streams logs for predefined applications. `google-fluentd.conf` can be modified to indicate additional logs that should be streamed.

Log-based metrics

Logs can be used to create log-based metrics. Stackdriver can accumulate logs that are defined by the filter every time a match appears. This data is then exposed to monitoring, and can be used further to create dashboards and alert policies.

As an example, logs containing a particular 404 error message can be counted during a period of 1 minute and exposed as a metric.

The log-based metric can either be system metrics or user-defined:

- **System Metrics**: These are predefined by Stackdriver Logging.
- **User-defined Metrics**: These metrics are created by a user on a project-by-project basis, based on the filtering criteria.

In the following screenshot, we can see an example of system and user-defined metrics:

Cloud audit logs

To understand better *who did what, where,* and *when*?, Cloud Audit Logs can be used. The logs are stored per project, folder, or organization, and are of the following types:

- Administrator activity
- System event
- Data access

The first two are enabled by default, and cannot be deactivated. The third one is disabled by default, as it can generate a massive amount of information. Audit logs are generated for most of the GCP services. To get the full list of services, refer to the following documentation: `https://cloud.google.com/logging/docs/audit/`.

The logs can be accessed from Log Viewer, just like any other log, but specific permissions are required to view them. The following are short descriptions of each type of audit log that we mentioned previously:

- **Administrator activity**: This contains information about actions on modifying resources' metadata or configuration. These may include, for example, the creation of a VM instance or changes to the permissions. To view the logs, Logging/Logs Viewer or Project/Viewer roles are required. To see only those logs under basic filtering, choose the `activity` log type.
- **System event**: This contains information on system events for Computer Engine. This may be, for example, the live migration of a VM instance. To view the logs, Logging/Logs Viewer or Project/Viewer roles are required. To see only those logs under basic filtering, choose the `system_events` log type.
- **Data access**: This contains information on the creation, modification, or reading of user-provided data. To view the logs, Logging/Private Logs Viewer or Project/Owner roles are required. To see only those logs under basic filtering, choose the `data_access` log type.

In the following screenshot, you can see an example of filtering for the administrator activity logs:

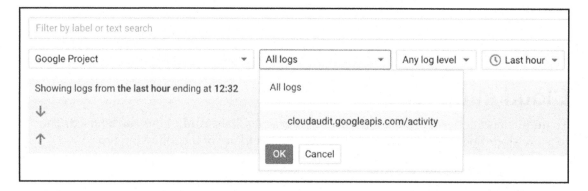

While there is no charge for administrator activity and system event logs, data access logs can incur additional charges when enabled. BigQuery has its own data access logs that are handled separately and cannot be disabled.

ACTIVITY

The audit logs can be also viewed from the **ACTIVITY** tab in the main GCP console screen, which is outside the Stackdriver console. From the main GCP console screen, click on **ACTIVITY** in the top-left corner, and this will bring you to the log list, as shown in the following screenshot:

DASHBOARD	ACTIVITY	
Today		
10:33 AM	Completed: Create network	google2182275_student@qwiklabs.net created
10:33 AM	Create network	google2182275_student@qwiklabs.net created
10:19 AM	Create dataset	google2182275_student@qwiklabs.net created
10:09 AM	Create Stackdriver alerting policy	google2182275_student@qwiklabs.net created
10:04 AM	Delete Stackdriver uptime check configuration	google2182275_student@qwiklabs.net deleted
10:03 AM	Create Stackdriver uptime check configuration	google2182275_student@qwiklabs.net created
10:03 AM	Create Stackdriver uptime check configuration	google2182275_student@qwiklabs.net created
10:01 AM	Create group	google2182275_student@qwiklabs.net created
9:55 AM	Completed: google.api.servicemanagement.v1.ServiceManager.Activate...	sd-provisioning-enabler@system
9:55 AM	google.api.servicemanagement.v1.ServiceManager.Activate...	sd-provisioning-enabler@system.gserviceaccount
9:55 AM	Completed: Create VM	google2182275_student@qwiklabs.net created
9:54 AM	Create VM	google2182275_student@qwiklabs.net created
9:49 AM	Update project	936076353769-dcb7hgk8cpl26aetfq99c7min7o6qfr
9:49 AM	Set IAM policy on project	936076353769-dcb7hgk8cpl26aetfq99c7min7o6qfr
9:49 AM	Completed: Set metadata on project	936076353769-dcb7hgk8cpl26aetfq99c7min7o6qfr
9:49 AM	Update project	936076353769-dcb7hgk8cpl26aetfq99c7min7o6qfr
9:49 AM	Set metadata on project	936076353769-dcb7hgk8cpl26aetfq99c7min7o6qfr

The logs are abbreviated, and can be filtered by categories, resources, and time periods. By selecting the entries, you can see further details. To narrow down the list of logs, you can use predefined filters, which you will find in the bottom-right corner. Select the filter and press **OK** to apply, as shown in the following screenshot:

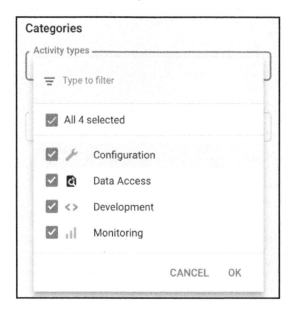

Retention

Retention defines how long the logs are stored in Stackdriver. After the stipulated period, the logs are removed. Depending on the log types, the retention time differs. Refer to the following list of log types and their retention periods:

- **Administrator activity**: 400 days
- **Data access**: 30 days
- **System event**: 400 days

Note that the logs can be exported and archived for longer periods. We have explained how to export logs in the *Exporting logs* section of this chapter.

APM

APM is a set of tools that developers use to give them some insight into how fast and how reliably they can run an application. It consists of three services:

- Trace
- Debugger
- Profiler

These tools are integrated into the code of the application. The application does not need to be hosted on GCP, but can run in any cloud or even on-premises, as long as connectivity is available. APM originates from Google's **Site Reliability Engineering (SRE)** team toolset. So, it is high time that we got into the shoes of SRE!

Trace

Stackdriver Trace allows you to track latencies in your microservices application. It shows you the overall time of the application responses, but can also show detailed delays for each of the microservices. This allows you to pinpoint the root cause of the latency.

The traces are displayed in the GCP console, and analysis reports can be generated. By default, it is installed on GAE standard, but it can be used with GCE, GKE, GAE flexible, and non-GCP machines. The tracing mechanism needs to be incorporated using the Stackdriver Trace SDK or API.

Debugger

This allows you to debug errors in the code of your application, without stopping the application. Developers can request a real-time snapshot of a running application, capturing the call stack and local variables. Debug logpoints can be injected into the code to display additional information. These can even be done in production, without affecting the end users.

By default, it is installed on GAE Standard, but it can be used with GCE, GKE, GAE Flexible, and non-GCP machines. It does not require a logging agent.

Profiler

Stackdriver Profiler shows you how many resources your code consumes. With the changes in the code in your application, there may be an unexpected rise in the demand for resources. Profiler allows you to pinpoint those issues, even in production. It uses a piece of code, called the **profiler agent** that is attached to the main code of your application, and it periodically sends information on resource usage. It currently supports Java, Go, and Node.js, and can be used with GCE, GKE, GAE Flexible, and non-GCP machines. The following screenshot presents an example Stackdriver Profiler with the CPU profile:

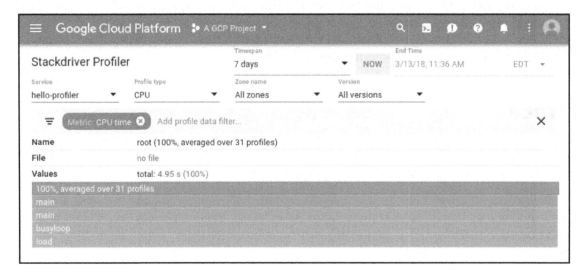

Source: https://cloud.google.com/profiler/docs/quickstart
License: https://creativecommons.org/licenses/by/4.0/legalcode

Error Reporting

Stackdriver Error Reporting allows you to collect and aggregate errors that are produced by your applications in a single place. The collected errors can be grouped and displayed in a centralized interface. This way, you can see how many crashes have occurred over a specific time period.

The service works in a very similar way to Stackdriver Logging, but it allows you to filter only the most important errors, and pinpoint the root cause of the crash. Error Reporting works with Google Functions, App Engine, GCE, GKE, and AWS EC2. It is, by default, enabled for the App Engine Standard environment. Multiple languages, such as Go, Java, .NET, Node.js, PHP, Python, and Ruby are supported. There are two ways to leverage error reporting:

- You can use the Stackdriver Logging API and send properly formatted error messages.
- You can call the dedicated Error Reporting API.

Information in Stackdriver Error Reporting is retained for 30 days.

Summary

In this chapter, we learned about Stackdriver and how to monitor GCP services, resources, and applications. There are three main functionalities:

- Monitoring
- Logging
- APM

To enhance monitoring and logging capabilities, install agents on the instances. Monitoring allows predefined metrics to be monitored. Logging allows you to create log-based metrics. Alert policies can be created on conditions, and they can send notifications to endpoints of your choosing. Tracing facilitates an understanding of the latency of your application components, including microservices and load balancers. Debugging allows you to look at a snapshot of the code that is causing an error, without stopping the application. Profiler shows how many resources are used by different components of the application. Finally, Error Reporting aggregates error logs of the application, and displays them on timescale charts.

In the exam, some questions may refer you to several case studies, with which you should be familiar, before you take the exam. These case studies explain fictitious business and solution concepts. In the next chapter, we will cover how to find these case studies, and we will look at an example case study and analyze it, in order to design an appropriate solution.

Further reading

If you want to learn more about Stackdriver, use the official Google documentation:

- **Stackdriver docs**: `https://cloud.google.com/stackdriver/docs/`
- **Monitoring agent**: `https://cloud.google.com/monitoring/agent/`
- **Logging agent**: `https://cloud.google.com/logging/docs/agent/`
- **Debugger**: `https://cloud.google.com/debugger/docs/setup/python`
- **Profiler**: `https://cloud.google.com/profiler/docs/about-profiler`
- **Error reporting**: `https://cloud.google.com/error-reporting/docs/setup/compute-engine`

Section 6: Exam Focus 6

This section will focus on an example case study and mock questions. This will help you to understand the exam in a more practical manner.

This section contains the following chapters:

- Chapter 16, *Case Studies*
- Chapter 17, *Test Your Knowledge*

16
Case Studies

As mentioned way back in `Chapter 1`, *GCP Cloud Architect Professional*, the Google Professional Architect exam involves referring to a certain set of case studies. Around 30% of the exam questions will relate to one or more of these case studies. Although you have access to these case studies before you sit the exam, you will not know which case studies will appear in the exam. However, you will have access to them in the exam, so there is no need to memorize each one! Think of it as Google being nice to us and giving us extra preparation material. During the exam, when you are asked a question about case study, you will have a split screen and will be able to view the case study and question simultaneously.

We will cover the following topics in the chapter:

- Exam case studies
- What are they looking for in the case studies?
- Example case study: TerramEarth, Dress4Win

Understanding how to approach exam case studies

The questions will clearly state the case study to which you need to refer. At the time of writing, in September 2019, there are three case studies available from the exam guide web page:

- **Mountkirk Games**:
  `https://cloud.google.com/certification/guides/cloud-architect/casestudy-mountkirkgames-rev2`
- **Dress4Win**: `https://cloud.google.com/certification/guides/cloud-architect/casestudy-dress4win-rev2`
- **TerramEarth**: `https://cloud.google.com/certification/guides/cloud-architect/casestudy-terramearth-rev2`

It is important to read over these case studies prior to the exam. In fact, you should make this a part of your study plan. Each case study refers to a business that needs to integrate with **Google Cloud Platform** (**GCP**). You will find a business overview and a solution concept, and it is your job to map these concepts and requirements into GCP services.

The main objective when looking through these case studies is to try to allocate keywords that you can map to GCP services. However, there is also a lot of information that is there simply to fill out the case study. It is important to separate what information is not needed and what is important. For example, if there is a requirement to build a reliable and reproducible environment, it might be wise to start thinking along the lines of Cloud Deployment Manager, which offers you a repeatable deployment process. Likewise, if the technical requirements suggest the company wants to be able to scale up or down based on demand, then we might be inclined to think of autoscalers, load balancers, and managed instance groups. Understanding the use case of each service is key to the case studies. The good thing is we get to review the case studies up front!

In this chapter, we will look at one of the aforementioned case studies in detail to try and show exactly what they are looking for from you in the exam and how you should look to process the information you receive and try to map it to relevant GCP services.

 While you are reading the case study, it is recommended to also refer to the GCP solutions page: https://cloud.google.com/solutions. These solutions give good examples of how use cases can be mapped to reference architecture.

What are they looking for in the case studies?

Let's look closely at one of the case studies presented by Google Cloud. We have selected Mountkirk Games. On the initial first pass of reading this case study, we can see that it's broken down into five distinct sections, so let's look at each in more detail:

- Company overview
- Solution concept
- Business requirements
- Technical requirements
- Executive statement

The case studies' text is referenced by the excerpts of each section. As a reminder, the full document can be viewed in the URLs mentioned at the start of this chapter.

Company overview

We will now look at the company overview:

> *Mountkirk Games makes online, session-based, multiplayer games for mobile platforms. They build all of their games using some server-side integration. Historically, they have used cloud providers to lease physical servers.*
>
> *Due to the unexpected popularity of some of their games, they have had problems scaling their global audience, application servers, MySQL databases, and analytics tools. Their current model is to write game statistics to files and send them through an ETL tool that loads them into a centralized MySQL database for reporting.*
>
> *Source:* https://cloud.google.com/certification/guides/cloud-architect/ca sestudy-mountkirkgames-rev2
> *License:* https://creativecommons.org/licenses/by/4.0/legalcode

So, what information can be taken from here that will help us form a solution architecture? Well, some things should be screaming out to you by now!

The first paragraph informs us that the core business is online games for mobile platforms. Immediately, we should be aware that mobile games platforms generate a large amount of real-time data and have a large number of devices connecting to them, all of which will come from different types of connections (Wi-Fi, 3G-5G, and so on). This is a pretty unique industry.

The second paragraph starts to identify some potential GCP services:

- Issues with scaling = instance groups
- Global audience = global load balancing
- MySQL databases = Cloud SQL, Cloud Spanner
- Analytics = Bigtable

The final paragraph of the company overview also gives away some key information. What do we think of when we see ETL? Dataflow? Yep! You got it! Additionally, it seems they are actually using MySQL to store analytical information. This doesn't seem efficient, and we have many better GCP offerings to provide this service.

Solution concept

We will now look at the solution concept:

> *Mountkirk Games is building a new game, which they expect to be very popular. They plan to deploy the game's backend on Google Compute Engine so they can capture streaming metrics, run intensive analytics, take advantage of its autoscaling server environment, and integrate with a managed NoSQL database.*
>
> *Source:* https://cloud.google.com/certification/guides/cloud-architect/ca sestudy-mountkirkgames-rev2
> *License:* https://creativecommons.org/licenses/by/4.0/legalcode

The solution concept only offers us a few lines of information, yet still provides us with key information. They are telling us that they are building a new game in a new way. If we refer to the company overview, they are used to dealing with third parties, but it seems that has been based on private clouds. They are now looking for a public cloud-first approach and have selected GCE. Again, we can map more services to keywords:

- Streaming/Dataflow
- Analytics/BigQuery
- Autoscaling/Managed Instance Groups
- NoSQL/Datastore

Business requirements

We will now look at the business requirements:

- *Increase to a global footprint*
- *Improve uptime - downtime is loss of players*
- *Increase the efficiency of the cloud resources we use*
- *Reduce latency to all customers*

> *Source:* https://cloud.google.com/certification/guides/cloud-architect/ca sestudy-mountkirkgames-rev2
> *License:* https://creativecommons.org/licenses/by/4.0/legalcode

The business requirements consist of only a few bullet points, but we can still uncover some information. We can see here that the company has requirements for availability and wants to be able to offer lower latency to customers. This might get us thinking of multi-region deployments, which provide higher availability than zonal resources, and a Cloud Content Delivery Network to accelerate access to websites and applications.

Technical requirements

We now have a number of technical requirements, which have been split into backend and game analytics platforms as follows:

Requirements for the game's backend platform:

- *Dynamically scale up or down based on game activity.*
- *Connect to a transactional database service to manage user profiles and game state.*
- *Store game activity in a time-series database service for future analysis.*
- *As the system scales, ensure that data is not lost due to processing backlogs.*
- *Run a hardened Linux distribution.*

Requirements for the game analytics platform:

- *Dynamically scale up or down based on game activity.*
- *Process incoming data on the fly directly from the game servers.*
- *Process data that arrives late because of slow mobile networks.*
- *Allow queries to access at least 10 TB of historical data.*
- *Process files that are regularly uploaded by users' mobile devices.*

Source: `https://cloud.google.com/certification/guides/cloud-architect/ca sestudy-mountkirkgames-rev2`
License: `https://creativecommons.org/licenses/by/4.0/legalcode`

What kind of services spring to mind when you read these requirements? There are some keywords or phrases on almost every line: scale up and down, transactional database, time-series database, analytics, data arriving late. We should map these to GCP services. For example, if we see analytics, we may think of BigQuery straight away.

You should also pay attention to specific sizes that are mentioned, as these can help rule out services. For example, we can see there is a requirement for at least 10 TB of data, insinuating we need a greater capacity. Cloud SQL has a limitation of 10,230 GB, so we need an alternative. Additionally, we need to accommodate a hardened Linux distribution. Does this mean we cannot use App Engine?

Executive summary

The final section of our case study is the executive summary:

> *Our last successful game did not scale well with our previous cloud provider, resulting in lower user adoption and affecting the game's reputation. Our investors want more key performance indicators (KPIs) to evaluate the speed and stability of the game, as well as other metrics that provide deeper insight into usage patterns so that we can adapt the game to target users. Additionally, our current technology stack cannot provide the scale we need, so we want to replace MySQL and move to an environment that provides autoscaling, low latency load balancing, and frees us up from managing physical servers.*
>
> *Source:* https://cloud.google.com/certification/guides/cloud-architect/ca sestudy-mountkirkgames-rev2
> *License:* https://creativecommons.org/licenses/by/4.0/legalcode

There is a clear message that scaling is the primary concern for the executives and this sums up a lot of what we have taken from the previous sections. How many times did we read words such as dynamic? They want to migrate to a managed service to remove the need to manage traditional infrastructure and to also provide low latency and load balancing to improve performance. We should, hopefully, be able to think of a high-level solution based on these requirements. Dataflow is a low-latency, serverless processing service. Could this be used as part of our solution?

Forming a solution

After the first pass, we have managed to extract a number of keywords and map them to specific GCP services. The next step is to try and form a solution out of this. How do these services link to each other to make a usable design that will relate to the requirements set out by the company? The exam will not ask you to make an end-to-end solution—it will ask you which services are more appropriate to meet the needs of the specific question, but having an idea of how to do this will also stand you in good stead as a GCP cloud architect.

The analytics platform

One of the key takeaways from the case study is that we will be dealing with mobile data streaming in at a high rate, and also some batch data. Let's take a quick look at the Google Solutions web page for guidance. If we look at the mobile guide at `https://cloud.google.com/solutions/mobile/mobile-gaming-analysis-telemetry`, we can see that there is actually a reference architecture for building a mobile gaming analytics platform. Let's focus on how we can handle real-time events from mobile devices. If we look at the following diagram, we can see that it mirrors our requirements:

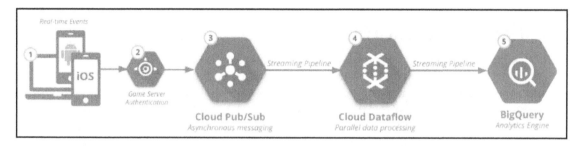

We can see the use of Cloud Pub/Sub helps us process data on the fly with its event-driven design. This is an ideal service to ingest real-time event streams and would be consumable by multiple destinations. Pub/Sub also acts as a queue to fetch new messages and push them on to the next service in the pipeline. This is performed instantly as the messages arrive.

We also have to accommodate batch data. Again, this reference architecture shows us exactly how to accomplish this. Mobile devices can upload their data to Cloud Storage, which is a cost-effective way to store object data:

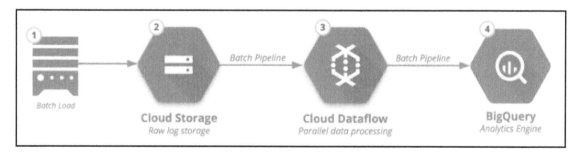

The next step in this process is Cloud Dataflow, which is acting as our data processing service. We can create separate pipeline jobs to process both real-time and batch data to ensure the data is well formed and matches the BigQuery schema. Dataflow has a time windowing trigger that allows it to process events based on the actual time they occur, as opposed to when they were sent or received.

Finally, BigQuery helps us with our analytics requirements and the reporting of large data and can query up to 10 TB of data. BigQuery is a managed service, and it can provide rapid scaling, both of which are demanded by the executive summary.

The backend platform

Our backend requirements are pretty clear. We need to provide autoscaling and store the game state. Due to security requirements, we have to run a hardened Linux image. We should note that, by hardened image, we mean an image that has been customized to limit potential vulnerabilities. The solution concept has already told us they plan to use Compute Engine instances for the backend, so the obvious choice to meet our scaling needs is to use instance groups. Additionally, this gives us the option to use a custom image to meet our security requirements. The following diagram shows a high-level diagram of this solution:

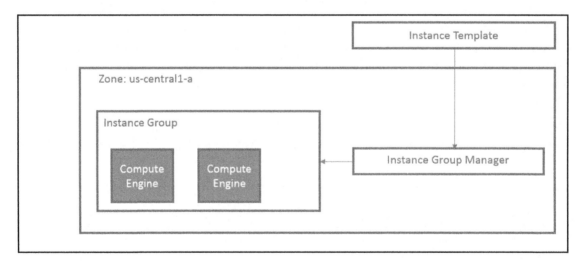

Autoscaling should be based on game activity. Managed Instance Groups offer autoscaling capabilities and will add or delete instances from a group based on load or, alternatively, we can scale based on custom metrics from Stackdriver.

Let's look at the requirements for our storage and find a service that fits best. One of the key requirements is to preserve the game state. Cloud Datastore is an excellent choice for this.

We can then pass the data on to Dataflow once again and connect to the same pipeline of services that we have for the analytics platform. Using Cloud Dataflow and BigQuery will again allow us to meet the technical requirements of this environment, such as using a time-series database, scalability, and processing backlogs.

Summary of Mountkirk

So, after mapping these services, we can be confident in the exam that we understand the business needs and how to use the appropriate services. You should, however, also be mindful not to expect a simple link between what we see in the case study and what the question is. It will not always be as simple as, for example, which storage service best fits the requirements? Some questions may be a reference to the case study but could add additional requirements that are not seen in the case study, for example, what IAM policy could Mountkirk use to isolate development and production? We have nothing in the case study relating to development, production, or IAM, but we should still expect to see questions like these.

Additional case studies

We would also like to look at the other two case studies available at the time of writing. We hope you now have a clear view of how to break down these case studies and understand that the key is to locate keywords that help us map to GCP services. We will not go into so much depth for the other two cases, but we hope you will begin to see links yourself and start to form the start of a solution as you read through the case studies.

TerramEarth

We will now look at the TerramEarth case study. Again, we will review what can be gleaned from the online documentation. At the end of the case study, we will provide an analysis. We would like you to write down the services that jump out to you as you are reading and compare your findings to our analysis:

Company overview:

TerramEarth manufactures heavy equipment for the mining and agricultural industries. About 80% of their business is from mining and 20% is from agriculture. They currently have over 500 dealers and service centers in 100 countries. Their mission is to build products that make their customers more productive.

Solution concept:

There are 20 million TerramEarth vehicles in operation, which collect 120 fields of data per second. Data is stored locally on the vehicle and can be accessed for analysis when a vehicle is serviced. The data is downloaded via a maintenance port. This same port can be used to adjust operational parameters, allowing the vehicles to be upgraded in the field with new computing modules.

Approximately 200,000 vehicles are connected to a cellular network, allowing TerramEarth to collect data directly. At a rate of 120 fields of data per second, with 22 hours of operation per day, TerramEarth collects a total of about 9 TB/day from these connected vehicles.

Existing technical environment:

TerramEarth's existing architecture is composed of Linux and Windows-based systems that reside in a single U.S. West Coast-based data center. These systems gzip CSV files from the field, upload via FTP, and place the data in their data warehouse. Because this process takes time, aggregated reports are based on data that is 3 weeks old.

With this data, TerramEarth has been able to preemptively stock replacement parts and reduce unplanned downtime of their vehicles by 60%. However, because the data is stale, some customers are without their vehicles for up to 4 weeks while they wait for replacement parts.

Business requirements:

- *Decrease unplanned vehicle downtime to less than 1 week.*
- *Support the dealer network with more data on how their customers use their equipment to better position new products and services.*
- *Have the ability to partner with different companies—especially with seed and fertilizer suppliers in the fast-growing agricultural business—to create compelling joint offerings for their customers.*

Technical requirements:

- *Expand beyond a single datacenter to decrease latency to the American Midwest and East Coast.*
- *Create a backup strategy.*
- *Improve the security of data transfer from equipment to the data center.*
- *Improve the data in the data warehouse.*
- *Use customer and equipment data to anticipate customer needs.*

Application 1: Data ingest

A custom Python application reads uploaded data files from a single server and writes to the data warehouse.

Compute:

- *Windows Server 2008 R2*
  - *16 CPUs*
  - *128 GB of RAM*
  - *10 TB local HDD storage*

Application 2: Reporting

An off-the-shelf application that business analysts use to run a daily report to see what equipment needs repair. Only 2 analysts of a team of 10 (5 West Coast, 5 East Coast) can connect to the reporting application at a time.

Compute:

- *Off-the-shelf application. License tied to a number of physical CPUs:*
  - *Windows Server 2008 R2*
  - *16 CPUs*
  - *32 GB of RAM*
  - *500 GB HDD*

Data warehouse:

- *A single PostgreSQL server:*
  - *RedHat Linux*
  - *64 CPUs*
  - *128 GB of RAM*
  - *4x 6 TB HDD in RAID*

Executive statement:

Our competitive advantage has always been in our manufacturing process, with our ability to build better vehicles at a lower cost than our competitors. However, new products with different approaches are constantly being developed, and I'm concerned that we lack the skills to undergo the next wave of transformations in our industry. My goals are to build our skills while addressing immediate market needs through incremental innovations.

Source: https://cloud.google.com/certification/guides/cloud-architect/casestudy-mountkirkgames-rev2
License: https://creativecommons.org/licenses/by/4.0/legalcode

Analysis

Again, there's a lot of information to take in here. But let's focus on getting the keywords and try to form a picture in our head about which services would be used.

Let's try to summarize what this is actually telling us. There are company vehicles distributed globally and the company collects valuable data locally. However, some models seem newer than others, and we can see that 200,000 vehicles are connected to a mobile network. This is IoT. We know we can use Cloud IoT Core to connect devices and stream data into Cloud Pub/Sub, and Pub/Sub can also handle delayed data. We will need something like Dataflow to process this data.

We can also deduce that the current setup is costing the company money due to the downtime of their vehicles, so we need to start to think about how GCP can benefit them. What cloud service could replace the FTP server? We could use streaming transport for those that are connected. Looking at the solution concept, we can see that we need to handle storage in the region of 9 TB/day. What kind of GCP storage offerings could help us here? Maybe we should be looking at Cloud Storage, as this offers PB storage and acts as a filesystem. We should also think about the means of transfer to reduce latency and look at multi-region buckets, because this is a global company that is looking to expand beyond a single data center. Cloud Storage could be an option to allow us to use gsutil to securely transfer from a machine to the cloud.

What other things jump out at you? Perhaps you'll now look at the technical requirements and notice that a Python application is used. Which GCP service could we use? If you are thinking about App Engine, then you are correct!

Finally, let's look at the executive summary. It's clear to see there is a requirement for managed services due to skill shortages. We have already met these requirements in our conceptual design by mapping the services.

Dress4Win

We will now look at the Dress4Win case study. Again, we will review what can be found from the online documentation. At the end of the case study, we will provide an analysis. We would like you to write down the services that jump out to you as you are reading and compare your findings to our analysis.

Company overview:

Dress4Win is a web-based company that helps their users organize and manage their personal wardrobe using a web app and mobile application. The company also cultivates an active social network that connects their users with designers and retailers. They monetize their services through advertising, e-commerce, referrals, and a freemium app model. The application has grown from a few servers in the founder's garage to several hundred servers and appliances in a colocated data center. However, the capacity of their infrastructure is now insufficient for the application's rapid growth. Because of this growth and the company's desire to innovate faster, Dress4Win is committing to a full migration to a public cloud.

Solution concept:

For the first phase of their migration to the cloud, Dress4Win is moving their development and test environments. They are also building a disaster recovery site because their current infrastructure is at a single location. They are not sure which components of their architecture they can migrate as is and which components they need to change before migrating them.

Existing technical environment:

The Dress4Win application is served out of a single data center location. All servers run Ubuntu LTS v16.04.

Databases:

- MySQL. 1 server for user data, inventory, and static data:
  - MySQL 5.7
  - 8 core CPUs
  - 128 GB of RAM
  - 2 x 5 TB HDD (RAID 1)
- Redis 3 server cluster for metadata, social graph, and caching. Each server is as follows:
  - Redis 3.2
  - 4 core CPUs
  - 32 GB of RAM

Compute:

- *40 web application servers providing microservices-based APIs and static content:*
  - *Tomcat - Java*
  - *NGINX*
  - *4 core CPUs*
  - *32 GB of RAM*
- *20 Apache Hadoop/Spark servers:*
  - *Data analysis*
  - *Real-time trending calculations*
  - *8 core CPUs*
  - *128 GB of RAM*
  - *4x 5 TB HDD (RAID 1)*
- *Three RabbitMQ servers for messaging, social notifications, and events:*
  - *8 core CPUs*
  - *32 GB of RAM*
- *Miscellaneous servers:*
  - *Jenkins, monitoring, bastion hosts, and security scanners*
  - *8 core CPUs*
  - *32 GB of RAM*

Storage appliances:

- *iSCSI for VM hosts*
- *Fiber channel SAN - MySQL databases:*
  - *1 PB total storage; 400 TB available*
- *NAS - image storage, logs, and backups:*
  - *100 TB total storage; 35 TB available*

Business requirements:

- *Build a reliable and reproducible environment with scaled parity of production.*
- *Improve security by defining and adhering to a set of security and Identity and Access Management (IAM) best practices for the cloud.*
- *Improve business agility and speed of innovation through the rapid provisioning of new resources.*
- *Analyze and optimize the architecture for performance in the cloud.*

Technical requirements:

- *Easily create non-production environments in the cloud.*
- *Implement an automation framework for provisioning resources in the cloud.*
- *Implement a continuous deployment process for deploying applications to the on-premises datacenter or the cloud.*
- *Support failover of the production environment to the cloud during an emergency.*
- *Encrypt data on the wire and at rest.*
- *Support multiple private connections between the production data center and cloud environment.*

Executive statement:

Our investors are concerned about our ability to scale and contain costs with our current infrastructure. They are also concerned that a competitor could use a public cloud platform to offset their upfront investment and free them up to focus on developing better features. Our traffic patterns are highest in the mornings and weekend evenings; during other times, 80% of our capacity is sitting idle.

Our capital expenditure is now exceeding our quarterly projections. Migrating to the cloud will likely cause an initial increase in spending, but we expect to fully transition before our next hardware refresh cycle. Our total cost of ownership (TCO) analysis over the next 5 years for a public cloud strategy achieves a cost reduction between 30% and 50% over our current model.

Source: https://cloud.google.com/certification/guides/cloud-architect/casestudy-mountkirkgames-rev2

License: https://creativecommons.org/licenses/by/4.0/legalcode

Analysis

The first thing you should notice in the requirements is that this is the only case study to mention different environments, such as testing and development environments. These are also the environments they wish to move first, as well as introducing DR. So, this is a gradual approach to cloud adoption. Availability and DR are easily accomplished in the cloud, but we should be aware of the services that offer this natively, for example, multi-regional storage buckets.

So, we know we have to keep these separated based on the business requirements, but how? Well, we want to have different projects for these environments, so we can begin to think back to `Chapter 13`, *Security and Compliance*, to allow the separation of duties. It's also clear that Dress4Win wants these environments to be repeatable automated deployments. Can you think of any GCP services that are aligned to this? Yep, exactly! Cloud Deployment Manager.

One of the other elements that jumps out is that the company are unsure what they can move to the cloud as is. Well, this is an easy win, and we can actually map a number of services. For example, MySQL will map to Cloud SQL or a number of miscellaneous servers, which could map directly to GCE. They have a Hadoop cluster, which can map to Dataproc, and they have a RabbitMQ messaging service, which can map to Pub/Sub.

For the rest of this case study, we would like you to take what you have learned from previous case studies and try to map more services. What about the security that is mentioned? Which GCP services allow encryption in transit and rest? What would allow the data center to connect to the GCP cloud over multiple connections?

We would be interested to hear your designs!

Summary

So, now you have an overview of what to expect in exams for the case studies. In this chapter, we broke down the Mountkirk case study section by section and identified the keywords that we can map to services. For the remaining case studies, we hope you have been able to go through each one in its entirety and also extract the keywords.

 Exam tip: Remember: there is no need to provide an end-to-end solution design to be successful in this exam, but understanding the use cases of each GCP service is a key objective.

Further reading

- **Solutions**: https://cloud.google.com/solutions/
- **More solutions**: http://gcp.solutions/
- **SRE**: https://landing.google.com/sre/books/

17
Test Your Knowledge

It is high time to test your knowledge on what you have learned. Here are two mock exams to help you. Good luck!

Mock test 1

1. Company X needs to keep their data available for auditing purposes for 5 years. Which storage option should they choose?

    (A) Google Cloud Bigtable
    (B) Google Cloud Multi-Regional Storage
    (C) Google Cloud Coldline Storage
    (D) Google Cloud Nearline Storage
    (E) Google Cloud BigQuery

2. Company X wants to choose a proper storage system for IoT sensor data. There are 2,000 sensors that send temperature data every second. Company X would like to perform further analysis of the accumulated data. Please select the most appropriate choice:

    (A) Google Cloud Bigtable
    (B) Google Cloud Datastore
    (C) Google Cloud Spanner
    (D) Google Cloud SQL

3. You have deployed a virtual machine instance to GCP in project X. Specific configuration and software has been installed on this instance. In order to share this image with other teams that only have access to project Z, what would you advise?

    (A) Create a snapshot. Use the snapshot to create a custom image. Share the image with the other projects.
    (B) Create a snapshot and store it on Google Storage.
    (C) Use a third-party tool to perform a file-level backup of the instance. Copy the image to Google Storage. Import the image to project Z.
    (D) Use Google Transfer Services.

4. Company X is looking to analyze data. They are using a hybrid cloud mixture of on-premises and GCP infrastructure and need to analyze both stream and batch data. Select the appropriate GCP service that will allow them to achieve this requirement:

    (A) Google Cloud Dataproc
    (B) Google Cloud BigQuery
    (C) Google Cloud Compute Engine and Airflow
    (D) Google Cloud Dataflow

5. Company X is using Hadoop to analyze data. They are using a hybrid cloud mixture of on-premises and GCP infrastructure. They want to move the data analysis to GCP, but they want to migrate it with minimal effort. Which service should they use?

    (A) Google Cloud Dataproc
    (B) Google Cloud Dataflow
    (C) Google Cloud Composer
    (D) Google Compute Engine

6. Customer X is storing data on Google Datastore. They are using a hybrid cloud mixture of on-premises and GCP infrastructure. Applications on both platforms are needed to access Datastore. Which solution should be used to enable access?

    (A) Use Google-managed keys for GCP instances. Use user-managed keys for on-premises instances.
    (B) Use Google-managed keys for all instances.
    (C) Use Google-managed keys for GCP instances. Use Firebase authentication for on-premises instances.
    (D) Use Google-managed keys for GCP instances. Use a third-party tool for on-premises instances.

7. Company X is using GCP with a number of configured projects. They have special requirements vis-à-vis billing visibility and management. Based on the following statement, select the appropriate answer: A CTO should be able to control the budget for different projects, while a project manager should be able to see billing information for their project only.

   (A) Set the billing administrator role to the CTO for all the projects that they manage. Set the billing viewer role to the project manager for their project.
   (B) Set the billing administrator role to the program manager for a random project. Set the billing viewer role to the project manager for their project.
   (C) Set the billing administrator role to the program and project managers.
   (D) Set the owner role to the program and project managers.

8. You are monitoring a service with uptime checks. The services are reported as unavailable from different GCP regions. You know that the service is up and running. How can you solve the monitoring issues?

   (A) Download the source IPs from the uptime check console and create an ingress firewall rule for the service.
   (B) Download the source IPs from the uptime check console and create an egress firewall rule for the service.
   (C) Use a third-party tool, outside GCP, to create the uptime checks.
   (D) Install Stackdriver monitoring agents on all instances that are hosting the service.

9. Company X is looking to create a development and production environment in GCP. What would be the best practice to separate those environments?

   (A) Create two separate projects for each environment. Give the development team access to the development project only. Give the operation team access to production only.
   (B) Create two separate projects for each environment. Give the development team and the production team access to both projects.
   (C) Create one project and two VPCs. Give the development team and the production team access to that project.
   (D) Create two separate Google accounts for each team.

10. Company X wants to perform an analysis of data coming from sensors. The data can arrive out of order. You need to make sure that the data is in the correct order. Which services should be used to minimize the effort?

    (A) IoT Core, Pub/Subs, and Dataflow
    (B) IoT Core, Pub/Subs, and Dataproc
    (C) IoT Core, Pub/Subs, and GKE
    (D) IoT Core, Pub/Subs, and GCE

11. Company X has deployed an application using App Engine. They want to release a new version of that application to production. They want to test that application on only a set of users. What is the most appropriate solution?

    (A) Deploy a new version of the application. Use traffic splitting to redirect part of the requests to the new version.
    (B) Deploy the application to a separate project, and direct the user to use a new URL to connect to it.
    (C) Migrate the application to GKE, and use blue-green deployment.
    (D) Migrate the application to GKE, and use rolling updates.

12. Company X is using the App Engine Flex environment. They have deployed a new version of the application. The application crashed. The code is stored in GitHub. How would the fastest recovery be performed?

    (A) Delete the new application and deploy a new application from GitHub.
    (B) Roll back the application to a previous release.
    (C) Split the traffic between the old and new releases, 10% to 90%.
    (D) Open a ticket to GCP Support to roll back the application to the previous release.

13. Company X is using Stackdriver to monitor their GCP environment. They want to store the logs and be able to analyze them. What would be the best solution for them?

    (A) Create a sink to Pub/Subs.
    (B) Create a sink to Spanner.
    (C) Create a sink to BigQuery.
    (D) Create a sink to Bigtable.

14. Company X is using a GKE cluster. They want to scale, due to an increasing demand for CPUs. What would be the most appropriate command to run?

   (A) Run the `gcloud container cluster resize` command to change the number of worker nodes.
   (B) Run the `gcloud container cluster resize` command to change the number of master nodes.
   (C) Run the `kubectl container cluster scale` command to change the number of worker nodes.
   (D) Run the `gcloud container cluster scale` command to change the number of worker nodes.

15. Company X wants to migrate their MySQL database to the cloud. They would like to use managed services. Select the most appropriate choice.

   (A) Use the Compute Engine instance and deploy MySQL.
   (B) Use the App Engine instance and deploy MySQL.
   (C) Use Cloud SQL.
   (D) Use Cloud Spanner.

16. Company X is creating an application that will analyze the comments on their Facebook profiles. They want to use the easiest way to analyze whether there are any negative comments. Which service should they use?

   (A) TensorFlow
   (B) Google AutoML
   (C) Google ML Engine
   (D) The Natural Language API

17. Company X wants to leverage ML in order to estimate the cost of the materials, based on past data. What type of model should they use?

   (A) Regression
   (B) Classification
   (C) Multi-class Classification Model

18. Company X wants to set alerts for project budgets. What is the best way to achieve this?

    (A) Create budget alerts with a desired percentage.
    (B) Create a ticket with Google Support to set hard quotas.
    (C) Create a cron job to check the billing and send an email if a threshold is exceeded.
    (D) Set a limit on credit cards that are attached to the account.

19. Company X wants to store data in Cloud Storage. The data will be accessed once every quarter. After a year, the data will be archived. Choose the most cost-effective solution.

    (A) Store the data in a multi-regional bucket. Set the auto-archiving policy to 365 days.
    (B) Store the data in a regional bucket. Set the auto-archiving policy to 365 days.
    (C) Store the data in a Nearline bucket. Set the object life cycle policy to move the data to the Coldline bucket after 365 days.
    (D) Store the data in the Nearline bucket. Create a cron job to move the data to the Coldline bucket after 365 days.

20. Company X wants to set up a static website. What is the fastest and most cost-effective solution?

    (A) Use Cloud Launcher to deploy Apache Server.
    (B) Use App Engine with a predefined web server.
    (C) Use Cloud Compute Engine and a start up script to install Apache Server.
    (D) Use Cloud Storage to host content.

Mock test 2

1. Company X wants a standardized redeployable Hadoop cluster, with options that a managed service doesn't offer. Which solution would suit?

    (A) A Cloud API
    (B) Deployment Manager
    (C) Dataflow
    (D) TensorFlow

2. Company X is looking to connect their backend platform to a managed NoSQL database service. There is an expectation that the databases could grow into PB scale. As an architect, they ask you which is the best GCP service to fit these requirements without needing to refactor any applications. What is the best fit?

   (A) MySQL
   (B) Bigtable
   (C) Firebase
   (D) Redis

3. Select the different types of service accounts (select three):

   (A) User-managed
   (B) Automated
   (C) Google-managed
   (D) G Suite
   (E) Google APIs

4. Company X has two projects, separated by separate VPCs that need to be able to communicate with one another. Which network service allows this?

   (A) VPC peering
   (B) Cloud load balancing
   (C) Dedicated interconnect
   (D) VPN

5. Company X is looking to use containers in the cloud. They want to continue to be developer focused, and have a code-first strategy. What is the best solution?

   (A) App Engine Standard
   (B) Containers on Compute Engine
   (C) Kubernetes Engine
   (D) App Engine Flexible

6. Your IT manager is looking at cloud vendor data storage services. His DBA has informed him that the principal requirements are strong consistency and high availability, with the potential to grow to PB scale. What is the best storage solution?

   (A) Cloud SQL
   (B) Cloud Storage
   (C) Cloud Datastore
   (D) Cloud Spanner

7. Company X needs to be PCI compliant. Which combination of GCP services would help to meet these requirements?

    (A) Stackdriver Monitoring, Stackdriver Trace, and Cloud Spanner
    (B) Stackdriver Monitoring, Stackdriver Logging, and BigQuery
    (C) Stackdriver Error Reporting, Stackdriver Debug, and Datastore
    (D) Stackdriver Tagging, Stackdriver Trace, and BigQuery

8. A storage engineer for Company X needs to migrate data from his AWS S3 bucket to his GCP storage bucket. What is the best solution for this?

    (A) Storage Transfer Service
    (B) Transfer Appliance
    (C) Online transfer
    (D) BigQuery data transfer

9. A company web page is serving users all over the globe. They want to make sure that users will always get content in the most efficient manner, regardless of where they are located. Which load balancing solution would best fit these requirements?

    (A) Network load balancing
    (B) Internal load balancing
    (C) HTTP(S) load balancing
    (D) TCP proxy load balancing

10. Company X is looking to the cloud to achieve autoscaling. They wish to deploy over multiple zones in a standardized manner, while also benefiting from load balancing. What GCP service best suits?

    (A) Deployment Manager
    (B) Managed instance groups
    (C) Google Compute Engine manager
    (D) Instance fleet

11. You are creating new firewall rules and wish to identify specific targets according to their use, for example, a web server. Which filter should you use?

    (A) Zones
    (B) Network tags
    (C) Instance groups
    (D) Targets

12. You have deployed an instance into the same VPC as already-existing instances. When you try to use SSH to connect to the external IP address, the connection is refused. Why might this be?

    (A) The FW rule to allow SSH is restricted to internal traffic only.
    (B) There is no external IP allocated to the instance.
    (C) You do not have the correct custom IAM role to initiate SSH.
    (D) You should use the Google API for external SSH.

13. At the moment, your IT department is seeing lots of bugs reported whenever a new software update is released for the company's internal timesheet application. These bugs were not spotted during QA. You have been asked to design a new strategy that will keep the bugs to a minimum, and regain confidence in the IT department. Which option best suits?

    (A) Advise that you should only deploy updates once per year.
    (B) Deploy only part of the update to production.
    (C) Perform the tests more times during QA.
    (D) Use canary deployment methods.

14. Your company is looking to connect their onsite networks to a GCP VPC, in order to dynamically exchange routes between each site. Which service would you advise?

    (A) Cloud Router
    (B) Cloud Interconnect
    (C) External peering
    (D) Cloud DNS

15. You plan to connect VPC networks using VPC peering. What network mode is best suited?

    (A) Auto mode networks
    (B) VPC VPN networks
    (C) Custom mode
    (D) Sub-networking mode

16. You have been tasked with researching different methods to extend your on-premises network to your GCP VPC network. You are reminded by your manager that your network bandwidth is 1 GBps. What would be the best option?

    (A) Dedicated interconnect
    (B) Partner interconnect
    (C) VPC interconnect
    (D) VPN interconnect

17. Company X wants to extend their data center to the cloud. You have been hired as an external consultant to advise on the best hybrid connectivity option. They advise you that they need access to private compute resources on GCP, but are not worried about encryption at the application level. What option best corresponds to their needs?

    (A) Cloud VPN
    (B) Partner Interconnect
    (C) Direct peering
    (D) Carrier peering

18. You want to serve all of your content with a low latency, worldwide. Which GCP service should you use?

    (A) Cloud CDN
    (B) Cloud VPN
    (C) Google CloudFront
    (D) Cloud Endpoints

19. You wish to load balance your systems based on incoming ports. What LB concept should you use?

    (A) Network load balancing
    (B) TCP load balancing
    (C) HTTP(S) load balancing
    (D) SSL proxy load balancing

20. You are looking to allow access to publish messages to a Cloud Pub/Sub topic. Your security team reminds you that you should be as granular as possible. Which type of IAM role should you use?

    (A) Primitive role
    (B) Predefined role
    (C) Custom role
    (D) Policy-based role
    (E) Topic role

Assessments

Answers to Mock Test 1

1. C: Coldline storage is the most cost-effective option. For more information, refer to `https://cloud.google.com/storage/`:

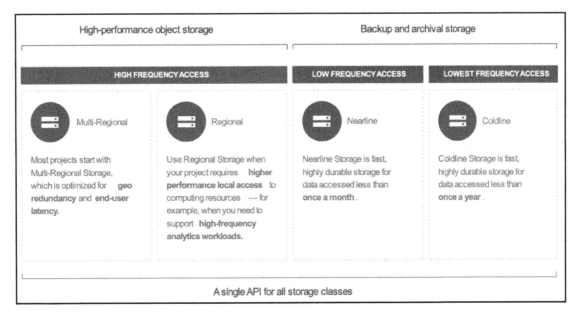

2. **A**: Bigtable is a petabyte-scale, fully managed NoSQL database service for large analytical and operational workloads. It is ideal for ad tech, Fintech, and IoT. Reference: `https://cloud.google.com/bigtable/`.

3. **A**: Custom images can be created from snapshots and shared across projects. Reference: `https://cloud.google.com/compute/docs/images/create-delete-deprecate-private-images`.

4. **D**: "Cloud Dataflow is a fully managed service for transforming and enriching data in stream (`https://cloud.google.com/solutions/big-data/stream-analytics/`) (real time) and batch (historical) modes with equal reliability and expressiveness – no more complex workarounds or compromises needed. And with its serverless approach to resource provisioning and management, you have access to virtually limitless capacity to solve your biggest data processing challenges, while paying only for what you use." Reference: `https://cloud.google.com/dataflow/`:

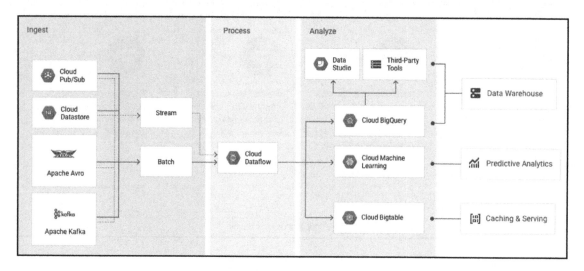

Source: https://cloud.google.com/dataflow/
License: https://creativecommons.org/licenses/by/4.0/legalcode

5. **A**: Cloud Dataproc is a fast, easy-to-use, fully managed cloud service for running Apache Spark and Apache Hadoop clusters in a simpler, more cost-efficient way. Reference: `https://cloud.google.com/dataproc/`:

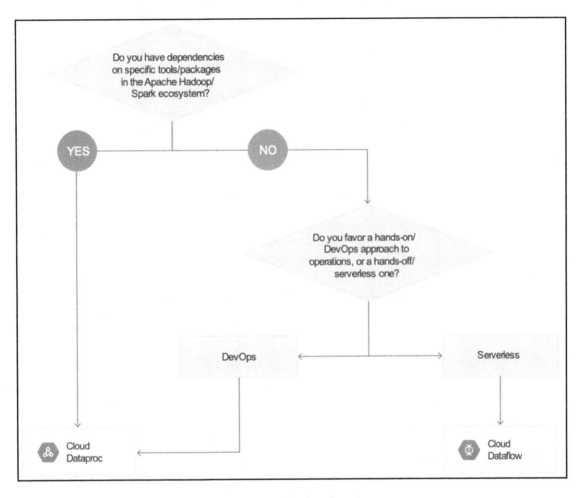

Source: https://cloud.google.com/dataproc/
License: https://creativecommons.org/licenses/by/4.0/legalcode

6. **D**: Refer to the following diagram to understand the best practices:

Source: https://cloud.google.com/iam/docs/understanding-service-accounts
License: https://creativecommons.org/licenses/by/4.0/legalcode

7. **A**: IAM best practice is to set minimum requited privileges. Reference: `https://cloud.google.com/blog/products/gcp/iam-best-practice-guides-available-now`.

8. **A**: You need to open firewall rules to allow uptime checks. Reference: `https://cloud.google.com/monitoring/uptime-checks/using-uptime-checks#get-ips`:

Uptime Checks ❷							Add Uptime Check ⋮	
							Download source IPs	
CHECKS	VIRGINIA	OREGON	IOWA	BELGIUM	SINGAPORE	SAO PAULO	POLICIES	ACTIONS
default	❶	❶	❶	❶	❶	❶	🔔	⋮

Source: https://cloud.google.com/monitoring/uptime-checks/#monitoring_uptime_check_list_ips-console
License: https://creativecommons.org/licenses/by/4.0/legalcode

*"Your use of uptime checks is affected by any firewalls protecting your service:
If the resource you are checking isn't publicly available, you must configure the resource's
firewall to permit incoming traffic from the uptime check servers. Refer to Getting IP
addresses* https://cloud.google.com/monitoring/uptime-checks/using-uptime-
checks#get-ips *to download a list of the IP addresses.*

> • *If the resource you are checking doesn't have an external IP address, uptime
> checks are unable to reach it."*

9. **A**: Based on best practice with the fewest possible privileges. Reference: https://
   cloud.google.com/docs/enterprise/best-practices-for-enterprise-
   organizations.

10. **A**: DataFlow will accommodate the processing of late data. DataFlow is a
    managed Apache Beam service.

    However, data isn't always guaranteed to arrive in a pipeline in time order, or to
    always arrive at predictable intervals. Beam tracks a watermark, which is the
    system's notion of when all data in a certain window can be expected to have
    arrived in the pipeline. Once the watermark progresses past the end of a window,
    any further element that arrives with a timestamp in that window is
    considered late data. Reference: https://beam.apache.org/documentation/
    programming-guide/.

11. **A**: Use traffic splitting to redirect a subset of traffic to the correct version of the
    application. Reference: https://cloud.google.com/appengine/docs/standard/
    python/splitting-traffic.

12. **B**: The fastest way is to roll back the application.

    "We don't want to mess around with our code, we need to fix this right now.
    Users are upset! Go back to the list of versions and check the box next to the
    version that was deployed first. Now, click the **MAKE DEFAULT** button located
    above the list. Traffic immediately switches over to the stable version. Crisis
    averted!

    That was easy.

    You can now delete the buggy version by checking the box next to the version
    and then clicking the **DELETE** button located above the list."

    Reference: https://cloud.google.com/community/tutorials/how-to-roll-
    your-app-engine-managed-vms-app-back-to-a-previous-version-part-1.

13. **C**: BigQuery datasets provide big data analysis capabilities. References:
    - `https://cloud.google.com/logging/docs/export/configure_export_v2`.
    - `https://cloud.google.com/logging/`.

14. **B**: gcloud container cluster resize is used for resizing the GKE cluster. Reference: `https://cloud.google.com/sdk/gcloud/reference/container/clusters/resize`.

15. **C**: "Cloud SQL is a fully managed database service that makes it easy to set up, maintain, manage, and administer your relational PostgreSQL and MySQL databases in the cloud". Reference: `https://cloud.google.com/sql/`.

16. **D**: Sentiment analysis inspects the given text and identifies the prevailing emotional opinion within the text, especially with a view to determining a writer's attitude as positive, negative, or neutral. Reference: `https://cloud.google.com/natural-language/docs/analyzing-sentiment`.

17. **A**: Reference: `https://developers.google.com/machine-learning/crash-course/descending-into-ml/linear-regression`.

18. **A**: "You can apply budget alerts to either a billing account or a project, and you can set the budget alert at a specific amount or match it to the previous month's spend. The alerts will be sent to billing administrators and billing account users when spending exceeds a percentage of your budget". Reference: `https://cloud.google.com/billing/docs/how-to/budgets`.

19. **C**: Reference: `https://cloud.google.com/storage/docs/lifecycle`.

20. **D**: Reference: `https://cloud.google.com/storage/docs/static-website`.

Answers to Mock Test 2

1. **B**: Deployment Manager. Requirements are a non-managed service and one that is standardized. Deployment Manager allows for repeatable deployments. Reference: `https://cloud.google.com/deployment-manager/`.

2. **B**: Bigtable and Redis are only noSQL options. The key word here is "refactor".

3. **A, C, E**: Reference: `https://cloud.google.com/iam/docs/service-accounts`.

4. **A**: VCP peering allows connectivity across two VPC networks regardless of whether or not they belong to the same project. Reference: `https://cloud.google.com/vpc/docs/using-vpc-peering`.

5. **D**: App Engine Flex is developer focused and has a code-first strategy. Reference: `https://cloud.google.com/appengine/docs/flexible/`.

6. **D**: Cloud spanner can scale into PT of data and fits the requirements for high availability and strong consistency. Reference: `https://cloud.google.com/spanner/`.

7. **B**: Stackdriver Monitoring, Stackdriver Logging, and BigQuery. Reference: `https://cloud.google.com/blog/products/gcp/oro-how-gcp-smoothed-our-path-to-pci-dss-compliance`.

8. **A**: Storage transfer service. Reference: `https://cloud.google.com/storage-transfer/docs/overview`.

9. **D**: TCP Proxy. Reference: `https://cloud.google.com/load-balancing/docs/tcp/`

10. **B**: Managed instance groups; specifically, regional managed instance groups let you improve availability by spreading instances across multiple zones with a region. Reference: `https://cloud.google.com/compute/docs/instance-groups/distributing-instances-with-regional-instance-groups`.

11. **B**: Tags that are put onto GCE instances can also be used to determine the FW rule on both inbound and outbound rules. If a web server is applied to a VM and added to the FW rule, then it will be impacted. Reference: `https://cloud.google.com/vpc/docs/firewalls`.

12. **A**: The default VPC rules have `default-allow-internal` specified, which permits incoming connections to a VM instance from others in the same network. Reference: `https://cloud.google.com/vpc/docs/firewalls#default_firewall_rules`.

13. **D**: Use canary deployment methods. Reference: `https://cloud.google.com/blog/products/gcp/how-release-canaries-can-save-your-bacon-cre-life-lessons?hl=de`.

14. **A**: A cloud router uses BGP to learn new subnets in your VPC and announces them on your on-premise network. Reference: `https://cloud.google.com/router/docs/concepts/overview`.

15. **C**: Custom mode networks. Reference: `https://cloud.google.com/vpc/docs/vpc`

16. **B**: Partner interconnect. Dedicated interconnect requires 10 GB, and the other options do not exist. Reference: `https://cloud.google.com/interconnect/docs/how-to/choose-type`.

17. **A**: Cloud VPN satisfies requirements. If application-level encryption is needed, then partner interconnect or direct interconnect should be considered. If there is a requirement to connect to G suite, then carrier peering should be considered. Reference: `https://cloud.google.com/hybrid-connectivity/`.

18. **A**: Cloud Content Delivery Network caches in numerous locations around the world, thereby yielding reduced latency. Reference: `https://cloud.google.com/cdn/docs/overview`.

19. **A**: Network load balancing can balance loads on your system based on the incoming address, port, and protocol type. Reference: `https://cloud.google.com/load-balancing/docs/network/`.

20. **B**: Predefined role. Reference: `https://cloud.google.com/iam/docs/overview`.

Other Books You May Enjoy

If you enjoyed this book, you may be interested in these other books by Packt:

Google Cloud Platform for Architects
Vitthal Srinivasan, Janani Ravi, Judy Raj

ISBN: 978-1-78883-430-8

- Set up GCP account and utilize GCP services using the cloud shell, web console, and client APIs
- Harness the power of App Engine, Compute Engine, Containers on the Kubernetes Engine, and Cloud Functions
- Pick the right managed service for your data needs, choosing intelligently between Datastore, BigTable, and BigQuery
- Migrate existing Hadoop, Spark, and Pig workloads with minimal disruption to your existing data infrastructure, by using Dataproc intelligently
- Derive insights about the health, performance, and availability of cloud-powered applications with the help of monitoring, logging, and diagnostic tools in Stackdriver

Google Cloud Platform Administration
Ranjit Singh Thakurratan

ISBN: 978-1-78862-435-0

- Understand all GCP Compute components
- Deploy and manage multiple GCP storage options
- Manage and utilize the networking resources offered by GCP
- Explore the functionalities and features of the GCP Container
- Understand the workings of GCP operations such as monitoring and error reporting
- Discover an immune GCP using its identity and security options

Leave a review - let other readers know what you think

Please share your thoughts on this book with others by leaving a review on the site that you bought it from. If you purchased the book from Amazon, please leave us an honest review on this book's Amazon page. This is vital so that other potential readers can see and use your unbiased opinion to make purchasing decisions, we can understand what our customers think about our products, and our authors can see your feedback on the title that they have worked with Packt to create. It will only take a few minutes of your time, but is valuable to other potential customers, our authors, and Packt. Thank you!

Index